St. Peter Denying Christ
by Gustave Doré (1832-1883)

MARK'S ACCOUNT OF PETER'S DENIAL OF JESUS

A History of Its Interpretation

Robert W. Herron, Jr.

with a Foreword by
William L. Lane

UNIVERSITY
PRESS OF
AMERICA

Lanham • New York • London

Library of Congress Cataloging-in-Publication Data
Herron, Robert W., 1955-
Mark's Account of Peter's Denial of Jesus :
A History of Its Interpretation / by Robert W. Herron :
with a foreword by William L. Lane.
p. cm.
Rev. ed. of the author's thesis (Ph. D.)—Rice University.
Includes bibliographical references and index.
1. Bible. N.T. Mark XIV, 54—Criticism,
interpretation, etc.—History. 2. Bible. N.T.
Mark XIV, 66-72—Criticism, interpretation, etc.—
History. 3. Jesus Christ—Denial by Peter. I. Title.
BS2585.2.H445 1991
226.3' 06' 09—dc20 91-26366 CIP

ISBN 0-8191-8352-0 (cloth : alk. paper)
ISBN 0-8191-8353-9 (pbk. : alk. paper)

 The paper used in this publication meets the minimum requirements of
American National Standard for Information Sciences—Permanence
of Paper for Printed Library Materials, ANSI Z39.48–1984.

DEDICATION

To
ROBERT WILBURN, SR.
&
JUANITA ELEANOR GREEN
HERRON

We stand a little taller,
we see a little farther,
but our foundation is no surer
than the shoulders which bear us.

Contents

Foreword

No Gospel has occupied scholars so intensively over the last decade as that of Mark. The publication of articles, collections of essays, dissertations, monographs, and full-length commentaries has continued unabated, making it increasingly difficult to control the secondary literature on the Gospel. An impression of the literary explosion which has occurred in the field of Markan studies within the last twenty to thirty years can be gained from a perusal of the index of journal articles, essays in collected works, and books published from 1954 through 1980 compiled by H.M. Humphrey (*A Bibliography for the Gospel of Mark, 1954-1980* [Studies in the Bible and Early Christianity, Vol. 1] New York: Edward Mellen Press, 1981). He lists 1599 titles that appeared during these 27 years. A review of the work published in Europe and the United States alone over the course of the past decade would expand his index considerably further.

It is not simply the quantity of the secondary literature which makes an entrance into Markan studies difficult. The task is aggravated by the absence of any consensus. Reading through the major literature confirms that specialists on Mark do not agree, and every year the number of contributors to the discussion increases. Markan studies are in a state of flux, and it is difficult to discern where they are going. The student of Mark, confronted with conflicting conclusions, will ultimately be driven back to a fresh consideration of the text of the Gospel itself and to the discussion it has prompted over the course of the centuries.

Robert W. Herron, Jr. is one of the new contributors to the discussion of the Gospel of Mark. After graduate studies in the Humanities, in which he distinguished himself, he entered the doctoral program in Religious Studies at Rice University. The present monograph draws attention to Mark's account of Peter's denial of Jesus. This study had its beginning in a study of the role of the disciples and of discipleship in the Gospel of Mark under the direction of Professor Werner H. Kelber. It was subsequently refined and given focus by concentration upon the history of interpretation of Mark 14:54, 66-72 under the direction of Professor Niels C. Nielsen, Jr.

MARK'S ACCOUNT OF PETER'S DENIAL OF JESUS

A representative survey of the history of the interpretation of this significant incident disclosed how diverse, even contradictory, are studies of the denial pericope. Professor Herron recognized that after listening to the discussion prompted by the text the interpreter of Mark is summoned to three tasks. The initial task is descriptive, asking "what" is the nature of the diversity. The second, more fundamental task is the analytical, asking "why" the range of interpretation was so broad. The final task is prescriptive, asking the crucial question of "how" the text should be understood. When he addressed himself to these three tasks he found exposed the extent of the impact of presuppositions and the choice of methodology upon the conclusions to which an interpreter arrives as he seeks to listen to the detail of the text.

The present study is a significant achievement. Professor Herron demonstrates the importance of the denial pericope for an understanding of the whole Gospel story in Mark. He further demonstrates the value of a history of interpretation approach to a unit of Markan text. The text of a Gospel pericope possesses both a literal-historical meaning and another corresponding level of significance, with theological and pastoral implications commensurate with the primary level of meaning. Pre-modern interpreters tended to neglect the literal-historical meaning in their concentration upon the spiritual significance of the text. Modern and contemporary interpreters, in an attempt to approach the text from a value-neutral, objective point of view, tend to neglect the theological and pastoral implication of the text. Professor Herron calls for an interpretation of the text in a manner commensurate with its intention. This presupposes a readiness to assess our own subjective points of view and the presuppositions with which we approach the text of the Gospel.

This is an important study of the interrelatedness of hermeneutics to the cultural, historical, and the theological factors which tended to shape the directions of biblical interpretation throughout the pre-modern, modern and post-modern periods. Professor Herron calls for a more deliberate commitment to balance the historical-critical search for the literary meaning of the text with the pre-modern concern for the spiritual significance of the text. This is a significant contribution to the current discussion of method for approaching the Gospel of Mark. Ultimately, he is calling for an approach to the biblical text which will not preclude a living encounter with its claim and witness.

William L. Lane, Dean
School of Religion
Seattle Pacific University

Preface

This book is an edited version of my doctoral dissertation. I am grateful to University Press of America for expressing confidence in me by publishing it. It represents an academic and spiritual pilgrimage too personal and boring to recount in detail, but which perhaps merits a brief explanation by way of background.

Through my graduate studies in religion I was introduced to many new and strange ideas. The whole of the modern enterprise complete with anti-supernatural-istic presuppositions and the positivistic historical-critical method of biblical inter-pretation took me by storm. Among the smaller pieces of the strange puzzle was the suggestion that the writer of the Gospel of Mark was written as a religious and political polemic against the disciples of Jesus and *their disciples* of a generation later. It went against my own pious religious upbringing, to be sure. But I worked through that and I still doubted it. I continued to work through it in research papers and out of personal interest, and I could not make it fit; it just did not "sound right." But I also could not adequately explain why. It is a technically argued thesis and contains much truth. The conclusions were wrong, but they and their proponents were larger than I.

Then I began to study the hermeneutics of the Church Fathers. There I found what I believe to be at least part of the answer. I combined two interests, the seemingly negative portrayal of the disciples in the Gospel of Mark with the hermeneutics of the Fathers. To make the combination work I chose one passage, the most negative in the text, Peter's denial of Jesus, and followed it through the history of the Church as thoroughly as time and talent would allow. The result is before you and I eagerly invite you to read it.

In summary, I concluded that while pre-modern exegetes were guilty of many errors of devotion and lacked many tools and skills which we value and benefit from as moderners, they possessed one advantage which too many modern exegetes have lost: a keen sense for the "spirit" of the text. As a rule modern scholars are forever looking for something "behind" the text: an historical base or an oral tradition or an author's motive. And while all of those things are important objects of study, they cannot replace the text itself in priority, or at least not without distorting the view. That is why I evaluated the literary critical approach so highly near the end of the study. It insists on bracketing out all the other modern, critical questions until the primary one is asked: what does the text say? Having addressed that as well as one can, one can then turn to the other issues.

The pre-modern exegetes were in many ways not as sophisticated (although they saw things more clearly than we sometimes allow). They usually thought they were looking for something behind the text, uncovering a deeper "spiritual sense." In fact they were near the surface. They frequently were too trusting of a text when it comes to historical veracity or too one-dimensional in their view of history. They frequently equated historical events with the textual record. But the result was that they took the text at "face value," and there they found hovering the "spirit" of the text, the point the author was trying to make, the larger meaning of the text. And this is awfully close to the job of the literary critic. Whether a text is historically accurate is an important but other question; likewise the question of whether the author had a discoverable motive.

To go on is to get into the thesis itself and to risk the error of oversimplification. But I would add this preview of my conclusion on the negative portrayal of the disciples and of Peter in particular. While it is true that Mark's presentation of the disciples and Peter is harsh, they are not unredeemable; nor were they meant to be. It is of course possible to overinterpret the story and conclude that Mark is engaged in a vendetta against the disciples and a later generation of Jerusalem representatives. As Martin Hengel (*Studies in the Gospel of Mark* [London: SCM Press Ltd., 1985] 157) dryly notes: "Unbridled redaction criticism makes everything possible in this way."

To add a poignant comment by Raymond Brown (*CBQ* 39 [1977] 285): If the author intended to polemicize against the disciples, he "was one of the most incompetent writers of all times, since almost all his readers have interpreted him to say the opposite of what he intended about the Eucharist, about Peter, and about the resurrection." And the testimony of all the simple folk through history who have read the story cannot be dismissed. The "spirit" of the story will not allow such an interpretation. The Gospel is a mirror in which the believing reader finds him/herself here and there. And while the Gospel condemns all unbelief and moral failure, it also offers, even begs for repentance. *We are the disciples;* some of us have been in the courtyard with Peter. One is free to guess why the story was written as it was. As moderners we feel compelled to explore the historical events behind the portrait. But the story *as it is* is powerful, and invites identification with the disciples even in their failures and denials. I am convinced of it.

The production of a book is a massive undertaking. I think no one can produce one alone; certainly I have not. The list of creditors grew long very fast, even if those on it insist they are misplaced. An edited version of my dissertation in book form would be presumptuous if I failed at least in attempting to acknowledge some of the folks whose help is most conspicuous.

This study first took recognizable shape while I served as Research Fellow at the Institut zur Erforschung des Urchristentum in Tübingen, Germany. I am grateful to them for the use of their facilities, and also to Professors Martin Hengel, Hans Küng and Otto Betz who, each in a different way, provided insight and encouragement.

My second year Greek class in the Spring of 1988 helped me through some of the Greek texts which appear in the appendices. Teachers really can learn as much from their students as they from us. I thank Robert Fisher, Ruth Lindsey and Gary Smith for helping me put the manuscript in form to send to the publisher, and hasten to accept full responsibility for any errors herein.

Dr. Niels C. Nielsen, then chair of the Department of Religious Studies, Rice University, also served as the chair of my thesis committee, and his assistance and counsel brought me over what seemed at the time insurmountable obstacles. Dr. Clyde Manschreck also served on the committee and worked very closely with me to see the project through to completion.

Dr. William L. Lane wrote the Foreword. It is but one more on a long list of gracious favors bestowed on a student who felt undeserving of his friendship and collegiality. He has been a mentor in the very best fashion, and I thank him once more.

I have dedicated the book to my parents for good reasons which they know.

My two children, Trey and Tiffany, were too young to appreciate the sacrifices they made that I might pursue this venture. I am still in the process of making it up to them. And lastly, I thank my wife, Diane. She will protest my claim that this book is as much hers as mine; but I know.

Robert W. Herron, Jr.
Lee College
June 1991

ACKNOWLEDGEMENTS

The author wishes to gratefully acknowledge the use of the following material and assistance:

Father David Hurst, editor of Bede's works in *Corpus Christianorum Series Latina* for his translation of the Latin text of Bede;

John Phillips of the Department of Philosophy and Religion at the University of Tennessee at Chattanooga for translations of the Latin texts of the *Glossa ordinaria* and Pseudo-Jerome;

Permission from both the author and the original publisher for the excerpt from Norman R. Peterson, "When is the End Not the End? Reflections on the Ending of Mark's Narrative (16:8)," *Interpretation* (1980) 34: 151-66;

Permission from the publishers for the selection from D. W. and T. F. Torrance, *Calvin's Commentaries: A Harmony of the Gospels: Matthew, Mark and Luke and The Epistles of James and Jude,* translated by A. W. Morrison, vol. 3, Grand Rapids: Wm. B. Eerdmans (1972) 169-73;

Unless otherwise indicated all Scripture references are from the Revised Standard Version Bible, © 1946, 1952, 1971 by the Division of Christian Education of the National Council of the Churches of Christ in the USA. Used by permission.

Chapter 1
Introduction

MARKAN STUDIES are quite multi-faceted, overlapping many disciplines, and with vectors sometimes paralleling, sometimes intersecting, sometimes pointing in opposite directions. The present study was conceived as several concerns progressed and intersected. A modern student's study of the Gospel of Mark typically begins with William Wrede's "messianic secret" and touches the milestones along the way to the present: Karl Ludwig Schmidt, Ernest Lohmeyer, and Willi Marxsen's redaction criticism with its indelible impact on Markan studies.[1] Such was my pilgrimage.

But historically there is more to Markan studies than the twentieth century. The Gospel of Mark, though neglected, was nevertheless revered, and there are studies of Mark before our era. The different historical contexts produced different hermeneutical principles. The same passage would be understood differently in the fifth century than in the sixteenth; differently in the East than in the West.

In one sense, therefore, *this study is very narrowly focused. It concentrates on one passage, Mark 14:54, 66-72,* in the shortest and, until the nineteenth century, the most neglected Gospel. There is not even a commentary to be found on Mark until the late fifth century. And much of what is written from then until the nineteenth century is brief and inaccessible. While this study is not exhaustive, it does attempt to be "representative."

On the other hand, a study of this passage and *in this way* becomes very broad. It began when it became clear how diverse, even contradictory, studies of this passage were. The first question is "descriptive" and asks "what" is the nature of the diversity? The second and more basic question is "analytic." It asks "why?" And in order to answer why the interpretations were so many and so varied, it seemed necessary to do a "history of interpretation." The study is a representative span of all Church History. The third question is "prescriptive." It asks "how" the text should be understood.

1

While it true that a methodology has a significant bearing on one's interpretation, why one chooses a methodology becomes important as well. And perhaps more revealing is why one's choice of a methodology frequently seems to matter very little. In other words, one's theological and philosophical presuppositions frequently loom so large as to force a methodology "around" virtually predetermined conclusions. If so, the questions of how and what kind of interpretation can/should be sought must be addressed. And finally, how does one contribute to the ongoing discussion?

It is hoped that some contribution can be made to the understanding of the passage under study. But that can be attempted only after taking a hard look at the impact of presuppositions and methodologies on conclusions. It will be necessary, therefore, to "do" history, philosophy, hermeneutics, and biblical criticism.

The Context of the Study

In order to appreciate a history of interpretation of this passage, one should think of it as the center of a series of concentric circles. The outer, most encompassing circle is the study of the Gospel of Mark, which has changed drastically in the last one hundred years.[2] One of the themes, or inner circles, occupying Markan scholars in that time is that of discipleship.[3] That in turn has yielded a vast array of interpretations of the person of Peter, and also on the pericope of Peter's denial of Jesus (Mark 14:54, 66-72).

Peter is the first (1:16) and last (16:7) disciple mentioned, both times by name.[4] Peter is not only the first named upon the "making" of the Twelve (3:14-16), but he figures as the chief disciple in almost every episode which involves this group.[5] A typical example is the author's reference to "Simon and those who were with him" as the ones who pursued Jesus into his prayerful solitude (1:36). On more than one occasion Peter serves as a spokesman for the disciples as, for example, with the plea "We have left everything and followed you" (10:28-30) and also in the expression of surprise at the withering of the fig tree (11:20-22). Even within the "inner group,"[6] it is Peter who is presented as compelled to speak at the Transfiguration (9:2-13) and who becomes the object of rebuke in Gethsemane (14:32-42).

Although all the disciples promise never to forsake Jesus, it is Peter who says so "vehemently" (14:31); and thus when all do forsake Jesus (14:50), the author brings Peter back into the story plot to narrate his denial (14:54, 66-72). On the other hand, the messenger's offer of a reunion with Jesus is offered to "the disciples, *even* Peter" (16:7). It is possible to conclude that in the narrative, as goes Peter so go the disciples, except that Peter's fate is of necessity written large.[7] Although Peter is one of the "round" or "colorful" characters in the narrative, the colors are decidedly dark.

It is no surprise then that whatever solution one posits for the Gospel's many questions, Peter's role is usually considered vital. Peter is "the most fully developed character in the entire story other than Jesus."[8] This is true especially because of the scene of Peter's denial which, notes Auerbach, "fits into no antique genre."[9] Weeden locates the core of an erroneous christology in the person of Peter (esp. his "confession" in 8:27-33),[10] and actually concludes that the evangelist "portrays Peter as a dunce."[11] Günther Klein has argued that the entire incident of Peter's denial is non-historical and that its creation served a larger anti-Petrine movement designed in part to debunk the Apostle as the primary witness of the resurrection.[12] "The disciples are 'round' characters because they have conflicting traits," say Rhoads and Michie. "Their contrast with Jesus is sharpest when, by use of the framing device, the narrator places Jesus' trial and Peter's trial side by side."[13]

The importance of understanding the denial pericope for an understanding of the whole Gospel story can hardly be overestimated. It is clearly one of the boldest, darkest swatches in the entire weave.

Thesis

We have taken seriously the warning of Josef Ernst regarding the story of Peter's denial: "Das Thema ist in letzter Zeit gründlich abgehandelt worden, so daß es auf den ersten Blick überflüssig erscheint, es erneut aufzugreifen."[14] Interpretations, especially those of the modern period, are very diverse. It seems unwise to try to make an additional advance until some stock has been taken of the past and present. *This is the contribution of a history of interpretation: so to order the past and present interpretations that future interpretations will make sense.* Our study of the denial pericope in Mark will yield the following results:

1. whether and to what extent one's interpretation of this story is "contextual" and reveals one's own theological presuppositions and *Sitz im Leben* as much as that of the passage;

2. whether and to what extent one's methodology tends to determine how this passage is viewed and the results of an investigation;

3. whether and to what extent there is any correlation between one's theological presuppositions and/or historical situation and the methodology used;

4. a reevaluation of this passage in light of this history of interpretation will suggest that a text possesses both a literal-historical meaning and a deeper spiritual significance (theological and pastoral implications) which is commensurate with that meaning. Whereas the premodern exegetes erred on the side of neglect of the literal-historical meaning, and exaggerating and *eis*egeting the spiritual meaning of the text, the modern exegetes tend to err on the side of neglecting the theological and pastoral implications of the text. A balance between these can be ascertained with greater accuracy when:

a) One listens to the collective wisdom of the voice of the church, not with a view toward obtaining a lowest common denominator, but in an effort to establish the parameters of common sense and probability. Exegetes of every age have tended to regard their point of view as superior to all others, sometimes to the exclusion of all others. Might this include the modern point of view as well? Religionists have recently begun to question how limited a specifically "western" approach can be and have begun to entertain the validity of a Latin American, third-world, feminist, or eastern reading of the text. This would be beyond our scope. But if a wider "synchronic" reading of the text is self-evidently necessary and helpful, how much more salutary is a continuous "diachronic" reading of the text?

b) One employs a multi-methodological approach which seeks to avoid the extremes and tunnel vision inevitable when one methodology is used to the exclusion of all others;

c) One recognizes that a completely objective, scientific approach is elusive. We regard it as self-defeating to proffer a superficial, illusory "objectivity," excluding at the outset questions of truth and meaning. It seems as though the modern historical critical method, in an attempt to approach its subject from a value-neutral, objective point of view, has only succeeded in more carefully cloaking its own varied values and presuppositions. As Walter Wink notes: "It is clear that the 'objective standpoint' is none other than the historically conditioned place where *we* happen to be standing, and possesses no neutrality or detachment at all."[15] Since subjectivity cannot be abandoned, it is wiser to be honest about assessing our own subjective point of view and the presuppositions with which we approach the text.

The Value of an Historical Survey

An historical survey has an almost inevitable tendency to be tedious and pedantic. If these less enviable characteristics cannot be avoided, hopefully they will be counterbalanced by the more positive attributes of this approach.

An historical survey helps to put modern interpretations into perspective; it makes the modern voice less a solo and more a voice in a choir. I do not know if it is endemic of every age and culture, or merely common. But I somehow acquired the "prejudice of modernity"; viz., the view that time brings progress, and what is progressive cannot be instructed or corrected by what is earlier, older, less advanced. C. S. Lewis admitted a similar weakness, what he called "'chronological snobbery,' the uncritical acceptance of the intellectual climate common to our own age and the assumption that whatever has gone out of date is on that account discredited."[16] One criterion Lewis used to avoid the insidious effect of "chronological snobbery" is worth noting:

> You must find why it went out of date. Was it ever refuted (and if so by whom, where, and how conclusively) or did it merely die away as fashions do? If the latter, this tells us nothing about its truth or falsehood. From seeing this, one passes to the realization that our own age is also "a period," and certainly has, like all periods, its own characteristic illusions. They are likeliest to lurk in those widespread assumptions which are so ingrained in the age that no one dares to attack or feels it necessary to defend them.[17]

We will be interested in knowing why a particular interpretation of this passage is no longer fashionable and why another has become so.

An historical survey points out the interrelatedness of hermeneutics to cultural, historical and theological contexts. Earlier biblical interpreters were influenced by philosophical assumptions which we probably cannot, nor should, accept. Nevertheless, says Patrick Henry, "they were aware of the 'hermeneutical problem,' that is, of the difficulties of determining the meaning of ancient texts."[18] Recognition of that, of their answers to the problems, even of how they formulated the questions, will help in the appreciation of our own context. We concur with S. Kealy:

> Only with an understanding of the philosophical and cultural development behind the modern approach to the Bible can that method be properly appreciated and its limitations recognized e.g. [sic] much of the 19th century source criticism was a reaction to the extremes of Strauss who considered Mark a hypochondriac, while Bultmann and Barth were reactions to the impact of World War I on the European scene.[19]

An historical survey challenges the "absoluteness" of the modern historical critical method. Walter Wink, in his little book *The Bible in Human Transformation,* speaks of "The Bankruptcy of the Biblical Critical Paradigm":

> Biblical criticism...is bankrupt solely because it is incapable of achieving what most of its practitioners considered its purpose to be: so to interpret the Scriptures that the past becomes alive and illumines our present with new possibilities for personal and social transformation.[20]

There seems to be a growing consensus that criticism has "arrived at something of an impasse."[21] An historical survey helps to place the present "impasse" at a distance, to make it part of a wider horizon. Henry suggests that what we can learn from this process is that most of the ancient and medieval biblical interpreters were churchmen, pastors and monks, not university professors. Their relationship with the world around them and its people was much more intimate. The relevance of what they were doing and why was much clearer; the relationship of the Bible to the community was assumed. "It might turn out that the 'strangeness' of the interpretations of many centuries ago is a result not only of their different philosophical assumptions but also of their being directed to a community of all sorts and conditions of persons, and not simply to students and professors."[22] In brief: "a history of interpretations helps to avoid superficiality in reading, widens one's horizon in studying a gospel, and opens up the unsuspected depths of a profound many-sided work like Mark."[23]

Method and Procedure

Our procedure will be as follows: The sources are divided into two periods, what we have called the premodern and the modern. We have chosen this division because Mark's Gospel was overshadowed and neglected until the nineteenth century by the belief that it was only an abstract of Matthew. The works of Karl Lachmann, C. H.

Weisse, and H. J. Holtzmann altered that view, proposing that Mark was the earliest Gospel and therefore was the most reliable source for reconstructing the historical Jesus.

Sources were chosen on the basis of three criteria in order: (a) *Comments on Mark's Gospel,* since our concern is with Mark's version of the story. It is true that some commentaries on Mark seem still more interested in Matthew or Luke (as, e.g., Euthymius). Nevertheless, with the exceptions of Origen's comments on Matthew's version of the pericope to provide a contrast with Victor of Antioch, and Calvin's *Commentary on the Harmony* as the best example of Reformation exegesis on the passage, we have entertained only those sources which addressed Mark's version of the story. Hence, many "synoptic" treatments of the pericope are excluded; (b) *Importance,* as judged by the consensus of the scholarly community and the impact on later works; and, (c) *Representativeness* of respective periods, schools, or movements.

For Chapters Two through Six we engage in description and analysis. It is necessary first to describe as exactly as possible what an author has said. Secondly, it is necessary to offer some analysis of why he said this. For some authors this will be more obvious than for others, but we will begin by asking after his religious and theological background, who influenced him, what methodology he employed and why, and how and to what extent he reflects or contrasts his social and cultural environment.

For Chapters Seven and Eight we engage in prescription. We hope to offer some guidelines for using several modern methodologies simultaneously, but also incorporating some of the insights of history, thereby preventing the weaknesses of any one methodology used to exclusion.

We will not be so presumptuous as to suggest that ours is a definitive interpretation. But we do claim that, owing to the advantages of the historical survey approach, this study:

a) advances the discussion and understanding of Mark 14:54, 66-72;

b) has implications for the broader understanding of the theme of discipleship and of Mark's Gospel broadly;

c) underscores the importance of presuppositions in relation to methodology in biblical hermeneutics and urges that more attention be given to clarification and refinement of basic presuppositions in choosing and using a methodology.

Endnotes for Chapter One

[1]William L. Lane, "From Historian to Theologian: Milestones in Markan Scholarship," *RevExp* 75 (1978) 601-17; idem, "The Gospel of Mark in Current Study," *SWJT* 21 (1978) 7-21; Howard Clark Kee, "Mark as Redactor and Theologian: A Survey of Some Recent Markan Studies," *JBL* 90 (1971) 333-6; idem, "Mark's Gospel in Recent Research," *Int* 32 (1978) 353-68; J. D. Kingsbury, "The Gospel of Mark in Current Research," *RelSRev* 5 (1979) 101-7; R. S. Barbour, "Recent Study of the Gospel According to St. Mark," *ExpTim* 79 (1968) 324-329.

[2]The opinion of Mark as a mere "abbreviator" can be traced to Augustine (Philip Schaff, ed., *Saint Augustine*, NPNF 6 [Grand Rapids: Eerdmans, 1979] 78). That opinion began to change with Karl Lachmann's publication ("De Ordine narrationum in evangeliis synopticis," *TSK* VIII [1835] 570ff) demonstrating that Mark was independent of Matthew and Luke. C. H. Weisse *(Die evangelische Geschichte Kritisch und philosophisch bearbeitet* [2 vols.; Leipzig: Breitkopf & Härtel, 1838]) and H. J. Holtzmann *(Die Synoptischen Evangelium: Ihr Ursprung und geschichtlicher Charakter* [Leipzig: Breitkopf & Härtel, 1863]) mark the furthering of Lachmann's thesis and the solidifying of *the "Markan Hypothesis."* Mark came to be viewed as both the earliest and, for that reason, the most historically reliable account of the life of Jesus.

W. Wrede *(Das Messiasgeheimnis in den Evangelien* [Göttingen: Vandenhoeck & Ruprecht, 1901; 1963]; English tr. by J. C. G. Greig, *The Messianic Secret* [London: James Clarke, 1971]) and his theory of *the "messianic-secret"* marks the next dramatic turn. By asserting that Mark manipulated the material to present a non-messianic figure as the Messiah for ecclesiological reasons, he laid the groundwork "for a view of Mark as interpreter rather than as archivist or neutral reporter" (Kee, "Mark's Gospel in Recent Research," 353).

But cultivation of that ground fell to form criticism (M. Dibelius, *Die urchristliche Überlieferung von Johannes dem Täuer* [Tübingen: J. C. B. Mohr, 1911]; idem, *Die Formgeschichte des Evangeliums* [Tübingen: J. C. B. Mohr, 1919]; English tr. by B. L. Woolf, *From Tradition to Gospel* [New York: Charles Scribner's Sons, 1934]) and K. L. Schmidt in particular *(Der Rahmen der Geschichte Jesu* [Berlin: Trowitzsch, 1919; 1964]). Schmidt won the day with his opinion that Mark was a collection of individual stories which were "formed" in the period of oral transmission and whose placement in the Markan story was of secondary importance, if important at all (281). Schmidt's conclusion, literally the last sentence of his book, is that there is "kein Leben Jesu im Sinne einer sich entwickelnden Lebensgeschichte, keine chronologischen Aufriß der Geschichte Jesu, sondern nur Einzelgeschichten, Perikopen, die in ein Rahmenwerk gestellt sind" (317). The attempt to ascertain the *Sitz im Leben* of the Gospel tradition was furthered by E. Lohmeyer *(Galilaa und Jerusalem* [Göttingen: Vandenhoeck & Ruprecht, 1936]) and R. H. Lightfoot *(Locality and Doctrine* [London: Hodder & Stoughton, 1938]).

The next significant stage of development was that of redaction criticism (See G. Bornkamm, G. Barth, H. J. Held, *Tradition and Interpretation in Matthew* [Philadelphia: Westminster, 1963]; H. Conzelmann, *The Theology of St. Luke* [New York: Harper & Row, 1960]). Willi Marxsen (*Der Evangelist Markus Studien zur Redaktionsgeschichte des Evangeliums* [Göttingen: Vandenhoeck & Ruprecht, 1956]; Paginations taken from the English tr. by R. A. Harrisville, *Mark the Evangelist: Studies on the Redaction History of the Gospel* [Nashville: Abingdon, 1969]) was programmatic for the view of Mark as a creative theologian whose arrangement and manipulation of the stories were more important than the stories themselves, because "a literary work or fragment of tradition is a primary source for the historical situation out of which it arose, and is only a secondary source for the historical details concerning which it gives information" (*Ibid.*, 24, cited by Marxsen from R. Bultmann, "The New Approach to the Synoptic Problem," *JR* 6 [1926] 341).

[3]Of the issues dominating Markan studies since Marxsen, perhaps three stand out: christology, discipleship, and pursuit of the Gospel's *Sitz im Leben*, in that order. They are, of course, intricately related. The discussions of discipleship in Mark can be placed into four categories: messianic secret, a traditional-positive apostleship, theological polemic, and *typology per contrarium*.

According to F. J. Moloney, "All other discussions of Marcan discipleship begin with [Wrede's 'messianic secret']" ("Vocation of the Disciples in the Gospel of Mark, *Salesianum* 3 [1981] 490). The incomprehension of the disciples was for Wrede Mark's explanation of why Jesus was never confessed as Messiah during his lifetime. Wrede's explanation, as Ralph Martin summarizes (*Mark: Evangelist and Theologian* [Grand Rapids: Zondervan, 1972] 93) is different: "Jesus was never confessed as Messiah in his lifetime because he never was Messiah." Others who continue the discussion along the lines of the "messianic secret" are T. A. Burkill (*Mysterious Revelation* [New York: Cornell University Press, 1963]; idem, "The Hidden Son of Man in St. Mark's Gospel," *ZNW* 52 [1961] 189-213), G. Schmahl (*Die Zwölf in Markusevangelium* [Trier: Paulinus, 1974]; idem, "Die Berufung der Zwölf im Markusevangelium," *TTZ* 81 [1972] 203-13), and U. Luz ("Das Geheimnismotiv und die markinische Christologie," *ZNW* 56 [1965] 9-30).

There are a number of scholars who have seen in Mark's text evidence of a more *traditional apostleship*. In this view much of discipleship failure is rooted in the historical events, and the disciples are for Mark appropriate models for all future followers of Jesus. See the works of S. Freyne (*The Twelve: Disciples and Apostles. A Study in the Theology of the First Three Gospels* [London: Sheed & Ward, 1968]; idem, "At Cross Purposes: Jesus and the Disciples in Mark," *Furrow* 33 [1982] 331-9; idem, "The Disciples in Mark and the *maskilim* in Daniel," *BTB* 5 [1975] 67-77), J. Donaldson ("'Called to Follow'. A Twofold Experience of Discipleship in Mark," *BTB* 5 [1975] 67-77), and K. Stock (*Die Boten aus dem Mit-Ihm-Sein. Das Verhältnis zwischen Jesus und den Zwölf nach Markus*, AnBib 70 [Rome: Biblical Institute

Press, 1975]; idem, "Gliederung und Zusammenhang in Mk 11-12," *Bib* [1978] 481-515).

The line of interpretation which has probably received the most attention (both positively and negatively) is that which discerns in Mark's presentation of the disciples a polemic against a theology espoused by an alternative tradition within the community. Three key figures in this development are Alfred Kuby ("Zur Konzeption des Markus-Evangeliums," *ZNW* 49 [1958] 52-64), J. B. Tyson ("The Blindness of the Disciples in Mark," *JBL* 80 [1961] 261-8, see esp. 263 n. 6 for his acknowledged indebtedness to Kuby), and T. J. Weeden (*Mark—Traditions in Conflict* [Philadelphia: Fortress, 1971]) who on p. 25 credits Tyson with having "performed an invaluable service for Markan scholarship by...opening up a fresh, new way to view the Markan treatment of the disciples." W. Kelber (*The Kingdom in Mark. A New Place and A New Time* [Philadelphia: Fortress, 1974] xi) credits Weeden with having "brought the discipleship phenomenon in Mark into focus." Thus the beginning of this line of reasoning, so far as I can tell, is traceable to Kuby. For additional studies of this type see T. J. Weeden ("The Heresy that Necessitated Mark's Gospel," *ZNW* 59 [1968] 145-58), W. Kelber ("Mark 14:32-42: Gethsemane. Passion Christology and Discipleship Failure," *ZNW* 63 [1972] 166-87; idem, *The Oral and the Written Gospel. The Hermeneutics of Speaking and Writing in the Synoptic Tradition, Mark, Paul, and Q* [Philadelphia: Fortress, 1983]).

The fourth category consists of scholars who feel that although Mark presents the disciples in a negative manner, his motive is not polemical. *Typology per contrarium* is a term we have borrowed from D. J. Hawkin ("The Incomprehension of the Disciples in the Marcan Redaction," *JBL* 91 [1972] 491-500) to describe those views which to one degree or another view the negative portrayal of the disciples as a literary device by which the reader is given a negative example with which both to identify and improve on. Compare now the works of R. C. Tannehill ("The Disciples in Mark: The Function of a Narrative Role," *JR* 57 [1977] 386-405), E. Best (*Following Jesus: Discipleship in the Gospel of Mark* [Sheffield: JSOT, 1981] 14; idem, "Discipleship in Mark: Mark 8:22-10:52," *SJT* 23 [1970] 323-37; idem, "Mark 3:20, 21, 31-5," *NTS* 22 [1975-76] 309-19; idem, *Mark: The Gospel as Story* [Edinburgh: T & T Clark, 1983]; idem, "Mark's Use of the Twelve," *ZNW* 69 [1978] 11-35; idem, "Peter in the Gospel According to Mark," *CBQ* 40 [1978] 547-58; idem, "The Role of the Disciples;" idem, *The Temptation and the Passion*, SNTSMS 2 [Cambridge, 1965]), and Augustine Stock (*Call to Discipleship: A Literary Study of Mark's Gospel* [Wilmington, DL: Michael Glazier, 1982]; idem, "Literary Criticism and Mark's Mystery Play," *Bible Today* 100 [1979] 1909-15).

[4]Martin Hengel (*Studies in the Gospel of Mark* [SCM Press, 1985] 51; also 156, n. 75) says "this is an *inclusio*, through which the evangelist deliberately wants to stress this disciple in a quite special way."

[5]R. P. Meye (*Jesus and the Twelve: Discipleship and Revelation in Mark's Gospel* [Grand Rapids: Eerdmans, 1968] 228) thinks Mark equates the disciples and the Twelve. This is a disputed point. Hengel (*Studies*, 51) says: "As the spokesman of the Twelve Peter not only acknowledges the messiahship of Jesus but is also sharply rejected by him (8.29, 32f.); he is an embodiment of the disciples' lack of understanding and their failure."

[6]The "inner group" sometimes consists of Peter, James, and John (5:37) and sometimes these three plus Andrew (3:16-18; 13:3).

[7]Judas seems to be an exception. He is the only disciple depicted as Jesus' "enemy." As Dewey (Peter's Curse and Cursed Peter," in *The Passion in the Gospel of Mark* ed. by Werner Kelber [Philadelphia: Fortress, 1976] 108 n 39) notes, "Judas does not get the same kind of attention: being the last listed of the Twelve (3:19), he is forgotten until needed to identify Jesus (14:44-45) and then just as quickly is forgotten again (Mk must remind us that he is 'one of the Twelve,' 14:10, 20, 43)."

[8]T. E. Boomershine, *Mark, The Storyteller: A Rhetorical-Critical Investigation of Mark's Passion and Resurrection Narrative* (Ann Arbor, MI: University Microfilms, 1974) 138.

[9]Eric Auerbach, *Mimesis: The Representation of Reality in Western Literature*, tr. by W. R. Trask (Princeton: University Press, 1953) 45.

[10]Weeden, *Mark*, 54ff.

[11]*Ibid.*, 123.

[12]Günther Klein, "Die Verleugnung des Petrus. Eine traditionsgeschichtliche Untersuchung," *ZTK* 58 (1961) 285-328; idem, "Die Berufung des Petrus," *ZNW* 58 (1967) 1-44.

[13]D. Rhoads and D. Michie, *Mark as Story: An Introduction to the Narrative of a Gospel* (Philadelphia: Fortress, 1982) 123.

[14]J. Ernst, "Noch Einmal: Die Verleugnung Jesu Durch Petrus (Mk 14, 54.66-72)," *Catholica* 30 (1976) 207.

[15]W. Wink, *The Bible in Human Transformation* (Philadelphia: Fortress, 1973) 3.

[16]C.S. Lewis, *Surprised by Joy, The Shape of My Early Life* (New York: Harcourt, Brace & World, 1955) 207.

[17]*Ibid.*, 207-8.

[18]P. Henry, *New Directions in New Testament Studies* (Philadelphia: Westminster, 1979) 58.

[19]S. P. Kealy, C.S.Sp., "Reflections on the History of Mark's Gospel," *Proceedings: Eastern Great Lakes Biblical Society* (1982) 47-8; idem, *Mark's Gospel: A History of Interpretations* (New York: Paulist Press, 1982).

[20]Wink, *Bible in Human Transformation*, 2.

[21]Kealy, "Reflections," 48.

[22]Henry, *New Directions*, 59.

[23]Kealy, *Mark's Gospel*, 3.

Chapter 2

The Apostolic and Patristic Eras

Assimilation of Mark by Matthew and Luke[1]

Although the debate over the dates of the Synoptic Gospels is endless, one can say with reasonable certainty that the writers of the Gospels according to Matthew and Luke used the Gospel of Mark as their chief source before the end of the first century.[2]

The Gospel of Matthew.[3] In general Matthew represents a more Jewish presentation of the Gospel.[4] Scholars have long noted the five large didactic sections which would make the work useful as a church manual, but which also seem to parallel the five books of Moses.[5] Matthew goes to great lengths to show how Jesus' life and ministry fulfilled Old Testament prophecies. Matthew's Jesus issues a New Law which "fulfills" the Old Law of Moses (Chapters 5-7). Matthew incorporates almost all of Mark's Gospel but re-presents it along the lines indicated, frequently smoothing out possible misinterpretations.[6]

In recounting Mark's story of Peter's denial of Jesus,[7] Matthew retains the intercalation[8] of Jesus's trial by indicating that Peter followed Jesus into the courtyard (Mt. 26:58) but does not pick up the story until after Jesus' trial (Mt. 26:69-75). Interestingly enough, Matthew omits Mark's mention on both ends of the intercalation that Peter was "warming himself" (Mark 14:54; 67). Most scholars recognize this as a device of Mark's to remind the reader that he is picking up the story of the denial where it was left off, with Peter outside in the courtyard *while* Jesus' trial was taking place simultaneously.

Beyond this Matthew stipulates that it was "another maid" than the first who accosted Peter and elicited his second denial (26:71). He clarifies Mark's words as to how the guards knew Peter was a Galilean: "for your accent betrays you" (26:73). And he omits any mention of a second crowing of the cock. In Matthew's account "immediately the cock crowed" after Peter's third denial. Such is the strong evidence

13

that Mark's Gospel was the first work which possessed the kinds of awkward details Matthew would clarify.[9]

The Gospel of Luke.[10] The Gospel of Luke is the first part of a two-volume work, Luke-Acts.[11] In contrast to Matthew, Luke has a more universal appeal. It is the Gospel to the nations, and more than any other Gospel it highlights the plight of the poor, the Gentile, and women.[12] It is sometimes called the "Social Gospel."

In his incorporation of Peter's denial he chooses not to follow Mark in his intercalation. When he records that Peter followed Jesus into the courtyard (22:54-55), he continues on with the story of Peter unbroken (22:56-62) before recounting Jesus' trial (22:63-71). In Luke's story, the occasion for Peter's second denial was not the accusation of a maidservant (either the same or another), but of a man (22:58). He also omits Mark's mention of a second cock crowing, recording only one crowing after the third denial, "immediately, while he was still speaking" (22:60). At this point he adds a detail unique to himself, namely, that "the Lord turned and looked at Peter" (22:61).[13]

The significance of both the similarities and differences received debate very early on as our discussion of interpretations below indicates. Although the closing of the canon prohibited further reinterpretations such as Matthew's and Luke's, on the other hand "the process continued to this day in the biblical and theological interpretations and commentaries which have been produced without ceasing."[14]

Synoptic Parallel of the Account of Peter's Denial of Jesus. Following is a Synoptic parallel of Peter's Denial. Underlined words indicate significant deviations by Matthew and Luke from Mark's account. The text is that of the *Revised Standard Version.*

MATTHEW 26	MARK 14	LUKE 22
57) Then those who had seized Jesus led him to Caiaphas the high priest, where the scribes and the elders had assembled.	53) And they led Jesus to the high priest; and all the chief priests and the elders and the scribes were gathered.	54) Then they seized him and led him away, bringing him into the high priest's house.
58) But Peter followed him at a distance, as far as the courtyard of the high priest, and going inside he sat with the guards *to see the end.*	54) And Peter had followed him at a distance, right into the courtyard of the high priest; and he was sitting with the guards, *and warming himself at the fire.*	Peter followed at a distance; 55) and when they had kindled a fire in the middle of the courtyard and sat down together, Peter sat among them.

69) Now Peter was sitting outside in the courtyard. And a maid came up to him, and said,

"You also were with Jesus the Galilean." 70) But he denied it before them all, saying, "I do not know what you mean." 71) And when he went out to the porch, *another maid* saw him, and she said to the bystanders, "This man was with Jesus of Nazareth." 72) And again he denied it with an oath, "I do not know the man." 73) After a little while the bystanders came up and said to Peter, "Certainly you are also one of them, *for your accent betrays you.*" 74) Then he began to invoke a curse on himself and to swear, "I do not know the man."

And immediately the cock crowed.

66) And as Peter was below in the courtyard, one of the maids of the high priest came; 67) and seeing Peter warming himself, she looked at him, and said, "You also were with the Nazarene, Jesus." 68) But he denied it, saying, "I neither know nor understand what you mean." And he went out into the gateway. 69) And *the maid* saw him, and began again to say to the bystanders, "This man is one of them." 70) But again he denied it.

And after a little while again the bystanders said to Peter, "Certainly you are one of them; for you are a Galilean." 71) But he began to invoke a curse on himself and to swear, "I do not know this man of whom you speak." 72) *And immediately the cock crowed a second time.*

56) Then a maid, seeing him as he sat in the light and gazing at him, said,

"This man also was with him." 57) But he denied it, saying, "Woman, I do not know him."

58) And a little later *some one else* saw him and said, "You also are one of them."

But Peter said, *"Man, I am not."*

59) And after an interval of about an hour still another insisted, saying, "Certainly this man also was with him; for he is a Galilean." 60) But Peter said, "Man, I do not know what you are saying." *And immediately,* while he was still speaking, *the cock crowed.* 61) *And the Lord turned and looked at Peter.*

75) And Peter remembered the saying of Jesus, "Before the cock crows, you will deny me three times." And he went out and wept bitterly.	And Peter remembered how Jesus had said to him, "Before the cock crows *twice,* you will deny me three times." And he broke down and wept.	And Peter remembered the word of the Lord, how he had said to him, "Before the cock crows today, you will deny me three times." 62) And he went out and wept bitterly.

Tradition of Mark's Dependence on Peter

The earliest form of the tradition about Mark's dependence on Peter is found in the well-known Papias fragment recorded by Eusebius:

> The Elder [John] said this also; Mark who had been Peter's interpreter, wrote down carefully as much as he remembered, recording both sayings and doings of Christ, not however in order. For he was not a hearer of the Lord, nor a follower, but later a follower of Peter, as I said. And he [Peter] adapted his teachings to the needs of his hearers as one who is engaged in making a compendium of the Lord's precepts.[15]

As one scholar points out, apart from Matthew's and Luke's use of Mark, Papias' statement "is, in fact, the first certain evidence of anyone even knowing about this gospel."[16] It was known and read, however. And how important it was to the growing church is indicated by the growing traditions about Mark's Gospel.

That Papias says Mark wrote down what Peter "remembered" indicates that Mark may have written the Gospel after Peter's death. That is specifically stated in the Anti-Marcionite Prologue[17] and Irenaeus.[18] A later tradition in Clement says that Peter was alive at its writing, but indifferent about the project.[19] Later Eusebius retells Clement's version to the effect that Peter endorsed the project.[20] Finally, Origen indicates that Peter actually commissioned the writing.[21]

Clearly the tradition was embellished. As written accounts became ever more precious to the Christian community, it became more important to validate a writing. This validation in Mark's case took the form of accounting for his Gospel as not an incidental endeavor, but an apostolic project. Peter's hand gets ever heavier because of the importance of the apostolic witness.

Even granting the embellishment of the tradition, it remains the case that the kernel of the tradition has much to commend it. Papias is probably fewer than fifty years removed from Mark's writing, and his source, the "elder," is earlier still. Moreover, as Martin Hengel notes, the Papias tradition "represents the markedly *critical comments* of an author who rated oral traditions even higher than written works. The connection between Peter and Mark, which in fact goes back to the first century and is attested independently of the presbyter in I Peter 5:13, cannot be a later invention in order to secure 'apostolic' authority for the Gospel."[22]

To this may be added the observation that many of the details in Mark are told from Peter's perspective, and Peter figures as an important historical character in the account in numerous ways—things which almost every modern commentator underscores. The tradition of Mark's dependence on Peter has fallen into disfavor in recent years.[23] But the evidence has not changed, only the interpretation of the evidence. Nevertheless, our study does not necessitate a final decision on Markan authorship.

As pervasive as the tradition was in the Patristic era, it is astonishing that so little was written on Mark's Gospel. Although Origen is said to have written a commentary on every book of the Bible, no extant commentary can be found on Mark.[24] The pericope of the denial is not recorded in the Gospel of Peter, nor in any of the Nag Hammadi documents.[25] Apart from its inclusion in Tatian's *Diatesseron*, which provides no significant treatment,[26] it was the fifth century before a commentary on Mark was written. The pericope of the denial from Mark's perspective is treated here for the first time.

Victor of Antioch

Authorship. Although this commentary is attributed to Cyril of Alexandria in some extant texts, in far more is it attributed to Victor, Bishop of Antioch. Many scholars seem satisfied with that affixation. But even if that could be determined more accurately, it actually tells us only a little more about the author, since almost nothing is known of Victor himself.[27] Several catenae on Luke have passages taken apparently from a now lost commentary of his on that Gospel.[28] But it is his own extant commentary on Mark for which he is remembered, for it was apparently the first on Mark's Gospel.[29]

Victor's work is usually called a catena,[30] and there is some justification for this, though the manner in which he uses his sources leaves this open to interpretation. Not only was this a popular, perhaps even standard genre of antiquity, but Victor himself states his method in the foreword (*hupothesis*), namely to collect the comments of others on the Gospels of Matthew, Luke, and John which he regarded pertinent to Mark:

> Many have put together reflections on the [Gospel] according to Matthew and on the [Gospel] according to John the son of thunder, and a few [have done so] on the [Gospel] according to Luke; but [since] absolutely no one, to my knowledge, has expounded on the [Gospel] according to Mark (at least I have heard of nothing to the present, having been busily making a diligent gathering of works) I have sought the occasional and scattered sayings of the teachers of the Church, to collect them and construct a concise commentary.[31]

Harold Smith has identified over ten of Victor's sources.[32] Infrequently the author will identify his source, including Origen, Eusebius, Titus, Apollinarius, Chrysostom, and Theodore of Mopsuestia.[33] But more often, as in our passage, a source is identified by no more than "but he says" (*ho men phesi*) or "but another says" (*allos de phesi*), perhaps thereby conforming to some literary custom. Victor never identifies Cyril of Alexandria as one of his sources, though he cites him frequently, especially in our passage. This may partially account for the attribution of the work to Cyril.

At any rate, "ideas concerning authorship differed entirely from those of modern times; especially when Holy Scripture was to be commented on."[34] This will perhaps also account for the fact that Victor, though infrequently taking the trouble to acknowledge when "another says" (*allos phesi*), will more frequently *not* do so, or if he does, go on to delete what he judges inappropriate, add the words of yet another Father, or continue at length with his own contribution. Burgon describes his method:

> His general practice is slightly to adapt his Author's language to his own purpose; sometimes, to leave out a few words; a paragraph; half a page. Then, he proceeds to quote another Father probably; or, it may be, to offer something of his own. But he seldom gives any intimation of what it is he does.[35]

Victor's two chief sources for his commentary on "Peter's Denial" are Chrysostom and Cyril of Alexandria. In comparing Victor's rendition to his sources[36] it is clear that although a catena reads awkwardly to a modern, Victor is wearing no straightjacket. If the Synoptics afford any comparison at all, Victor goes to more trouble to indicate when he is relying on someone at all, then takes greater liberty to embellish or otherwise improve those comments for his own purpose. Thus, the two most prominent works on Victor to our knowledge also agree that "the writer is not a catenist in the ordinary sense."[37] More pointedly, "the author of a compilation is an Author still."[38] It is possible to detect a flavor, even a "theology," from Victor's work. Thus while it is possible to identify his sources and compare his work to them, they cannot be equated; it can be said of Victor that the whole is more than the sum of its parts.

Transmission of the Text. It should perhaps be pointed out briefly that the question of Victor's use of his sources is not nearly so perplexing as the work of his copyists. There exist four published editions of Victor's work: (1) a 1580 Latin version by Theodore Peltanus; (2) a 1673 Greek text by Peter Possinus (though Victor's commentary in this edition is woven together with two additional anonymous commentaries in an attempt to produce one work); (3) a 1775 Greek text by C. F. Matthaei based on certain manuscripts apparently to be found only in Moscow; (4) an 1840 Greek text by J. A. Cramer, who published eight volumes of catenae on the New Testament, volume one of which includes Victor's commentary uninterrupted by any other source.[39] There is a wide variation in the editions, notes Burgon, not so much in respect of various readings, or serious modifications of his text; (though the transpositions are very frequent, and often very mischievous;) as resulting from the boundless license which every fresh copyist seems to have allowed himself chiefly in *abridging* his author.— To skip a few lines: to omit an explanatory paragraph, quotation, or digression: to pass *per saltum* from the beginning to the end of a passage: sometimes to leave out a whole page: to transpose: to paraphrase: to begin or to end with quite a different form of words;—proves to have been the rule.[40]

Fortunately Cramer's edition is regarded as "by far the fullest and most satisfactory exhibition of the Commentary of Victor of Antioch which has hitherto appeared."[41] We have adopted his text. As regards authorship and text, therefore, it will take us far afield to do any more than recognize the difficulties and then treat the text as though it possessed at least a modicum of authorial and textual authenticity.

Date, Purpose, and Place in History. There is little evidence to help one fix a date of composition with accuracy. Burgon's argument from the dates of known sources seems as reasonable as any, namely that

...since Chrysostom, (whom Victor speaks of as [*ho en hagiois*], [p. 408] and [*ho markarios*], [p. 442]) died in A.D. 407, it *cannot* be right to quote '401' as the date of Victor's work. Rather would A.D. 450 be a more reasonable suggestion: seeing that extracts from Cyril, who lived on till A.D. 444, are found here and there in Victor's pages. We shall not perhaps materially err if we assign A.D. 430-450 as Victor of Antioch's approximate date.[42]

The purpose for the writing seems forthright enough. Victor, having found no singular exposition on the Gospel of Mark, determined to construct one following the method stated in his "foreword" (*hupothesis*, the translation of the pertinent section of which is found above). The curiousness of the intense interest on Mark and especially his association with Peter coupled with the total lack of actual interaction with his work has been noted. Why he should have been so neglected is unexplainable, unless Augustine's sentiments about Mark's offering so little unique from Matthew and Luke had actually been held for some time, perhaps even unconsciously.

The location of the writing may very well have been Antioch, as the analysis of the commentary's character below will demonstrate. And Antioch herself influenced Christendom beginning with the first generation of believers, being famous for launching and supporting Paul on his missionary journeys and for bestowing on the "Christians" their (undoubtedly derisive) appellation (Acts 11:26). During this era Antioch ranked third behind Rome and Alexandria in size and importance. Among her notable bishops are Peter (which tradition is unproved) and Ignatius.[43]

After the fifth century Antioch began to decline in importance and influence. In addition to finding itself in opposition to a strict Nicean theology, the tradition there had other theological tendencies which belabored Trinitarian and incarnational terminology and often produced scholars and ideas which the church eventually defined as heretical. But the fourth and fifth centuries were Antioch's heyday, and up until then she enjoyed extraordinary prestige.[44] It is not surprising then that, although not altogether judged orthodox, works emanating from there also met with great success. According to Burgon, Victor's commentary is one example.

> ...it can scarcely require to be pointed out that Victor's Commentary,—of which the Church in her palmiest days shewed herself so careful to multiply copies, and of which there survive to this hour such a vast number of specimens,—must needs anciently have enjoyed very peculiar favour. It is evident, in fact, that an Epitome of Chrysostom's Homilies on S. Matthew, together with *Victor's compilation on S. Mark,*—Titus of Bostra on S. Luke,—and a work in the main derived from Chrysostom's Homilies on S. John;—that these four constituted the established Commentary of ancient Christendom on the fourfold Gospel.[45]

Antiochene Theology and Victor's Commentary

Antiochene and Alexandrian Hermeneutics. The Church at Antioch, as has been noted, exhibited considerable influence on early Christianity. A theological seminary of sorts was founded there about the late third and fourth centuries.[46] It spawned several schools of like kind throughout Syria. In fact, the term "school of Antioch" is frequently used to describe the theological tendencies of the Church in Syria, which tendencies seem largely explainable by a strong Jewish heritage which was so cautious in describing the Person of Jesus that its view of the Trinity is associated with Sabellianism and its view of Christ with Nestorianism.[47]

As a "school of thought," however, it is inevitably contrasted with Alexandria, especially as regards its hermeneutical approach. "Its tendency was Aristotelian and historical, in contrast with the more Platonic and mystical tradition characteristic of Egypt."[48] Again, influenced largely by Judaism,[49] "Antiochene exegesis of Scripture was historical, and unlike Alexandrian, looked not for a hidden meaning in the text, but for the sense intended by the inspired writer."[50]

The "School of Alexandria," of course, harks back to Philo of Alexandria and his principles of allegorization, who in turn strongly influenced Clement of Alexandria. But "only in the time of Origen does the school emerge into the clear light of historical knowledge...and it is he who sets forth most thoroughly and adequately the principles of Christian allegorization."[51] For example, the Septuagint version of Proverbs 22:20 reads:

> Do thou portray them *threefold* in counsel and knowledge, that thou mayst answer words of truth to those who question thee.[52]

Interpreting this in light of Paul's trichotic description of man in 1 Thessalonians 5:23, Origen concluded that Scripture, too, had a trichotic structure. The "body, soul, and spirit" of a man correspond respectively to the literal, moral, and allegorical-mystical senses of Scripture. But Origen almost never makes use of the "moral" sense. And the "literal" or "historical" sense only served as a vehicle for the "allegorical" meaning which Origen wanted to see. Why could the literal meaning not be trusted? Because...

> wherever in the narrative the accomplishment of some particular deeds, which had been previously recorded for the sake of their more mystical meanings, did not correspond with the sequence of the intellectual truths, the scripture wove into the story something which did not happen, occasionally something which could not happen, and occasionally something which might have happened but in fact did not.[53]

Discrepancies Between Accounts. Thus, in his Commentary on John, Origen states that the discrepancies between the Gospels are further evidence that an historical exegesis is impossible.[54] One is left with choosing one testimony against the others arbitrarily, or to affirm that the truth to be gleaned is not in the literal interpretation.

In contrast, Victor frequently attempts to reconcile apparent discrepancies, as in the case of the cock-crow.

> And the Evangelist says, that when he denied once, the cock crowed, but when he denied a third time, then [the cock crowed] a second time, describing more exactly the weakness of the disciple, and [that] he was utterly dead with fear. He had learned these things from his teacher. For he was a disciple of Peter. Thus that which is in Matthew and Mark [is] in harmony; even if it appears to be contradictory. For since at each [series of] "crowing" the cock was accustomed to crow both a third and fourth time, Mark makes clear that the sound neither gripped [him] nor led him to remembrance. So that both are true. For before the cock had completed the first crowing, he denied a third time. And not even when reminded of the sin by Christ did he dare to weep openly. But another says, "Matthew says simply and indefinitely 'before the cock crows,' [while] Mark in customary fashion added that which was omitted saying the prevailing sound of the cock [was heard] by all just as also the broad day [is] clear to all." Therefore, he says, the Evangelist interpreted the [words]: "before the cock-crow," specifying the second and making it clearer to all, not contradicting the others.[55]

The following should be noted: (1) Although Victor does not clearly indicate it, approximately 80% of this material is taken from Chrysostom.[56] In doing so he indicates that that which troubled Chrysostom also presented itself as a difficulty to him. Moreover, Victor found Chrysostom's answer satisfactory. They share the

Antiochene "school of thought." (2) Victor is evidence of how thoroughly held was the tradition that Mark was Peter's "disciple." (3) The ancients took note of one of Mark's "characteristics," namely, that his accounts are frequently rendered more fully and in greater detail than are Matthew's.

Allegory. Origen wrote no commentary on Mark that we know of, but in his Commentary on Matthew he expounds on Peter's Denial in a manner consistent with the principles described above. Origen does not dwell on the "historical" event of the denial. He rather reads with an eye toward discerning the "spiritual" meaning. Thus, Caiaphas "is the word of Jewish service."[57] And the court of Caiaphas the High Priest represents "all teaching contrary to Jesus." Thus,

> whoever is in the court of Caiaphas the High Priest cannot confess Jesus as Lord, unless he shall have gone out from his court, and have come outside of all teaching contrary to Jesus.[58]

Likewise, the night and the darkness represent a spiritual blindness of sorts, and the cock-crow represents a "messenger" of spiritual awakening.

> Fully considering Peter's denial, we say that "No one can call Jesus Lord, except in the Holy Ghost," and "the Holy Ghost was not yet" in men "because Jesus was not yet glorified." Therefore it was not possible either for Peter being as he was then to confess Jesus; nor yet was he to be blamed for not confessing Jesus...[59]

Therefore, although Peter's "historical" action is described, the principal thing is the "spiritual" significance. All the physical circumstances are allegorized and brought to bear in explaining Peter's actions:

> For consider that Peter sitting without, separated from Jesus and in the court of the High Priest, denied Jesus before all, and again a second time likewise he denied, not having gone *outside the door,* but wanting to go out, yet not having yet gone out. But also the third time, when those who stood by said, "Truly thou art one of them" and he began to call a curse on himself and swear "I know not the man," he was still not *outside.* And all his denials were made *in the night and in the darkness,* before the *coming of day and the sign of day,* the cock-crow, which rouses those who are willing from their *sleep.*[60]

Origen is known for his tendency to "universalism."[61] That tendency surfaces here. In making a pastoral application of this passage Origen compares the denials of other men to Peter's denial:

> Perhaps also all men when they deny Jesus in such a way that the sin of their denial may admit of healing, appear to deny Him before cock-crow, the Sun of righteousness not having been born to them nor drawing nigh in His rising.[62]

Thus, Origen concludes,

> So long as the signal of day was not, Peter in denying did not remember Jesus' words. But after the messenger of day called to him, then he remembered the word of Jesus who said to him, "Before the cock crow, thou shalt deny Me thrice." When he remembered Christ's word he was no longer in the court of the High Priest, nor beside his door, but outside; otherwise he would not have wept.[63]

Again, in contrast Victor reads the passage with an historical eye. He describes Peter's entrance into the court with a flare for detail, even if that detail must be gotten outside of Mark.

> Peter's fervor [was] great; not even after seeing the others fleeing did he flee; but he stood [his ground?] and entered; and John was [there], too, since he was known [to the high priest?].[64]

He describes the procedures of the Sanhedrin as "only an appearance of a court of justice." The chief priest, for example,

> does not cast the vote himself, but demands [it] from them, as though upon confessed sins and manifest blasphemy, and he anticipates the hearers saying, "For you yourselves heard the blasphemy," not only forcing and negatively influencing, but furthermore constraining those present to produce a vote against him as speaking blasphemy and making himself God.[65]

According to Victor, the chief priest had to stoop to theatrics: "He led them all on by rending his vestments. For it was a custom for them to do this, when they heard something which they deemed as blasphemies."[66]

Of particular interest is a comparison of Origen's method of interpreting the maid and others who confront Peter with Victor's method. Says Origen:

> I think the first maid of the High Priest, who makes Christ's disciples to deny, is the synagogue of the Jews according to the flesh, who have often compelled believers to deny; the second maid is the assembly of the Gentiles, who also were persecuting Christians and forcing them to deny; the third group, those standing in the court, are the ministers of various heresies, who also compel to deny Christ's truth.[67]

Victor engages in no such allegorization. In fact, he feels obligated to address the "historical" discrepancy, and that in Antiochene fashion:

> The blessed Peter was weak according to the prediction, and denied the Savior and Lord of all, and not once, but three times, and he made the denial confirmed by an oath on account of a word of a servant girl, and forgetting [i.e., not remembering] by reason of all the confusion the word of the Lord:

"He who denies me before men, I will deny him before my Father." For behold, he had denied before all; and again, whether this [same] servant girl, as Mark says, or whether another, as Matthew says, she discloses that he might be one of the disciples, for he did not ascertain this exactly by the recollection of Scriptures, since it was not necessary for saving faith; [especially] When Luke says that it was not a servant girl, but a man [who] emphatically asserts, that he was also with Jesus. Indeed, while such [information] is not essential [for salvation], it agrees with what has been previously stated, that Peter denied a second time with an oath not to have known the man.[68]

One sees here the tendency to "literalism." The "maidservants" do not represent anything other than themselves. But "whether it was the same maidservant as Mark says or another as Matthew says," is not a matter to quibble over. Indeed, the "School of Antioch" was known for discriminating between the more and less inspired parts of Scripture.[69] One Antiochene, Junilius, "sets up three classes of books, those of perfect authority, those of moderate authority, and those of none."[70] Is not Victor here making such a discrimination? He recognizes the historical discrepancy but refuses to allegorize it. He relegates it to that which is "not crucial to saving faith."

Pastoral Emphasis. The absence of an Alexandrian allegorical approach does not mean Victor cannot see "types" and make pastoral applications. Peter becomes a "type" of Christians who fall and are restored. Restoration is indicated chiefly in that "Peter wept bitterly, as Christ gave heed to him; therefore having turned he did not miss the mark, for he had remained, indeed was, a genuine disciple."[71] But it seems that both the restoration and Peter's inclination to repentance is predicated upon his participation in the sacrament: "before Christ was seized and Peter denied, he was a partaker of the body of Christ and of his precious blood, and thusly fell, and obtained the forgiveness of repentance."[72] Somehow participation in the sacrament afforded a security from forfeiture of one's salvation. Repentance was the "medicine of salvation" for the healing of spiritual wounds.[73]

Victor seems to dwell on this point in order to counter the influence of "the pure ones." Were it not for Theophylact it might be difficult to identify this group. But insofar as Theophylact follows Victor very closely, often word for word, we can with some degree of confidence trust Theophylact when he alludes to the "Novatianists."[74] From Victor's point of view, they merited a poignant attack regarding the nature of postconversion sins and repentance:

For the compassionate God has provided repentance as a medicine of salvation, which the pure ones endeavor to dispense with saying themselves to be pure; not considering that everyone who has such [ideas?] in himself is full of iniquity. For no one is pure from iniquity, as it is written. Furthermore, let them not be ignorant: that before Christ was seized and Peter denied, he was a partner of the body of Christ and of his precious blood, and thusly fell, and obtained the forgiveness of repentance. Therefore let them not accuse the gentleness of God, [but] be reminded by the one who clearly says, "the lawlessness of the transgressor shall in no way cause him harm, in the day in which he shall turn from his lawlessness."[75]

The reader may justly conclude that he, too, should not "accuse the gentleness of God." Indeed, the flavor of Victor's entire treatment of Peter's denial is that while some discrepancies in the accounts can be accounted for, they are largely "not necessary for saving faith." The crucial thing is that "we learn of the failures of the saints through the Scriptures, in order that we should be imitators of their repentance. For the compassionate God has provided repentance as a medicine of salvation."[76]

Summary

In his monograph *The Historical-Critical Method,* Edgar Krentz says, "The attempt of the school of Antioch to use only the historical-grammatical sense failed."[77] This judgment stands in stark contrast to the opinion of Robert M. Grant in *A Short History of the Interpretation of the Bible,* which is that "...in the long run the literal historical method [of Antioch] became the principal exegetical method of the Christian Church."[78] Neither is entirely correct, nor entirely wrong.

The history of Christian exegesis in the premodern era, especially in the West, was clearly dominated by a search for the spiritual sense, usually in support of dogma. The rest of our survey to follow is evidence of this. But this spiritual sense so characteristic of premodern exegesis was vaguer than usually portrayed, nor did it so completely rule out the concern for history that Krentz could justifiably characterize the results of the premodern effort as "the casual and almost accidental critical judgments in the premodern phase of biblical studies."[79]

Victor's commentary and the entire "Antiochene Method" were very influential on Biblical exegesis, especially in the East, but apparently also on the Reformation. A comparison of Theophylact's commentary (Appendix E) demonstrates a strong dependency on Victor (Appendix A), frequently citing the ideas in Victor, infrequently the very words. They agree that the discrepancy between Matthew, Mark, and Luke regarding Peter's second accoster is irrelevant. Furthering Victor's argument, Theophylact says, "Do they not agree in the significant and essential (thing) of our salvation? Did one say that the Lord was crucified, but another, [that he was] not?"

Theophylact also agrees hardily with Victor's theory about the cock-crow consisting of several crowings, "thereupon to fall into a kind of sleep, and again after some time to begin another 'crowing.'" And finally, Theophylact identifies the "pure ones" whom Victor so harshly criticized. They are the Novatianists, who "should be ashamed for refusing to receive [back into fellowship] those who sinned with the baptism and the partaking of the mysteries." Victor's "sacramental theology" is here echoed by Theophylact. Partaking of the body and blood provides a security against the forfeiture of one's salvation.

In general Victor's commentary tended to be more popular in the East, although Kealy has demonstrated the influence of Victor's commentary in so broad a cross section as Gregory the Great, Bede, Euthymius, and others.[80] And a perusal of John Calvin's commentary on this passage (Appendix G) justifies a strong suspicion that he knew Victor and the Antiochene school. Victor was frequently cited by the exegetes of a generation or two ago, those who felt an obligation to touch base with history.[81]

Neither Victor nor the Antiochene method can fairly be compared to the modern historical approach. But, as our analysis of Victor shows, neither can premodern be equated with precritical. Clearly an entirely different presuppositional framework determines how the questions are put and the answers evaluated. But Victor is a representative figure in the history of interpretation, one that is concerned with the intent of the author, the parameters of logic, and the hand of a providential God in history.

Endnotes for Chapter Two

[1]This section addresses the "assimilation" of Mark by Matthew and Luke, not their "interpretation" of him or the full theological implications of their use of him. The reasons are three: (1) To have done otherwise would have shifted the focus away from Mark to the theological emphases of Matthew and Luke; (2) This study attempts to be a "history" of interpretation, and to focus on Matthew's and Luke's use of Mark would seem to necessitate opening up the "biblical" discussion of the Synoptic problem and the theologies of the respective gospels; (3) Most of the more obvious discrepancies and contrasts are addressed by the fathers. They and their comments on Mark's account were more germane to our study than the Synoptic accounts per se.

[2]We are assuming Markan priority. A standard treatment of the evidence for the priority of Mark is presented by B. H. Streeter (*The Four Gospels* [London, 1953] 151-98) and D. Guthrie (*New Testament Introduction* [Downers Grove: IVP, 1970] 121-88). The exceptions to this widely held thesis are best represented by W. R. Farmer (*The Synoptic Problem* [New York, 1964]), who argues for Matthean priority, and R. L. Lindsey ("A Modified Two-Source Document Theory of the Synoptic Dependence and Interdependence," *NovT* 6 [1962] 239-63), who argues for Lukan priority. More recently H. Stoldt (*History and Criticism of the Marcan Hypothesis* [Edinburgh: T & T Clark, 1980]) presents a case against Markan priority, and Martin Hengel (*Studies in the Gospel of Mark* [London: SCM Press, 1985]) presents the most persuasive argument to date for the traditional view that Mark was based on Petrine testimony.

[3]Major studies discussing the purpose, destination, and place of origin for Matthew are G. D. Kilpatrick, *The Origins of the Gospel According to St. Matthew* (Oxford: Clarendon: 1946); Krister Stendahl, *The School of St. Matthew and Its Use of the Old Testament* (Philadelphia: Fortress, 1954); Robert H. Gundry, *Matthew: A Commentary on his Literary and Theological Art* (Grand Rapids: Eerdmans, 1982).

[4]B. F. Westcott, *Introduction to the Study of the Gospels* (Boston: Gould & Lincoln, 1888); N. Hillyer, "Matthew's Use of the Old Testament," *EvQ* 36 (1964) 12-26; Robert H. Gundry, *The Use of the Old Testament in St. Matthew's Gospel, with Special Reference to the Messianic Hope* (Leiden: E. J. Brill, 1967).

[5]G. D. Kilpatrick, *Origins*, 136; R. H. Fuller, *A Critical Introduction to the New Testament* (London: Duckworth, 1966) 117.

[6]Vincent Taylor, The Gospels (London: Epworth, 1945) 81; R. H. Gundry, *Use of the Old Testament*, 184; Will Marxsen, *Introduction to the New Testament* (Philadelphia: Fortress, 1968) 153.

[7]See the parallel just below on page 14.

[8]For a discussion of the literary device of intercalation see David Rhoads and Donald Michie, *Mark as Story* (Philadelphia: Fortress Press, 1982) 51.

[9]For studies on Matthew's denial pericope see G. Murray, "Saint Peter's Denials," *DRev* 103 (1985) 296-8; Raymond E. Brown, "The Passion According to Matthew," *Worship* 58 (1984) 98-107; and, Birger Gerhardsson, "Confession and Denial before Men: Observations on Matt. 26:57-27:2," *JSNT* 13 (1981) 46-66.

[10]H. J. Cadbury, *The Making of Luke-Acts* (London: S.P.C.K., 1958); N. B. Stonehouse, *The Witness of Luke to Christ* (Grand Rapids: Eerdmans, 1951); H. Conzelmann, *The Theology of St. Luke* (New York: Harper, 1960); Norval Geldenhuys, *Commentary on the Gospel of Luke* (Grand Rapids: Eerdmans, 1975).

[11]F. F. Bruce, *The Acts of the Apostles* (Grand Rapids: Eerdmans, 1952) 2;

[12]Donald Guthrie, *New Testament Introduction* (Downers Grove: IVP, 1970) 90-2.

[13]For studies on Luke's denial pericope see M. L. Soards, "'And the Lord Turned and Looked Straight at Peter': Understanding Luke 22,61," *Bib* 67 (1986) 518-9; Raymond E. Brown, "The Passion According to Luke," *Worship* 60 (1986) 2-9; E. LaVerdiere, "The Passion-Resurrection of Jesus according to St. Luke," *Chicago Studies* 25 (1986) 35-50; R. Michiels, "Het passieverhaal volgens Lucas" [The Passion Narrative according to Luke] *Collationes* 30 (1984) 191-210.

[14]Sean P. Kealy, *Mark's Gospel: A History of its Interpretation* (New York: Paulist Press, 1982) 11.

[15]The passage is taken from Eusebius' *Ecclesiastical History,* III, 39, 15. The original text may be found in Kurt Aland, ed., *Synopsis Quattuor Evangeliorum* (Stuttgart: Württemburgische Bibelanstalt, 1964) 531. The translation we have used is that of H. E. W. Turner, "The Tradition of Mark's Dependence upon Peter," *ExpT* 71 (1960) 260.

[16]E. R. Kalin, "Early Traditions About Mark's Gospel: Canonical Status Emerges, the Story Grows," *CurTM* 2 (1975) 332.

[17]The so-called Anti-Marcionite Prologue reads: "...Mark declared, who is called 'stumpy-fingered,' since he had short fingers in proportion to the rest of his body. He was Peter's interpreter. After Peter's death he wrote this gospel in Italy." The original text may be found in Aland, *Synopsis,* 532. This translation is that of Kalin, "Early Traditions," 333.

[18]The Irenaeus passage, *Against Heresies,* is found in Eusebius, *Ecclesiastical History,* V, 8, 2, and reads: "Matthew also produced a written version of the gospel [in addition to the apostolic *preaching* Irenaeus had just discussed], written among the Hebrews in their own language [i.e., Aramaic], while Peter and Paul were preaching in Rome and establishing the congregation there. After their death Mark, Peter's disciple and interpreter, delivered to us in writing the things Peter had preached [the section goes on to speak of Luke and John]." The original text may be found in Aland, *Synopsis,* 533. This translation is that of Kalin, "Early Traditions," 334.

[19]The Clement passage, *Hypotyposes*, Book 6, is found in Eusebius, *Ecclesiastical History*, VI, 14, 6, and reads: "When Peter had preached the word publicly in Rome and by the Spirit proclaimed the gospel, the large crowd in attendance urged Mark, inasmuch as he had followed him for a long time and remembered his words, to write down what he had said. And when he had finished he gave the gospel to those who had made the request. When Peter learned of it he neither hindered nor promoted it." The original text may be found in Aland, *Synopsis*, 539. This translation is that of Kalin, "Early Traditions," 335.

[20]Eusebius, *Ecclesiastical History*, II, 15, 1: "The light of piety shone so brightly on the minds of Peter's hearers that they were not content with a single hearing or with an oral presentation of the divine message. With every imaginable exhortation they kept on asking Mark (whose gospel we have), since he was Peter's follower, to leave them a written record of the teaching they had received orally, and they didn't give up until they had prevailed upon him. This is the reason for the writing of the scripture known as the Gospel According to Mark. And they say the when what had happened became known to the apostle by revelation of the Spirit, he was pleased with the zeal of the men and he approved the scripture for reading in the churches." The original text may be found in Aland, *Synopsis,* 539. This translation is that of Kalin, "Early Traditions," 336.

[21]The Origen passage, *Commentary on Matthew*, Book 1, is found in Eusebius, *Ecclesiastical History*, VI, 25, 4: "As we learn in the tradition concerning the four gospels which are indisputable in the church of God under heaven, the first one written was the gospel according to Matthew....The second was the gospel according to Mark, who wrote as Peter instructed him...." The original text may be found in Aland, *Synopsis*, 540. This translation is that of Kalin, "Early Traditions," 337.

[22]Hengel, *Studies,* 47.

[23]See, e.g., Ralph P. Martin, *Mark: Evangelist and Theologian* (Grand Rapids: Zondervan, 1972) 11-16.

[24]Kealy, *Mark's Gospel*, 21.

[25]A translation of the Gospel of Peter may be found in Edgar Hennecke, ed., *New Testament Apocrypha*, 2 vols. (Philadelphia: Westminster, 1963) 179-87; and also, Montague Rhodes James, ed. & tr., *Apocryphal New Testament* (Oxford: Clarendon Press, 1975) 90-4. Cf. also James M. Robinson, ed., *The Nag Hammadi Library* (San Francisco: Harper & Row, 1977).

[26]On the Diatesseron see Samuel Hemphill, *The Diatessaron of Tatian* (London: Hodder & Stoughton, 1888) 45-6; Smith, *DCB* IV:794-804; Carl H. Kraeling, *A Greek Fragment of Tatian's Diatessaron From Dura* (London: Christophers, 1935).

[27]Victor is not acknowledged at all in the following recognized authorities on Antioch: Virginia Corwin, *St. Ignatius and Christianity in Antioch* (New Haven: Yale University Press, 1960); Glanville Downey, *A History of Antioch in Syria from*

Seleucus to the Arab Conquest (Princeton: Princeton University Press, 1961); John Mason Neale, gen. ed., *A History of the Holy Eastern Church*, vol. 5: *The Patriarchate of Antioch* (New York: AMS Press, 1976). John W. Burgon (*The Last Twelve Verses of the Gospel According to S. Mark* [Oxford and London: James Parker and Co., 1871] 59-60) says of Victor that there is...

> scarcely a Commentator of antiquity about whom less is known. Clinton (who enumerates cccxxii "Ecclesiastical Authors" from A.D. 70 to A.D. 685) does not even record his name. The recent "Dictionary of Greek and Roman Biography" is just as silent concerning him. Cramer (his latest edition) calls his very existence in question; proposing to attribute his Commentary on S. Mark to Cyril of Alexandria. Not to delay the reader needlessly,—Victor of Antioch is an interesting and unjustly neglected Father of the Church.

But Burgon quotes no authority for his assertion. It may be that he became the unsurpassed authority on Victor and this commentary owing to his careful investigations into the extant manuscripts. His knowledge of them is impressive. It led him to conclude (274) that, in spite of the many lacunae, conflations, and numerous (erroneous) ascriptions...

> I yet distinctly ascertained, and am fully persuaded that the original work was *one*,— the production, no doubt, of "Victor, Presbyter of Antioch," as 19 out of the 52 MSS. declare.

It is nevertheless the case that one must be willing to accept Burgon's opinion on this matter, for his presentation of the evidence is less than convincing. Our references to "Victor," therefore, refer to the author of the Commentary on Mark with which we are working. We think this author was likely an historical figure named Victor who was a Bishop at Antioch. But we can make no more certain a claim than that the author reflects Antiochene theology, nor is it necessary to our task.

[28]Harold Smith, "The Sources of Victor of Antioch's Commentary on Mark," *JTS* 19 (1918) 352.

[29]It is commonly asserted (as, e.g., by Kealy, *Mark's Gospel*, 21) that Origen wrote a commentary on every book of the canon, and he may have. But if he or anyone else wrote a commentary on the Gospel of Mark, it seems that these commentaries suffered more neglect than the Gospel itself. At least Victor states plainly in his "Preface" that he knew of none, and I have found no evidence to disprove him.

[30]A catena is a document in which an editor compiles material in chain like fashion. It was apparently a fairly common practice of antiquity, and also of the early church, to gather as many comments as possible on a particular topic and record them seriatim.

[31]J. A. Cramer, S.T.P., ed., *Catenae Graecorum Patrum in Novum Testamentum*, vol. 1: *Catenae in Evangelia S. Matthaei et S. Marci* (Oxford, 1840) 263. My English

translation to selected passages from the "Preface" and the chapter "Concerning Peter's Denial" is found below in Appendix A. All of the citations of Victor's Commentary on Mark in this dissertation are my English translation of the Greek text; all paginations refer to Cramer's Greek text, *Catenae*, vol. 1.

[32]Smith, "Sources," 354.

[33]*Ibid.*, 353.

[34]Burgon, *Last Twelve Verses*, 276. It seems as though when the expression "he says" (*phesin*) occurs without an article, the implied author is God. See on this Donald Guthrie, *New Testament Theology* (Downers Grove, IL: IVP, 1981) 969; C. K. Barrett, *The First Epistle to the Corinthians* (London: Black, 1971) 149; M. Black, *Romans* (London: Oliphants, 1973) 135.

[35]*Ibid.*, 276.

[36]For his exposition on Peter's Denial Victor drew from Chrysostom's Homilies, the 84th on Matt. 26:51-54 and 85th on Matt. 26:67-68. The English translation can be found in Philip Schaff, *NPNF* 10 (Grand Rapids: Wm. B. Eerdmans, 1983) 501-10. Victor's citation of a passage of commentary dealing with Peter's Denial from Cyril of Alexandria's Commentary on Luke is apparently only extant in a Syriac edition edited by Payne Smith. I have been unable to obtain this source. A partial translation of this passage (on Peter's Denial) can be found in Smith, "Sources," 357. It is sufficient to allow a comparison of Victor's source to his use of it.

[37]Smith, "Sources," 353.

[38]Burgon, *Last Twelve Verses*, 269.

[39]For full citation see note 31 above.

[40]Burgon, *Last Twelve Verses*, 272-3.

[41]*Ibid.*, 271.

[42]*Ibid.*, 278. See, however, the opinion of H. B. Swete (*Commentary on Mark* [Grand Rapids: Kregel, 1977] cxv) who says: "A conjecture which placed it a century later would perhaps be nearer to the truth."

[43]F. L. Cross and E. A. Livingstone, eds., *The Oxford Dictionary of the Christian Church* 2nd. ed. (Oxford University Press, 1977) s.v. "Antiochene Theology," 65; John M'Clintock and James Strong, eds., *Cyclopaedia of Biblical, Theological, and Ecclesiastical Literature* (Grand Rapids: Baker Book House, 1968) s.v. "Antioch," I:266-9.

[44]Cross, *ODCC*, 65-6; M'Clintock, *CBTEL*, I:266-9.

[45]Burgon, *Last Twelve Verses*, 287.

[46]M'Clintock, *CBTEL*, I:269.

[47]Cross, *ODCC*, 65-6.

[48]*Ibid.*

[49]Robert M. Grant with David Tracy, *A Short History of the Interpretation of the Bible* (Philadelphia: Fortress Press, 1984) 63-72.

[50]Cross, *ODCC*, 65.

[51]Grant, *Interpretation*, 52, 56.

[52]*Ibid.*, 59.

[53]Origen, *De Principiis*, 4.2.9., as quoted in Grant, *Interpretation*, 57.

[54]Origen, *Commentary on the Gospel of John*, 10.3, as quoted by Grant, *Interpretation*, 58.

[55]Cramer, *Catenae*, 432-3.

[56]Smith, "Sources," 364-70; Chrysostom, *NPNF* 10:501-10.

[57]Origen, *Commentary on the Gospel of Matthew*, section 105, cited in Harold Smith, *Ante-Nicene Exegesis of the Gospels* vol. 6 (London: S.P.C.K., 1928) 11.

[58]Origen, *Matthew*, 114, cited in Smith, *Ante-Nicene*, 12.

[59]Origen, *Matthew*, 114, cited in Smith, *Ante-Nicene*, 12.

[60]Origen, *Matthew*, 114, cited in Smith, *Ante-Nicene*, 12-3. My emphases.

[61]Clyde L. Manschreck, *A Short History of Christianity in the World* 2nd. ed. (Englewood Cliffs: Prentice-Hall, 1985) 49-52.

[62]Origen, *Matthew*, 114, cited in Smith, *Ante-Nicene*, 13.

[63]Origen, *Matthew*, 114, cited in Smith, *Ante-Nicene*, 15.

[64]Cramer, *Catenae*, 429.

[65]*Ibid.*, 431.

[66]*Ibid.*

[67]Origen, *Matthew*, 114, cited in Smith, *Ante-Nicene*, 14.

[68]Cramer, *Catenae*, 431-2.

[69]Cross, *ODCC*, 66. o62

[70]Grant, *Interpretation*, 71.

[71]Cramer, *Catenae*, 430.

[72]*Ibid.*

[73]Victor's phrase "a medicine of salvation" recalls a phrase in Ignatius' Letter to the Ephesians 20:2: "...breaking one bread, which is *the medicine of immortality*, the antidote that we should not die, but live for ever in Jesus Christ." Cf. the Greek text in Kirsopp Lake, *Apostolic Fathers*, 2 vols. (Cambridge: Harvard University Press, 1977) I:195.

[74]See Alan Richardson (*A Dictionary of Christian Theology* [Philadelphia: Westminster Press, 1976] 235) for a discussion of the Novatianists. We feel confident that Theophylact correctly identifies the Novatianists as those against whom Victor

is directing his remarks. However, the concern for a life of Christian purity and the seriousness of post-conversion sins was perennial. Cp., e.g., the works of the Shepherd of Hermas (1 Hermas, or "Visions;" 2 Hermas, or "Commands;" 3 Hermas, or "Similitudes;" these texts can be found in *The Lost Books of the Bible* [New York: Bell Publishing Co., 1979] 197-269). The "Parable of the Tower" (1 Hermas 3, and 3 Hermas 9) is obsessed with whether "repentance [is] allowed to all those stones which are thus cast away, and were not suitable to the building of the tower" (1 Hermas 3:78). While Hermas allows for repentance of post-conversion sins, there is an unresolved tension: "For the repentance of the righteous has its end; the days of repentance are fulfilled to all the saints; but to the heathen, there is repentance even unto the last day" (1 Hermas 2:15).

[75]Cramer, *Catenae*, 430.

[76]*Ibid.*

[77]Edgar Krentz, *The Historical-Critical Method* (Philadelphia: Fortress Press, 1975) 7.

[78]Grant, *A Short History,* 72.

[79]Krentz, 6.

[80]Kealy, *Mark's Gospel,* 28-30.

[81]As, e.g., Henry B. Swete, *Commentary on Mark* (Grand Rapids: Kregel Publications, [1913] 1977) cxiv-cxv.

Chapter 3

Middle Ages

The Venerable Bede

In the year 597 Pope Gregory the Great sent Saint Augustine of Canterbury to England to convert the fair-haired heathen.[1] With the marginal success of this and other missionary efforts (by the Irish[2] and Theodore of Tarsus accompanied by Hadrian of Africa in 669), England enjoyed a century or so of relative peace and spiritual and cultural enlightenment. Almost co-extensive with these results is the Venerable Bede, born 673, who lived and left a legacy.[3]

Given over to the monastery at Wearmouth by his family at the age of seven,[4] he distinguished himself in religious servitude. When he was twelve, the monastery at Jarrow was built approximately five miles away, and Bede was sent there with several monks.[5] Choosing to remain a part of the community, he became a deacon at the age of nineteen and a priest at the age of thirty. He says he spent his entire life in the vicinity of these two communities,[6] Jarrow and Wearmouth, which actually constituted one monastery[7] in Northumbria (Northern England), legends of travels to Rome and elsewhere notwithstanding.

Owing to his prodigious writings and manifest expertise in many areas, "Bede could be the polyhistor of his time."[8] He has been called the Father of Carolingian Schools, of English Letters, of English History, of English Exegesis, even the Father of all the Middle Ages.[9] He is perhaps best known to our age for *The Ecclesiastical History of the English People*.[10] It is this work which is almost singular in its testimony of early English history, religious and otherwise. It is available today in many English editions.

But he was not always remembered so. Bede was honored throughout the Middle Ages for his Biblical exegesis.[11] In fact, Bede's testimony to his own great lifework warrants the conclusion that "Bede was not only, or even primarily, a historian."[12]

In the autobiographical appendix to his famous *Ecclesiastical History* Bede says:

> From the time I became a priest until the fifty-ninth year of my life I have made it my business, for my own benefit and that of my brothers, to make brief extracts from the works of the venerable fathers on the holy Scriptures, or to add notes of my own to clarify their sense and interpretation.[13]

Bede's estimation of his work is perhaps too modest, for his collections of "extracts" are quite extensive, as are his own contributions. And his production of commentaries constitutes by far the greatest portion of his extant works.[14] Nevertheless, "in modern scholarship," says Roger Ray, "they have suffered remarkable, I would say regrettable, neglect."[15] His works are available only in Latin. There is no exhaustive treatment of either his commentaries or his hermeneutical method.[16]

In Marci euangelium expositio. As the citation above indicates, Bede devoted himself to Biblical exegesis. For some of the books on which he commented there were no predecessors. As there is no evidence he knew Victor of Antioch, and none of his acknowledged sources come from any commentaries on the Gospel of Mark, his *In Marci Euangelium* would fall into this category. "His purposes were therefore either to furnish traditional commentary derived from established sources but put in a simplified form for his English students or to fill for them the gaps in which no commentary yet existed."[17]

In the case of *In Marci Euangelium*, Bede says in the prologue that it was composed many years, *plurimos annos,* after the commentary on Luke. According to C. E. Whiting,

> In the accompanying epistle to Acca [Bishop of Hexham], Bede said that he had compiled this commentary not only at his exhortation, but at that of many other brethren; and he had done his best to collect whatever he could find on the subject in the Fathers.[18]

Whiting also ascertained that it was "certainly written after his book on Samuel" and therefore must "be later than 716."[19] Perhaps this relatively late date accounts for the fact that although "the commentary on Mark includes large blocks of the Lucan commentary," nonetheless, says Brown, "this commentary manifests some of Bede's finest and most mature exegesis."[20]

Principles of Exegesis. Any history of Biblical interpretation is bound to ascertain that the Antiochene approach was the exception, the attempt to find multiple levels of meaning in the text the rule. A handbook espousing the Antiochene method, the *Instituta regularia divina,*[21] was written by Junilius about 551. There is evidence that it was in England in Bede's day. But there is no evidence that Bede used it. In fact, had he known it, M.L.W. Laistner argues he would have spurned it.

> He would certainly have disapproved of it strongly for more than one reason. His devotion to allegorical interpretation, as practiced especially by Gregory

I, would have made him frown on a literalist like Junilius. Again, Junilius' curious views on canonical and noncanonical Books in the Bible, views which, as Kihn has demonstrated, reproduce the teaching of Theodore of Mopsuestia, would have been strongly reprobated by so orthodox a man as Bede. In particular he would have rejected with indignation an author who excluded the Apocalypse from the prophetic Books *primae auctoritatis* and allowed it to be only *mediae auctoritatis.*[22]

Laistner's mention of allegorical interpretation brings us to Bede's hermeneutic. If an attempt to find multiple levels of meaning was the norm for ancient exegetes, categorizing and systematizing those attempts have proven difficult, and perhaps impossible in the case of Bede.

Although there were numerous "theories,"[23] two seem basic. Origen is usually identified as responsible for the "threefold sense" of Scripture: the literal (*somatikos*), moral (*psychikos*), and intellectual (*pneumatikos*). Cassian is given credit for developing the "fourfold sense:" historical, tropological, allegorical, anagogical. Bede, following Cassian, offered a fourfold interpretation of Psalm 147:12:

> According to the Psalm, *Praise the Lord, O Jerusalem; praise thy God, O Sion,* the four figures flow together into one, so that one and the same Jerusalem may be understood in four ways: according to *history,* the city of the Jews; according to *allegory,* the Church of Christ; according to *anagogy,* the City of God in Heaven; according to *tropology,* the soul of man.[24]

But it would be erroneous to think that Bede always, or even mostly, followed this fourfold sense. The situation seems to be simultaneously both more complicated and simpler than that. In his *Schemes and Tropes,*[25] Bede describes in great detail his understanding of the composition of Scripture. Of "schemes" he says: "Often for the sake of elegance (*decoris*) the arrangement of words in the Scriptures is found to be delineated (*figuratus*) otherwise than in common speech."[26] Jones calls these "figures of speech." Bede lists, describes, and illustrates seventeen schemes. "A trope is an utterance moved over from its usual significance to an unusual similitude for the sake of embellishment or by necessity."[27] Jones calls these "figures of thought." Bede listed thirteen "tropes," *of which allegory was only one*! Moreover, each trope has subspecies. As a species of trope, *allegory has seven subspecies*: irony, antiphrasis, enigma, charientismus, parhoemia, sarcasm, and asteismus. Jones concludes:

> In short, Bede taught his disciples in class that a fourfold meaning, which may be present in either things (facts, actions) or words, is not more or less than a polished and elevated way of expressing something which might have been said simply. There are seven species of allegory, which is itself only one of thirteen tropes, or figures of thought. Any one of the seven forms of allegory may be one of two kinds, of facts or of words, and each of these fourteen kinds

may bear one, two, three, or four senses, for each of which Bede does not hesitate to apply two or more names, one of which is, indeed, *allegoria* again, now in a minutely specific sense *if* it has any specific meaning at all.[28]

The point, I have gathered, is that the "senses of Scripture," at least for Bede, got lost in the detail, so that ultimately Bede cannot be said to have followed any program, at least not rigidly. To put it more positively, the attempt of the Fathers to elucidate the different levels of meaning of Scripture was a profession that the Bible could not be interpreted either literally or rigidly; "their methods of interpretation were intended to *free* the faithful readers from inherited claims of reason by attributing cogency to shifting points of view."[29] To the extent that any system, including an allegorical system, is followed rigidly, it undermines the legitimacy of this shifting point of view.

Ultimately Bede focused on this "immediacy" to which the text seemed to speak. As the exposition which follows below demonstrates, "Bede's method was not just allegorical and figural but mainly eclectic and pastoral. He used any device, or combination of devices, that might make the biblical text edifying to his audience... Exegetical theory...never forced Bede's hand."[30] Although Bede seems to have had an elaborate exegetical scheme worked out in theory, as Jones attests, in practice it seemed to boil down to the fact that Scripture frequently had more than a literal meaning which could be detected and expounded upon and given any number of names. And not even the literal or historical meaning was nor should be abandoned altogether.[31] For Bede, "exegesis was a never-ending quest for new points of view."[32] His interpretation of Mark 14:54, 66-72 affords an excellent spectrum of his method.

Critical Synthesis. "Critical synthesis" is how R. B. Palmer describes Bede's method of appropriating his sources.[33] Bede held a holy respect for the Church Fathers on the one hand and a profound sense of obligation to communicate the teachings of the Fathers to his audience on the other. They form two of Bede's theological presuppositions. This method of critical synthesis is his attempt to bring the two together.

As regards the respect for the Fathers, in his autobiographical appendix to *Ecclesiastical History,* Bede states,

> From the time I became a priest until the fifty-ninth year of my life I have made it my business, for my own benefit and that of my brothers, to make brief extracts from the works of the venerable fathers on the holy Scriptures, or to add notes of my own to clarify their sense and interpretation.[34]

Bede's focus on the Fathers derives from his understanding of the God-given role of "doctors" in Christian formation and instruction. His exposition of Romans 14:5 in *Octo Quaestionum Liber* goes as follows:

> ...the Apostle did not speak in the indicative mood, *abundat*, but in the imperative: "Let every man abound in his own sense." In this way he

commands that if we are not able to arrive at the more sublime secrets of the divine sacraments, yet we may humbly and devoutly serve the Lord in those which we truly understand and feel are understood and trustworthy. And thus will be fulfilled what he ordered, that every man should abound in his own sense, when we take care abundantly to perform those good works which we are taught to believe in and to do by the great doctors, to the end that, through the execution of those which we know, we may deserve likewise to attain a perception of those sublimities which we never did know.[35]

For Bede, therefore, every man could have an understanding of Scripture. But not every man would have the same depth of understanding or consistency. God has given the Church "great doctors" to expound the Scripture and preserve doctrine. This led to Bede's assuming the role of a communicator of their teachings to the common man, as will be explored below. Whether by "doctors" Bede meant not only the early Fathers but also local ministers is unclear. At any rate, the early Fathers were preeminent. And four dominate both his work in general and the Commentary on Mark in particular. "For him interpreting the Bible was almost the same thing as studying the works of Ambrose, Jerome, Augustine, and Gregory."[36]

Bede goes to great lengths, at least in the Commentaries of Luke and Mark, to indicate on whom he is depending here and there. In the preface to his *Commentary on Mark* he makes the following appeal to his readers:

> And I humbly pray the reader that, if he should deem these works of ours worthy of copying he should also carefully preserve in the transcribing the notation of those names which have been placed above in the margin, just as was admittedly done for the commentary on St Luke that we, with the help of God's grace, composed many years ago.[37]
> ...lest I be said to steal the sayings of my elders and compose these as my own.[38]

We have been careful to include these in our Appendix B. Each borrowing from a Father is indicated in the left margin with two letters: Ambrose by A...M, Augustine by A...V, Jerome (in Latin *Hier*onymus) by H...R, and Gregory by G...R (although Gregory is not actually represented in this pericope). The initial letter indicates the beginning of a citation, the second letter the end.[39] There are two places where Bede either failed to indicate dependency or, as is more likely, the marginal indicators have been lost in transmission.[40] The first half of the commentary on 14:54 is from Ambrose's *Explanation of Luke's gospel*; one sentence from the commentary on 14:70 is taken from Jerome's *Commentary on Matthew's gospel*. Each other instance of dependency is fairly clearly indicated in the Appendix B, both in the Latin and in the English translation.[41]

By modern standards the originality of his work may seem thereby compromised. But Bede (and many other Fathers) would have called the modern standard into question. As Brown so astutely notes, "Bede had no wish to be original, a quality authors and public have seen as praiseworthy since the nineteenth century; rather, he wished as he often said 'to follow the footsteps of the Fathers' in bringing the truth of the Scriptures and its interpreters to a dark age."[42] "Originality" (in the modern sense) would have been viewed as a vain and dangerous enterprise. Ascertaining truth to the salvation of souls was the primary objective. And that could most readily be done by studying those on whom the light of truth had clearly shone.

But neither can Bede be dismissed as "merely secondhand"[43] or "merely a *catena Patrum*."[44] There is a depth of understanding and acumen in Bede's appropriation of his sources which his presentation belies.[45] The Fathers were asking questions and proffering answers that Bede's parishioners and students would not have readily understood in their original form. Bede understood part of his pastoral role to be to so apportion and interpret the interpretations that his audience would be edified. This "simplicity, which may not be to our taste and for that matter was probably not always to Bede's," says Ray, "attests the intellectual capacity of his anticipated audience, *idiotae* and all, much more than the power of his own mind."[46]

Bede's exegesis, which at first glance seems to stand, as Willmes has said, "zwischen Rezeptivität und Selbststandigkeit,"[47] is actually a deeply reflective program on Bede's part. There seems to be wide agreement on this matter. Says Brown: "It is also clear that in both the anthological and original types he has made his own contribution, deciding which authority to follow, which opinion to incorporate and which to exclude, what comments to add, and what sort of synthesis to form."[48] Adds Ray: "It was his practice to deploy the clarified and inflected patristic texts according to didactic aims that make the resulting works his own."[49] The result, concludes Jenkins, is that "his mode of handling his materials entitles him to be considered as an original author."[50]

Pastoral Affirmation. Both Bede's view of the role of the Fathers and his role in transmitting their teaching are vectors pointing to the yet more important objective: "the modest one of providing for the *rudis lector* ['uncultivated reader'] a kind of preliminary introduction or summary based either directly or indirectly on their words."[51] Commenting on Proverbs 12:9 Bede says:

> Better is a stupid (*idiota*) and simple brother who, working the good things he knows, merits life in heaven, than one who being distinguished in learning of Scripture or even having filled the place of a "doctor" lacks the bread of love.[52]

Thus, while Bede commends the study of patristics in his commentary of Proverbs 13:23, he goes on to suggest that "apart from practical use, such studies may be wasted."[53] He is keenly aware of the "crudeness" of his countrymen. They do not know the languages nor understand the subtleties of theology. Hence, he approved of some worship and reading in English, having translated some texts into English himself.[54] While some are incapable of advancing in theological understanding (and the Church has an obligation to them), even those who are capable of receiving instruction must be brought along slowly; it is the nature of the ministry of nurturing. Thus, his commentaries were not directed primarily to the peasant, who may have been unable to read anyway, nor to monks, but to "a broad audience of professional churchmen."[55] It would be their obligation in turn to minister to their flocks.

For these reasons he admonishes those who would be pastors to be trained and to preach the Word of God sincerely and not for personal gain.[56] He saw no contradiction in a monk proclaiming the Gospel. Indeed, Bede seemed to view it as a discharge of his duty not only to preach but to have a general influence on the society, an ideal he probably inherited from Gregory the Great.[57] His monastic life was not isolated from, but integrated into, his community.[58]

As for his teaching, it was so presented that the neophyte had constantly before him the words of the "great doctors," but in small quantities and carried along with exposition.[59] As for his preaching, it was replete with illustrations and local flavoring. Jenkins demonstrates several examples where Bede omits some illustration from the Fathers "as being far removed from the experience of his own probable readers," and replaces it with "another homely English touch."[60]

Commaticum. It is this, more than a theory of exegesis, that most closely identifies Bede's "program." Bede called the procedure commaticum, a verse-by-verse commentary. The result was a reflective meditation on individual phrases and words designed to extract meanings relevant to personal and communal growth. It is true, as Brown notes, that "the process atomizes and fragments the text, allowing its thematic totality to be lost."[61] But it is not as though Bede was incapable of recognizing and underscoring larger themes and purposes.[62] Other writings (esp. Ecclesiastical History) clearly manifest this ability. It is that this process met the needs of his anticipated reading audience. He had "set himself the task of appropriating patristic exegesis to a Saxon church which needed to be drawn gently into the Christian mainstream."[63] At this history has judged him successful.

Turning to our passage specifically we see several examples where Bede ministered to his audience. Noting that the text of 14:54 says that "Peter had followed him at a distance," he reminds his reader,

...he would not have been able to deny him, if he had remained close to Christ.

Moreover, the reader should bear in mind that

...not only is Christ denied by one who says that he is not the Christ, but by him also who, while really a Christian, himself denies that he is so. For the Lord did not say to Peter, "You shall deny that you are my disciple," but "You shall deny me." Therefore he denied him when he denied that he was his disciple.

The role of the pastor-teacher is prefigured in the crowing of the cock. For Christians will naturally grow weary and sometimes fail, whereas the pastor-teacher's obligation is to stir them from their slumber:

> I think that by this cock must be understood some teacher who rouses us when we are asleep, and reproving our sleepiness says: "Come to your right mind, and sin no more."

Below we will discuss the allegorical interpretation of the fire with which Peter warmed himself. From a pastoral perspective, though, Bede admonishes his reader that there is a fire of zeal and charity and a fire of sin and culpability.

> Therefore, whoever has extinguished the perverse and culpable flame within himself can say to the Lord with the prophet: "For I have become like a wineskin in the smoke (literally, the winter), yet I have not forgotten thy statutes."

The reader must learn from Peter's failure, "How harmful are the communications of the wicked!" One can "not be penitent while detained in the court of Caiaphas." Nevertheless, Peter, for all his failure, is to be revered:

> For the fact that he was afraid is natural, that he followed him [a mark] of his devotion [to him], that he denied him [a mark] of his heedlessness, that he repented [a mark] of his faith.

The Role of Faith and Grace. This last touches on Bede's view of the role of faith and grace. One of the purposes of preaching was to enable the hearer to facilitate the divine response, to be open to the "Divine Spark." Thus, faith demands some impetus on the part of man, but ultimately it is insufficient in itself. The "transcendent reality" which ignites and sustains faith is God's grace. As Bede wrote in his *Commentary on Luke*:

> If God does not enlighten the hearts of the hearers, the preacher will labour in vain. If the means of proclamation are not based on divine grace, the preacher will not be able to thrust forth the javelin of his voice. The faith of the people does not merely come from the wisdom of the prepared sermon, but from the benefit of the divine calling.[64]

Even so, Bede's doctrine of Election is broad and encompassing. Though it requires an act of faith on the part of man, as Peter's removing himself from "the perverse and culpable flame" and from the "communications of the wicked" and "the court of Caiaphas," it nevertheless is dependent on the gracious advance of God which, judging from Bede's writings, excludes almost no one. Jones says Bede used Peter as an example of the principle of Election and Predestination in his *Commentary on Genesis*: "Peter was perfidious until the descent of the Holy Spirit—like the black crow, not the simple dove…; he is but one striking manifestation of the infinite Grace and Forgiveness of God."[65]

Historical-Critical Questions. If it is true that Bede is not to be viewed as a critic writing to and for critics but rather as a churchman writing for the formation of souls, it is also true that he "is neither wholly ignorant of, nor wholly indifferent to, critical problems."[66]

Mark's account of the Denial mentions two crowings. Although in the better texts the first crowing is not narrated, in all texts the second crowing is introduced *as a second crowing*. And in Bede's text the first crowing is included. On the words in 14:68, "And he went out into the gateway, and a cock crowed," Bede says:

> The other evangelists are silent about this crowing of the cock; yet they do not deny that it took place, just as some [of them] also pass over many other matters in silence which the others relate.

The discrepancy is thus accounted for by deferring to the evangelists' judgments about what to include in the text. There is no attempt to do as Victor or Theophylact who both offer suggestions about the cock crowing several times at each of several "crowings."

Regarding the discrepancy between Mark and Matthew over the identification of the second maid, Bede says:

> This maid should not be believed to be the same one who first accused him. For Matthew says most clearly: "And when he went out to the porch, another maid saw him, and she said to the bystanders," and so on.

Apparently just as Bede was willing to allow that Mark's account was the more complete in the case of the cock crow, so Matthew's account is the more complete in the case of the identification of the second maid. It is true that Mark says "the maid," using the definite article. Yet, according to Bede, "Matthew says most clearly… *another*…," specifying that *the* maid was not the *same* maid who saw him the first time. He does not address Luke's account here which implies that the second accoster was a man.

Bede explains why the bystanders could recognize Peter as a Galilean. Drawing on Matthew's account and Jerome's *Commentary on Matthew*, he says,

> This was not because the Galileans and the inhabitants of Jerusalem spoke a different language, for both were Hebrews, but "because each province and region had its peculiarities [in speaking] and could not avoid the sound of its local dialect." Hence in the Acts of the Apostles, when those on whom the Holy Spirit had rested were speaking in the tongues of all nations, among the others who had come together from the different regions of the world even those who dwelt in Judea are reported as having said: "Behold, are not all these

who are speaking Galileans? And how is it that we hear, each of us in his own native language?" And Peter, speaking to his brethren in Jerusalem, said: "And it became known to all the inhabitants of Jerusalem, so that the field was called in their language Akeldama." Why [did he say], "in their language," except that the same name sounded in one way to him, that is, the inhabitants of Jerusalem, and in another way to the Galileans?

Bede engaged in this lengthy explanation apparently because there was a point of contention about the word for "language" (Latin, *lingua*; Greek *dialectos*). At least in the Acts of the Apostles the word can mean both "language" (i.e., a different language) or "dialect" (i.e., of the same language). As a reminder that Bede, pastoral though he was, engaged in scholarly debate, we note his testy response to someone who called his judgment into question on this matter in his *Liber Retractationis*:

> I know that I have been blamed by some because I said that this sentence [sc. "Behold, are not all these that speak Galileans? And how have we heard every man our own tongue wherein we were born?"] could be understood in two ways, or rather inquired in what way it should be understood. To these I briefly reply that what I wrote about this same sentence in my previous volume, I did not put forth from my own understanding, but took from the words of a master holy and in all things unreprovable — Gregory Nazianzen.[67]

Allegory. While Bede is capable of appreciating the literal, historical meanings and the critical problems (as the above section demonstrates), he regards them as dry and lifeless without asking after the allegorical. In his Commentary on 1 Samuel Bede says,

> If we see the literal meaning of the Scriptures only, in the Jewish way, what reproof do we derive from them for our frequent sins, what consolation in the midst of the increasing troubles of the present day, what spiritual instruction to put us on our guard against error,...if we do not also know how to go on to the allegorical meaning, which touches us personally and revives us by rebuking, teaching, and consoling us?[68]

Earlier we established that allegory was not clearly definable. For our purposes it will be sufficient to say that types and allegories and many other designations refer broadly to a higher or spiritual meaning which the literal meaning only hints at.

After Bede makes a pastoral application of "Peter following at a distance," he then offers "another" (*Aliter*) interpretation from Augustine:

> The fact that Peter followed the Lord at a distance as he was going to his passion signified that the Church was going to follow [the Lord] indeed, that is, to imitate his sufferings, but in a far different manner; for the Church suffers on its own behalf but he [suffers] for the Church.

Of the fire with which Peter warmed himself, Bede says, "There is a fire of love, [there is] also [one] of avarice."

> ...the latter, kindled in the courtyard of Caiaphas by the prompting of the evil spirit, armed the culpable tongues of the unbelievers to deny and blaspheme the Lord. For the fact that the sanhedrin plotted evil deeds within the house of the chief of the priests is a type that foreshadowed the material fire that was kindled outside in the courtyard in the cold of the night...Being benumbed temporarily by this cold, the apostle Peter as it were desired to be warmed by the charcoal [fire] of the guards of Caiaphas because he sought the consolation of temporal advantage through fellowship with unbelievers.

The former fire of love, "coming down upon those who believed in the upper room on [Mount] Zion, taught them to praise God in other tongues." Peter experienced this fire even before Pentecost, when Providence recreated the terrible scene of that night, but under different circumstances:

> But right away, when he was regarded by the Lord, he both abandoned the fire of the wicked bodily and the lack of faith in his heart, and after the Lord's resurrection, being restored by the holy fire, he completely cleansed the mistake of his threefold denial by a threefold confession of faith. For then indeed after that memorable catch of fish was finished and when he came to the Lord with his fellow disciples and saw the charcoal fire there and fish lying on it and bread, immediately perceiving [the meaning] in his inmost heart, he was on fire [with the flames] of love.

Bede does not make this perception clear to his reader but only says that Peter "immediately perceived [the meaning] in his inmost heart." What did he perceive? Does this second "charcoal fire" symbolize the fiery trial of the sanhedrin *and Peter's trial in the courtyard?* If so, is the "bread" Jesus and the "fish lying on [the fire]" being consumed Peter!?

Circumstantiae. A particularly appealing aspect of Bede's allegorical or "higher" reading is notice of the *circumstantiae*, the belief that spiritual significance was revealed in "circumstances," the names of people, the places and times of events, and so on. In the *Commentary on Genesis* Bede says:

> The entire series of sacred utterance is replete with mystical figures, not only in words and deeds but times and places.

Bede did not invent this idea but inherited it from the rhetorical tradition.[69] But he found justification for it in Paul's dictum: "All things happened to them in figure, but they are written for our instruction" (1 Cor. 10:11):

> ..."all things," not only deeds or words which are contained in the sacred

Scriptures but truly also the relationships of places, hours, and seasons, and also the circumstances in which they are done or spoken.[70]

Bede repeats the principle frequently throughout his works, one of the clearest of which is in our text. In his commentary on Mark 14:71 Bede says:

Scripture is accustomed to point out the mystery of causes by the circumstances of the times. Hence Peter, who made his denial in the middle of the night, repented at cock crow. He also, after the Lord's resurrection, at daylight professed three times equally that he loved him, whom he had denied three times, because undoubtedly what he had erred through forgetfulness in the darkness he both corrected by recalling the hoped-for light and in the presence of this same true light he completely strengthened that in which he had wavered.

Likewise, Peter's very presence within the courtyard and with the guards reflects his spiritual condition. The need for a fire in the courtyard is testimony to the cold of the night which symbolizes the coldness of the unrepentant hearts.

Being benumbed temporarily by this cold, the apostle Peter as it were desired to be warmed by the charcoal [fire] of the guards of Caiaphas because he sought the consolation of temporal advantage.

A change of spiritual condition would have to be prefigured by a change in circumstances.

Peter himself among the faithless denied that he knew the man whom he had confessed to be the Son of God among his fellow disciples! But he could not be penitent while detained in the court of Caiaphas. He goes outside, as the other Evangelists narrate, so that being removed from the council of the impious he might wash away the filth of a timorous denial by unrestrained weeping.

One of the more striking examples of Bede's explanation of *circumstantiae* is a comment borrowed from Ambrose's *Explanation of Luke's Gospel* as to why it was a woman who first recognized Peter.

What does it mean that it was first a maid who revealed him, when there were doubtlessly men who could have more easily recognized him, unless that sex [women] would seem to have sinned in the murder of the Lord also, and that that sex would be redeemed by the Lord's passion? Therefore it was a woman who was the first to perceive the mystery of the resurrection and kept the commandments, so that she might do away with the error of the ancient transgression.

It seems to be a most interesting point among Bedan scholars that most of the kings of the time were won to Christianity through the testimonies of their wives. And several women influenced Bede's life, including abbesses, nuns, and common folk.[71] His daily contact with women was apparently more extensive than one would at first suppose. It was customary for the monasteries of the time to be "double monasteries," adjacent houses, one for the nuns and one for the monks. Such apparently was Bede's experience. In his *Commentary on Ezra* Bede offers his appraisal of the role of women.

> Fittingly are men's voices joined with the singing of women, for among women also there are those who, not only by their lives but even by preaching, can set fire to the hearts of others in praise of their Creator, no doubt on account of their feminine nature; as though by the very sweetness of their holy voices they assist in the work of building the temple of the Lord.[72]

A tentative conclusion might be that Bede regarded women as fully integrated into the plan of salvation. While many ancients, especially the Jews, regarded women as somehow especially responsible for the Fall, Bede found them also especially active in the events surrounding salvation. As a sex, women were not to be excluded from responsibility for "the murder of the Lord." Likewise, "that sex would be redeemed by the Lord's passion." Such *circumstantiae* were to Bede too important not to notice. Women were full participants in the Lord's passion, "and therefore it was a woman who was the first to perceive the mystery of the resurrection and kept the commandments." Bede is supporting Ambrose's suggestion that she no longer be regarded as bearing undue responsibility for the Sin. These things happened "that she might do away with the error of the ancient transgression."

Number Symbolism. Just as Bede inherited the principle of *circumstantiae,* so he also inherited the insight for spiritual symbolism in numbers, principally from Augustine. He frequently quoted one of Augustine's favorite texts, Wisdom of Solomon 11:20:

> But thou has arranged all things by measure and number and weight.

Indeed, says Isidore: "Take number from everything and everything perishes. Remove arithmetic from life and everything is confounded in blind ignorance, and men who do not know the method of calculation cannot be differentiated from animals."[73]

Bede would not let this be said of him. In fact, scholars tend to regard this enterprise as resulting in some of Bede's most fanciful exegesis. There are seemingly endless ways to add, subtract, multiply and divide numbers found in Scripture in order to derive spiritual insight. The measurements of Solomon's Temple are replete with symbolism. That it was built 480 years after the Exodus is to be explained that $480 = 4 \times 120$; 4 being the number of evangelical perfection (4 Gospels) and 120 representing both the age of Moses when he died and the number of recipients of the

Holy Ghost on Pentecost. The number 120 is a perfect spiritual number insofar as 120 = 10 x 12, both being perfect themselves, and because 120 is the sum of the first fifteen numbers (i.e., 1 + 2 + 3...+ 15 = 120).[74] The possibilities are nearly endless.

The interesting thing is that for number symbolism to have played so important a role elsewhere in Bede's exegesis, he refrains from pressing the interpretation in our passage. Peter, of course, denied the Lord three times. And 3 is elsewhere a significant number, the reason being, explains Bede, that it is the first "wholly integral" number.

> ...to be wholly integral, it must have a beginning, middle, and end. Among numbers this is the 3. It is made up of an odd and an even number. Three is the first really odd number. Even numbers are whole if they have equal parts on both sides; consequently 4 is the first wholly even number. The number 1 is the principle of numbers; it enjoys neither middle nor end. 2 must likewise be principle, for beginning and middle or beginning and end cannot exist together alone. The joining of the two principles results in the first whole number: 1 + 2 = 3.[75]

One would expect Bede to make more of this, but he is satisfied to say only that Peter "completely cleansed the mistake of his threefold denial by a threefold confession of faith." Although the denial was "complete," so was the restitution. Peter was whole.

Walafrid Strabo and the *Glossa ordinaria*

Born about 808, Walafrid was admitted at a very early age to the Benedictine Monastery at Reichenau, an island in Lake Constance. The name *Strabo* "was given to him because he squinted, but was by himself assumed as his name."[76] The major events of his life include his studies under Rabanus Maurus (826-829), who is also sometimes given credit for much of the *Glossa ordinaria*, and his friendship with the Emperor Louis the Pious and the Empress Judith. Their close relationship to him is exhibited in their appointing him tutor to their son Charles. Later Louis made him abbot of Reichenau (838) where, with the exception of a brief deprivation of his post from 840 to 842, he remained for the rest of his life and was, upon his death, buried there in 849.[77]

The *Glossa ordinaria.* Walafrid was well versed in classical literature and even earned fame as a poet. Even so, "his chief renown was won by the great exegetic compilation in which he had the major part, the *Glossa ordinaria*," says A. Hauck.[78] Unfortunately, it is almost certain that Walafrid had less a hand in its compilation than previously thought. "The myth of Walafrid Strabo's authorship dies hard," says Smalley, "since it is preserved in bibliographies and library catalogues."[79] In the case of Mark, the glossator is anonymous, a fact of little consequence for our passage since it contains no original material.

The work as a whole consists of the Latin text of the Bible surrounded by glosses in the margin and between the lines from the Church Fathers, chiefly Augustine, Jerome, Gregory, Isidore of Seville, and Bede, and sometimes contemporaries, Anselm of Laon, Rabanus Maurus, and perhaps Walafrid himself. Sometimes the authors are cited by name; more frequently they are not.

The *Glossa ordinaria* was reprinted several times during the eleventh to fifteenth centuries, sometimes in four volumes, sometimes in six. According to Hauck, "this, for nearly five centuries, served as the main source of Biblical science for the West, and was reissued again and again, usually with the work of Lyra, until the seventeenth century."[80] Schaff says the glosses came to be regarded as possessing the same authority as the Scriptures they elucidated.[81] Concludes Kealy: "Lectures on Scripture frequently took the form of 'glossing the Gloss.' Thus the 'Gloss' with the Bible became the standard textbook for students from about the time of Anselm of Laon."[82]

Exegesis of Mark 14:54, 66-72. For this passage the *Glossa* cites three sources: Bede is cited four times, though one of those is itself a citation from Ambrose (14:54) and another is partially a citation from Jerome (14:70). Jerome is cited twice by name at 14:54 and 14:68, but these are actually probably from a spurious source attributed to Jerome. There is an anonymous gloss at 14:68 which appears to be a paraphrase from Augustine, though it could have been gotten from Bede who also borrows this quote from Augustine.

One interesting point about how the *Glossa* was used is evident in the way it was constructed. In four instances in our passage a lengthy citation is interrupted with "etc., *usque ad*...," which can be translated "and so forth, as far down as..."[83] In other words, the glossator apparently assumed that his readers, chiefly theological students, would for the most part recognize the source being cited from a relevant sentence or two, and would be able to look up the complete commentary in the source itself.

Moreover, as Schaff points out, "the notes are brief and designed to bring out the 'inner sense.'"[84] Thus, (Pseudo-) Jerome is cited to explain:

> The courtyard is a worldly surrounding. [The] servants are demons. Fire is carnal desire, he who remains with which has not the strength to lament his sins.

The compiler appends to this remark a gloss from Bede to the effect that "there is [also] a fire of grace." Peter could be expected to repent only when the night had passed and he had removed himself from the "worldly surrounding." Hence,

> Peter denies (him) at night, at the cock's crow he repents. Him whom he had denied three times, on the third day he professed to love...he passed outside (as the other Evangelists tell it), so that isolated from the impious, he might more freely wash away the guilt of his denial by his tears.

It is clear, therefore, that the glossator of Mark and his audience were inclined toward mystical-allegorical exegesis. There is a notable lack of discussion about historical discrepancies and textual problems.

Theophylact

Very little is known of Theophylact, including his dates of birth and death.[85] He was the tutor of Prince Constantine Porphyrogenitus, son of the Roman Emperor Michael VII, Ducas Parapinaces (1071-1078).[86] He was the archbishop of Achrida and metropolitan of Bulgaria from 1078 until approximately 1107.[87] Secondary sources represent him as an extremely intelligent scholar, diligent churchman, and wise administrator. One of the chief characteristics of his letters is his frustration at the difficulty in nurturing the crude countrymen of his flock in the faith.[88]

Regarding the question of the Schism between the East and West, Theophylact adopted a conciliatory position. He speaks to the two issues of greatest dispute in his *Address on the Errors of the Latin Church* (which Schaff calls his "most interesting work"):[89] the procession of the Holy Spirit and the bread of the Eucharist. The former was judged to be the more serious question. Schaff notes that while Theophylact was unyielding in his defense of the Greek position over against the Latin, Theophylact nevertheless displayed even here a fairness and willingness to think the best in his comment that

> the error of the Latins may be due to the poverty of their language which compelled them to "employ the same term to denote the causality of the *communication* of the Holy Spirit and the causality of his *being*. The Latins, he observed, moreover, might retain the less accurate forms of expression in their homiletic discourses, if they only guarded against misconception, by carefully explaining their meaning. It was only in the confession of faith in the symbol, that perfect clearness was requisite."[90]

Regarding the bread of the Eucharist, the Latins insisted on unleavened bread, while the Greeks used leavened bread. Theophylact admitted that Christ used unleavened bread but argued that Christian liberty did not require a legalistic replication of such details. Nevertheless, concludes Schaff, "upon both these points of fierce and long controversy he counseled continual rememberance [sic] of the common Christian faith and the common Christian fellowship."[91]

Exegesis of Mark 14:54, 66-72. If the *Address on the Errors of the Latin Church* is his most interesting work, his fame rests with his commentaries, especially those on the Gospels.[92] Although he was dependent to a large extent on earlier Fathers, especially Chrysostom, he has nevertheless been praised for his own exegetical insight which "is so direct, precise, and textual, and his remarks are often so felicitous and to the point, that his commentaries have always been highly prized."[93]

Discrepancies. Theophylact's sound judgment and historical insight can be seen in his handling of the discrepancies between the accounts of Matthew and Mark. Regarding the identification of the servant girl he says:

And whether this same servant girl or another, she gazed directly at Peter having detected him. For Matthew says it was another [girl]; but Mark [says it was] the same one. But this [does] nothing to obstruct from us the truth of the Gospel; For do they not agree in the significant and essential [thing] of our salvation? Did one say that the Lord was crucified, but another, [that he was] not? Away; Be gone [with such thinking]!

Evidently it was important to him to keep a perspective about that which posed a serious question for scholarship and faith. He felt that the discrepancy between the identification of the servants was immaterial when compared with the scope and the nature of agreement between the Gospel accounts.

He was not unwilling to offer an historical explanation when he deemed it pertinent. And as Schaff points out, although Theophylact relies heavily on older writers, he "shows true exegetical insight, explaining the text clearly and making many original remarks of great value."[94] For example:

Now Matthew says indistinctly, "Before the cock crows"; but Mark elaborates [interprets], "Before [the cock] crows twice." For the roosters were accustomed, according to one school of thought, to crow several times, thereupon to fall into a kind of sleep, and again after some time to begin another "crowing." Therefore Matthew says, "Before the cock crows," by which he means "[Before] the completion of the cock-crow, you will deny me thrice."

This explanation of the cock crow underscores an understanding of the customs and behavior of the animal life which is only slightly less sophisticated than explanations by some modern scholars. A modern study of the crowing of roosters in Palestine confirms that there is indeed such a pattern of three crowings occurring approximately one hour apart and each lasting approximately five minutes.[95] Theophylact's source on this point is well informed.

Historical Exegesis. Theophylact's knowledge of the *Sitz im Leben* of the Gospel story is good and the information he supplies his reader valuable; "he conceived rightly the aim and method of exegesis, and the precision of his interpretation makes his commentaries still worthy of consideration."[96] There are perhaps not many who would agree with his suggestion that the young man of 14:51, 52 who fled away naked was "James, the brother of God...Who also received the See of Jerusalem from the Apostles after the ascension of the Lord." But he is relying on tradition at this point, and is careful to qualify the suggestion as only "probable" (*eikos*).

Theophylact explains to his reader why there is the mention in 14:53 of both a "high priest" and "chiefpriests," the latter being a plural of the former word.

Although the law required one to be high priest for life, there were many at that time who were buying the offices from the Romans each year. Therefore he says "chiefpriests," those having determined the limits of tenure for themselves, and disregarding the [legitimate] chiefpriesthood.

This agrees with the testimony of the Babylonian Talmud: "And as the candidate paid money in order to become high priest, they [the procurators] were in the habit of depriving the high priest of office every twelve months."[97] The office of the high priest was the subject of purchase and intrigue. In an assembly such as the one which tried Jesus there might be several former holders of the high priestly office, though only one would function as the officiating highest officer (cf. Luke 3:2).[98]

Pastoral Concerns. Although Theophylact's comments exhibit an adeptness in historical-critical matters, "at the same time they insist on practical morality."[99] Not even Peter's fall was without a moral lesson.

> God permitted him to suffer this on account of his (Apostolic) commission, in order that he might not be puffed up, and in order that he may also be sympathetic with those who [cause to?] stumble, having learned for himself the violence which is a weakness common to man.

It is for just such a reason that,

> The Novatianists should be ashamed for refusing to receive [back into fellowship] those who sinned with the baptism and the partaking of the mysteries.

> For behold Peter, having forgotten the undefiled body and blood, and having denied, was restored by repentance.

It is unclear if Theophylact was referring to any particular "sinners" at this point, a group with whom he perhaps had to deal in his tenure as archbishop. Moreover, Novatianism as a rigorist movement regarding the reconciliation of the lapsed seems to have died out by the end of the fifth century.[100] It may be that Theophylact was not referring so much to an active and clearly identifiable Novatianist movement as much as making a point regarding rigorism in general. That issue is perennial in the church. And Theophylact made his position on that issue clear:

> For they (i.e., the Evangelists) made the shortcomings of the saints a matter of public record, in order that we, if we should at any time stumble, should also have their examples in mind, and should through repentance hasten to be reconciled.

Linguistic Exegesis. It is probable that Theophylact's native language gave him an advantage regarding some of the more difficult points of the text. For the troublesome phrase in 14:72, *epibalon eklaien*, Theophylact offers two possibilities:

> ..."For 'breaking down' [*epibalon eklaien*]," he says, "he wept," by which he

intends to say, "covering [his] head [he began to weep]"; or perhaps rather, "he began [to weep] very violently."

While Theophylact failed to solve the question altogether, it is also true that his opinion on this (as with many other matters) still carries significant weight. His opinions are cited as authoritative by scholars such as Bengel and Lapide[101] and even by many modern sources such as Bauer-Arndt-Gingrich, Henry Barclay Swete, and Vincent Taylor.[102]

Deserving note lastly is Theophylact's description of Peter in 14:54 & 67. In both verses Mark makes reference to Peter "warming himself to the fire." This is a widely recognized literary technique of intercalation whereby the story of Peter's denial brackets Jesus' trial before the Sanhedrin. After reading of Jesus' trial, the reference to Peter "warming himself to the fire" in verse 67 reminds the reader of the same reference in verse 54. Hence, that which was happening to Jesus is to be understood as occurring simultaneously to Peter's experience in the courtyard. Theophylact makes only one comment about Peter in 14:54:

But Peter himself followed, exhibiting a warm love for the Teacher.

It sounds odd, but not so unusual as to question the statement at its face value. However, Theophylact's comment on 14:67 is odder still:

Peter was weak, even if he was also "warmer"...

It is possible, of course, to take this literally. Peter was "warmer" by virtue of his being near the fire. But it hardly deserves mentioning. And it makes no sense as a concomitant observation of "he was weak." Thus, while the adjective *thermoteros* can mean literally "warmer," it also has several metaphorical meanings, including "hasty, rash," and "zealous."

It is quite possible that Theophylact was playing on Mark's description of Peter's "warming himself to the fire" to create a double (triple?) entendre! The meaning could therefore be: Peter followed Jesus, exhibiting a "rash" or perhaps "zealous" love for the Teacher. And "he was weak, even if he was also *tempestuous*" or perhaps rather *"full of zeal."*

Euthymius Zigabenos

There is perhaps less known of Euthymius than of his contemporary Theophylact. He was an educated and capable Greek monk of the order of St. Basil. He lived in the convent of the Virgin Mary near Constantinople where he died around 1118.[103] He was favored by the emperor Alexius Comnenus (1081–1118) and his wife Anna.[104]

At the request of Alexius, he wrote a polemic against the Bogomiles, the medieval Bulgarian sect which held that God has two sons, the rebellious Satan and the obedient Jesus. But the effort turned into an extensive work against heresy in general, assailing not only the Bogomiles but Pantheists, Jews, Armenians, the Pope and the Latin church.[105] Called *The Panoply*,[106] the attack on the Roman Church, as in Theophylact, was concerned primarily with the procession of the Holy Spirit and the use of unleavened bread.[107]

One other work of his deserving mention is "The Dialogue with a Saracen Philosopher about Faith." It is a contrived debate in which a mythical Arab philosopher puts various questions to Euthymius about the Trinity, the Incarnation, the Eucharist, and the differences between Christianity and Muhammadanism. At the end of the debate the Saracen philosopher declares: "I have been defeated, I have been defeated. How great is the faith of Christianity! The teaching of Christianity is true. The Lord God declares it. Onward, servant of God, baptize me!"[108]

Exegesis of Mark 14:54, 66-72. Besides *The Panoply,* Euthymius wrote several commentaries on the Psalms and the Gospels. The former are much dependent on Chrysostom, the latter more independent. It is a scholarly consensus that the commentaries on the Gospels are superior to those on the Psalms, but there is disagreement about the quality of his commentaries compared to Theophylact. Philipp Meyer thinks him "inferior in exegetical precision to Theophylact";[109] Schaff thinks him his equal.[110] On the basis of his exegesis of Mark 14:54, 66-72, we agree with Meyer, though the amount of material is too small to form an accurate appraisal.

This is because unfortunately Euthymius regarded Mark so lowly that he hardly produced a separate commentary at all. He was not unwilling to address the discrepancies of the Evangelists, and such discrepancies did not appear to him insuperable. Notes Hagenbach:

> That one evangelist sometimes relates what is omitted by another, etc., he simply attributes to the circumstance that they did not exactly recollect all the facts, because they did not write until a considerable space of time had elapsed.[111]

However, according to Euthymius, Mark "agrees so closely with Matthew except where Mark is more complete,"[112] that a completely different commentary was not warranted. "His notes on Mark are therefore generally mere cross-references to those on Matthew; here and there, however, where Mark differs from Matthew or relates something which is peculiar to himself, useful comments will be found."[113] That occurs only once in the passage on Peter's denial. Euthymius thought the description of Peter "warming himself to the light" deserved further clarification:

> To the light, [i.e.] which came from the fireplace, so as to be seen by all those sitting together and all those in the courtyard; but concerning these [matters] it has been commented on there.

Otherwise, the reader is referred repeatedly to the sixty-fourth, sixty-fifth, or sixty-sixth chapters in the commentary on the Gospel according to Matthew.

On two occasions he tells his reader that in addition to finding commentary on a parallel verse in Matthew he will find comment on additional material. Thus, in 14:69-72a he adds,

..and read the exegesis of this there: "and entering within [he] sat with the attendants [in order] to see the end."

And again in 14:72:

Concerning this and also the other [matters] it has been commented on. Not only concerning the statement [that] he forgot by reason of fear and weakness, but also this: "Whoever should deny me before men, him also will I deny before my Father who is in heaven."

Euthymius is an important example of the influence of Augustine's opinion about Mark's being the abbreviator of Matthew. Euthymius' Commentary on Mark is subsequently only an abbreviation of his Commentary on Matthew.

Summary

Although our representation is not exhaustive, Bede and Strabo from the West, and Theophylact and Euthymius from the East, it indicates that the Antiochene method seems to have won the day for the Orthodox Church, while the Alexandrian method prevailed in Rome.

This provides an interesting point of contrast between Medieval and Reformation exegesis of this passage. As the discussion to follow shows, the Reformers denigrated the search for the "spiritual sense." The "literal sense" was none other than the revelation of God in Jesus Christ in history. This sense possessed its own spiritual significance. Thus, while the allegorical enterprise probably cannot be said to have caused the Reformation, its demise became a cause to champion among the Reformers. It is also interesting to note that Calvin's exegesis of this passage, while fresh and original, seems to depend more on Victor than any of the Medieval scholars. The same can be said for à Lapide and Quesnel for that matter, although here the kinship is in the spirit of the commentary rather than verbal dependency.

Endnotes for Chapter Three

[1]G. H. Brown, *Bede the Venerable* (Boston: Twayne, 1987) 3-5; E. W. Watson, "The Age of Bede," in *Bede: His Life and Times,* ed. A. Hamilton Thompson (New York: Russell & Russell, 1966) 39; Jean Leclercq, "Saint Bede and Christian Expansion," *WS* 7 (1985) 6; See also Henry Mayr-Harting, *The Coming of Christianity to England* (New York: Schocken Books, 1972) 62.

[2]Bertram Colgrave, *The Venerable Bede and His Times,* Jarrow Lecture 1958 (Gallowgate, Newcastle: J. & P. Bealls, n.d.) 6.

[3]C.E. Whiting, "The Life of the Venerable Bede," in *Bede,* ed. Thompson, 1.

[4]Brown, *Bede,* 14-6.

[5]Colgrave, *The Venerable Bede,* 3.

[6]Bede, *Ecclesiastical History,* V. 24; Cf. Leclercq, "Saint Bede," 19; Brown, *Bede,* 15; Whiting, "The Life of the Venerable Bede," in *Bede,* ed. Thompson, 5.

[7]Brown, *Bede,* 10.

[8]*Ibid.,* 9.

[9]*Ibid.,* Preface; Herbert Dunelm, "Introduction," in *Bede,* ed. Thompson, xv; Charles W. Jones, "Bede's Place in Medieval Schools," in *Famulus Christi,* ed. Gerald Bonner (London: SPCK, 1976) 261; See also Jones' "Some Introductory Remarks on Bede's Commentary on Genesis," *SacEr* 19 (1969-70) 115. o62

[10]*The Ecclesiastical History of the English People. Bede's Ecclesiastical History of the English People.* Edited and translation by Bertram Colgrave and R. A. B. Mynors (Oxford: Clarendon Press, 1969).

[11]Claude Jenkins, "Bede as Exegete and Theologian," in *Bede,* ed. Thompson, 152.

[12]J. Campbell, "Bede," in *Latin Historians,* ed. T.A. Dorey (London: Routledge & Kegan Paul, 1966) 159.

[13]Brown, *Bede,* 14-5.

[14]M.L.W. Laistner and H.H. King, *A Hand-List of Bede Manuscripts* (Ithaca, NY: Cornell University Press, 1943); See also Laistner's "The Library of the Venerable Bede," in *Bede,* ed. Thompson, 237-66.

[15]Roger Ray, "What do we know about Bede's Commentaries," *RTAM* 49 (1982) 6.

[16]*Ibid.,* 7; Jones, "Genesis," 131.

[17]Brown, *Bede,* 21.

[18]Whiting, "The Life of the Venerable Bede," in *Bede,* ed. Thompson, 21.

[19]*Ibid.*

[20]Brown, *Bede,* 56; Jones, "Genesis," 115.

[21]M.L.W. Laistner, "Antiochene Exegesis in Western Europe during the Middle Ages," *HTR* 40 (1947) 19-31.

[22]*Ibid.,* 29.

[23]Jones ("Genesis," 136, n60) cites T. Homes Dudden, *Gregory the Great* II, p. 309: "After him [Gregory] doctors maintained a threefold (Paschasius), a fourfold (Aquinas), a sevenfold (Angelom of Luxeuil), and [sic] eightfold (Odo of Cluny), and even an infinite sense of Scripture."

[24]*Ibid.,* 137; See also Brown, *Bede,* 47-8.

[25]*De arte metrica et de schematicus et tropis,* ed. C. B. Kendall, CCSL 123 A (Turnhout, Belgium: Brepols, 1975) 59-171. Part II translated by G. H. Tanenhaus, "Bede's *De Schematicus et Tropis* — A Translation," *Quarterly Journal of Speech* 48 (1962) 237-53.

[26]Jones, "Genesis," 141.

[27]*Ibid.,* 142.

[28]*Ibid.,* 145.

[29]*Ibid.,* 135.

[30]Ray, "Bede's Commentaries," 10.

[31]Brown, *Bede,* 47.

[32]Jones, "Genesis," 133.

[33]R. B. Palmer, "Bede as a Textbook Writer: A Study of his 'de arte metrica,'" *Speculum* 34 (1959) 584; Ray, "Bede's Commentaries," 11-2.

[34]Brown, *Bede,* 14-5.

[35]Jones, "Genesis," 147-8.

[36]Ray, "Bede's Commentaries," 10. 02

[37]M. L. W. Laistner, "Source-Marks in Bede Manuscripts," *JTS* 34 (1933) 350.

[38]Brown, *Bede,* 44.

[39]Laistner, "Source-Marks," 350; E. F. Sutcliffe ("Quotations in the Ven. Bede's Commentary on S. Mark," *Biblica* 7 [1926] 428): "He tells the reader that he has been careful to note in the margin (*eminus e latere*) the initial letters of names (*primas nominum letteras*) of the writers whose words he makes his own (PL 92, 304), in order to indicate the beginning and the end of each quotation (*ubi cuiusque patrum incipiat, ubi sermo quem transtuli desinat, intimare*)."

[40]As both Laistner ("Source-Marks," 350) and Sutcliffe ("Quotations," 428-9) point out, it was believed for many years that these notations had been lost. Although they have been largely recovered by these men, there are still lacunae.

[41]I am indebted to David Hurst, who is editor of several volumes of Bede's work in the Corpus Christianorum Series Latina, including *In Lucae evangelium expositio* and *In Marci evangelium expositio*, CCSL 120 (Turnhout, Belgium: Brepols, 1960), for a translation of Bede's commentary on Mark 14:54, 66-72. He pointed out to me Bede's sources in this section.

[42]Brown, *Bede*, 20.

[43]Ray, "Bede's Commentaries," 11.

[44]Jenkins, "Bede as Exegete and Theologian," in *Bede*, ed. Thompson, 170.

[45]*Ibid.*

[46]Ray, "Bede's Commentaries," 12.

[47]A. Willmes, "Bedas Bibelauslegung," *Archiv für Kulturgeschichte* 44 (1962) 291.

[48]Brown, *Bede*, 44.

[49]Ray, "Bede's Commentaries," 11.

[50]Jenkins, "Bede as Exegete and Theologian," in *Bede*, ed. Thompson, 170.

[51]*Ibid.*

[52]*Ibid.*, 166.

[53]*Ibid.*, 165.

[54]T. R. Eckenrode, "The Venerable Bede and the Pastoral Affirmation of the Christian Message in Anglo-Saxon England," *DRev* 99 (1981) 273.

[55]Ray, "Bede's Commentaries," 11.

[56]Eckenrode, "Pastoral Affirmation," 261.

[57]*Ibid.*, 272.

[58]*Ibid.*, 265.

[59]Ray, "Bede's Commentaries," 11.

[60]Jenkins, "Bede as Exegete and Theologian," in *Bede*, ed. Thompson, 171, 188-9.

[61]Brown, *Bede*, 44.

[62]*Ibid.*, 44-5.

[63]Ray, "Bede's Commentaries," 12.

[64]Eckenrode, "Pastoral Affirmation," 262; See also p. 260 for Bede's comments in his *Commentary on Mark*: "It is essential that the word of the preacher comes first, and then divine help will ensue to enlighten and inspire the heart of the listener"; and also: "The uneducated were eager to learn the Divine Enlightenment so that they would be refreshed...but lacking preachers who would spread the tidings, they found no one to show them the way."

[65]Jones, "Genesis," 124.

[66]Jenkins, "Bede as Exegete and Theologian," in *Bede*, ed. Thompson, 170.

[67]*Ibid.*, 158.

[68]David Hurst, "Venerable Bede and the Scriptures," *WS* 7 (1985) 69.

[69]Ray, "Bede's Commentaries," 17, esp. fn. 60.

[70]Brown, *Bede,* 45.

[71]Bede Foord, "Bede the Venerable and Venerable Women," *WS* 7 (1985) 51.

[72]*Ibid.*, 61.

[73]Jones, "Genesis," 118.

[74]Jenkins, "Bede as Exegete and Theologian," in *Bede,* ed. Thompson, 175.

[75]Jones, "Genesis," 119.

[76]Philip Schaff, *History of the Christian Church, IV: Medieval Christianity* (Grand Rapids: Wm. B. Eerdmans, 1950) 729.

[77]*Ibid.*, 729-30; Albert Hauck, s.v. "Walafrid Strabo," *The New Schaff-Herzog Encyclopedia of Religious Knowledge* (Grand Rapids: Baker Book House, 1957) 238.

[78]Hauck, 238.

[79]B. Smalley, *The Study of the Bible in the Middle Ages* (New York: Philosophical Library, 1952) 57.

[80]Hauck, 238.

[81]Schaff, 730.

[82]Kealy, *Mark's Gospel,* 39

[83]For the complete text of (Pseudo-) Jerome interrupted by the "etc. *usque ad...,*" see Appendix D. For the complete text of Bede thus interrupted, see Appendix B.

[84]Schaff, 730-1.

[85]Schaff, *Christian Church* 4:644.

[86]*Ibid.*; also see *ODCC,* 1364.

[87]*Ibid.*, 4:644.

[88]*S-HRE,* s.v. "Theophylact" by Philipp Meyer, 11:407.

[89]Schaff, *Christian Church,* 4:645.

[90]*Ibid.*

[91]*Ibid.*

[92]*Ibid.*, 644.

[93]*CBTEL,* s.v. "Theophylact," 10:336.

[94]Schaff, 4:644.

[95]See H. Kosmala, "The Time of the Cock-Crow," *ASTI* 2 (1963) 118-20; 6 (1968) 132-4.

[96]*S-HRE*, 11:407.

[97]William Lane (*The Gospel According to Mark,* NIC [Grand Rapids: Eerdmans, 1974] 531) cites The Babylonian Talmud *Yoma* 8b.

[98]*Ibid.*, 543-4.

[99]*ODCC*, 1364

[100]Alan Richardson, ed., s.v. "Novatianism" by H. E. W. Turner, *A Dictionary of Christian Theology* (Philadelphia: Westminster, 1976) 235.

[101]Johann Albrecht Bengel, *Gnomon of The New Testament* Vol. 1 o62 (Edinburgh: T. & T. Clark, 1859) 568; Cornelius à Lapide, *The Great Commentary of Cornelius à Lapide,* tr. by Thomas W. Mossman Vol. 1 (Edinburgh: John Grant, 1908) 439.

[102]BAGD, 289-90; Swete, *Commentary on Mark* (Grand Rapids: Kregel, 1977) 366; Vincent Taylor, *The Gospel According to St. Mark* (London: Macmillan, 1952) 576-7.

[103]Philipp Meyer, s.v. "Euthymius Zigabenus," *S-HRE* 4:216; Schaff, *Christian Church,* 4:648.

[104]Schaff, *Christian Church,* 4:648.

[105]*Ibid.*

[106]Hagenbach, *Christian Doctrines,* 2:112.

[107]*S-HRE*, 4:216.

[108]Adel-Théodore Khoury, "Gespräch über den Glauben zwischen Euthymios Zigabenos und einem Sarazenischen Philosophen," *ZMR* 48 (1964) 203. Both this citation and the title of Euthymius' work mentioned at the beginning of the paragraph are my English translation of Khoury's German translation which is taken from Migne's *PL* 131.

[109]*S-HRE*, 4:216.

[110]Schaff, *Christian Church,* 4;648.

[111]Hagenbach, *Christian Doctrines,* 2:167.

[112]For the Greek text of this citation see Swete, *Mark,* cxvi.

[113]*Ibid.*

Chapter 4

Reformation and Post-Reformation

The Seeds of a Reformation View of Scripture

The Reformation had a significant impact on Biblical hermeneutics. It marks a genuine shift in methodological approaches. It would be difficult to say if the results of Reformation exegesis were due more to a change in presuppositions or in methodology. It may be that the shift in methodology was due to a shift in presuppositions. But the change was not as sudden in coming as is sometimes supposed. Klaas Runia has identified at least three historical developments during the Middle Ages which helped set the stage for the Reformation and mark a certain continuity with the two eras.

Recovering the Literal Sense of Scripture. Although Medieval hermeneutics is chiefly characterized by the fourfold interpretation, the literal meaning was never completely obscured.[1] Thomas Aquinas, as one example, had already clarified in his *Summa Theologica* that "all interpretations are based on one, that is the literal form, from which alone we can argue."[2] Nicholas of Lyra, of whom Luther was at first critical,[3] also pursued the significance of the literal form and thus, according to Runia, paved the way for Luther. Runia cites an often quoted jingle:

Si Lyra non lyrasset
Lutherus non sallasset.
(If Lyra had not sung,
Luther would not have danced.)[4]

Recovering the Primacy of Scripture over the Magisterium. An important difference between the Medieval and Reformation views is that of the relation of the

Scripture to the Church. The view, clearly articulated by the Reformers, that the authority of Scripture was primary to that of the Church, was a source of irreconcilable differences between the Reformers and Rome.[5] Before the Reformation William of Ockham had tactfully written that "what is not contained in the scriptures or cannot with necessity and obvious consistency be deduced from the contents of the same, no Christian needs to believe."[6] Moreover, in the case of a (hypothetical) contradiction between the magisterium and Scripture, the final authority and infallibility rests with Scripture. Neither Ockham in particular nor medieval scholarship in general was prepared to surrender final ecclesiastical authority. Nevertheless, says Runia, "this view of scripture also paved the way for Luther.[7]

Recovering the Ministry of Study. The way was paved for the Reformers intellectually by "the new humanism" in the fourteenth (in Italy) and fifteenth (in Germany and the rest of Europe) centuries. Figures such as Laurentius Valla, Johannes Reuchlin, and Desiderius Erasmus gave fresh impetus to the study of Scripture, especially with their emphasis on the study of the Biblical languages of Hebrew and Greek.[8]

While these developments help explain why the Reformation was possible, they do not explain why the Reformers thought it necessary. For that, one would have to explore a vaster array of factors than we are able. Runia suggests it was the developing notion that the Bible rather than the Church was the way to God. The pendulum swung the other direction.[9]

The Hermeneutics of the Reformers

Luther and many others of the Reformers felt free to evaluate the books of the canon in light of their testimony of Christ. According to Luther,

> John's Gospel and St. Paul's epistles, especially that to the Romans, and St. Peter's first epistle are the true kernel and marrow of all the books. They ought properly to be the foremost books, and it would be advisable for every Christian to read them first and most, and by daily reading to make them as much his own as his daily bread. For *in them you do not find many works and miracles of Christ described*, but you do find depicted in masterly fashion how faith in Christ overcomes sin, death, and hell, and gives life, righteousness, and salvation. This is the real nature of the Gospel as you have heard.[10]

Luther is often quoted for his dissatisfaction with James because it was, in his opinion, "an epistle of straw, for it has nothing of the nature of the gospel about it."[11] Perhaps he felt the Synoptic Gospels focused too much on the "many works and miracles of Christ" and thereby neglected a more direct theological message. Whatever the explanation, Luther did not write a commentary on the Synoptic Gospels or on Mark. Hardly anyone did.[12] By far the most important was Calvin's commentary on the *Harmony*, to which we shall shortly turn our attention. It seems appropriate to address first the hermeneutical principles which characterized the Reformation movement.

History Grounds Scripture. This is not the most important principle for the Reformers, but it provides the best point of contrast with their Medieval forerunners. They became convinced that the highly prized "spiritual sense" of Scripture had been abused and misused as a way of reading into the text preconceived meanings. In the view of the Reformers, the literal historical meaning of the text does not conceal some true spiritual meaning behind or above it; it *is* the spiritual meaning of the text. It is by the simplest, most natural grammatical-historical sense of the text that God has communicated the profoundest, most supernatural message. Said Luther in his controversy with Erasmus:

> Let us rather take the view that neither an inference nor a trope is admissible in any passage of Scripture, unless it is forced upon us by the evident nature of the context and the absurdity of the literal sense as conflicting with one or another of the articles of faith. Instead, we must everywhere stick to the simple, pure, and natural sense of the words that accords with the rules of grammar and the normal use of language as God has created it in man.[13]

Thus, Luther was not unwilling to admit allegory provided it was the clear intention of the author to have his words allegorized. But otherwise one should not search for a spiritual meaning beyond the historical meaning. Again, "our first concern will be for the grammatical meaning, for this the truly theological meaning."[14]

Tradition Bears Witness to Scripture. Again, while not the most important, this hermeneutical principle of the Reformers also provides an important point of contrast. "The Roman church," explains Ronald S. Wallace, "believed that the Church had given birth to the Word; thus the primacy, in the act of interpretation, lay not with the Word but with the Church."[15] The entire Reformation movement seemed united on this point, that the Church finds its existence in Scripture. Any discrepancy between the two is a moot point for discussion. Scripture corrects all our opinions and judgments. Says Calvin:

> We do not with perverted ardor and without discrimination rashly seize upon what first springs to our minds. Rather, after diligently meditating upon it, we embrace the meaning which the Spirit of God offers. Relying upon it, we look down from a height at whatever of earthly wisdom is set against it. Indeed, we hold our minds captive, that they dare not raise even one little word of protest, and humble them, that they dare not rebel against it.[16]

What, then, of tradition and the fathers? They are very valuable. Wrote Calvin to one Grynaeus,

> Since in this life we cannot hope to achieve a permanent agreement in our understanding of every passage of Scripture, however desirable that would be, we must be careful not to be carried away by the lust for something new, not to yield to the temptation to indulge in sharp polemic, not to be aroused to animosity or carried away by pride, but to do what is necessary and to depart from the opinions of earlier exegetes only when it is beneficial to do so.[17]

Calvin and others of the Reformers seemed uninterested in pointless iconoclasm of tradition. Calvin felt himself particularly bound to Augustine. The hermeneutical principles which follow, of scripture interpreting scripture, with the illumination of the Spirit and the focus of Christ, determine not only which interpretations the Reformers themselves were allowed to proffer but also which interpretations of any age were permissible. A Christ-centered, literal interpretation based on grammatical-historical exegesis was the goal. In this light, explains Grant, a Christian "can make use of the fathers insofar as they were competent exegetes. Of legal authority they retain none."[18]

The Spirit Illuminates Scripture. This and the principles to follow are more central to the Reformation hermeneutical enterprise. If Scripture is prior to the Church's decrees about it and if its real significance is grounded in its historical-literal meaning, then it follows that any Christian may read and interpret the Bible with efficacy. The message of Scripture is not a mystery to be deciphered by the clerical specialist nor to be excavated from the hard or bland surface meaning. According to Luther, "there is not on earth a book more lucidly written than the Holy Scripture."[19] Assuming an ability and willingness to study the history in which Scripture is grounded, the difficulty in interpreting Scripture lies not in Scripture but in our hearts. Explains Luther:

> There are two kinds of clarity in Scripture, just as there are also two kinds of obscurity: one external and pertaining to the ministry of the Word, the other located in the understanding of the heart.[20]

And,

> It ought above all to be settled and established among Christians that the Holy Scriptures are a spiritual light far brighter than the sun itself, especially in things that are necessary to salvation.[21]

But the objective clarity of Scripture can only illuminate that reader whose heart will not block that light. This requires the work of the Holy Spirit to change the individual by experience and then to illumine the meaning of Scripture. "For the Spirit is required for the understanding of Scripture, both as a whole and in any part of it."[22] Again, religious experience does not bring understanding, but to the one who thirsts after Christ in the Bible, the Holy Spirit will quench it. "God must say to you in your heart, This is God's word."[23]

Scripture Interprets Scripture. But this work of the Holy Spirit does not mean that the work of the interpreter is entirely subjective. Scripture cannot mean anything we want it to mean. But it cannot mean anything which the magisterium or tradition might dictate either. And that is the whole point. "The Bible is not one standard of authority among others, as it was for medieval Catholicism," explains Grant. "It is the sole standard."[24] And the true work of the Spirit is to open our hearts to the objective self-revelation of Scripture. "Scripture is its own light," says Luther. "It is a great thing when Scripture interprets itself."[25]

This principle probably includes the technical rule already utilized by the fathers that the unclear and doubtful passages of Scripture are to be interpreted in light of those passages which are clear and certain.[26] But Luther meant more than this. It is that Scripture possesses a clarity in and of itself. And the Spirit is not something which is given to the magisterium of the Church (contra Rome) or to individuals (contra the Enthusiasts). The Spirit comes in and through the Scripture itself. In one passage directed against the Enthusiasts Luther says,

> God gives no one his Spirit or grace except through or with the external Word which comes before. Thus we shall be protected from the Enthusiasts, that is, from the spiritualists who boast that they possess the Spirit without and before the Word and who therefore judge, interpret, and twist the Scriptures or spoken Word according to their pleasure.[27]

The Spirit is the author of Scripture. And God only gives His Spirit in and through Scripture. For this reason Luther even used the phrases "self-interpretation of Scripture" and "interpretation of scripture through the Holy Spirit" interchangeably.

Christ Orients Scripture. This objective, historical-literal meaning of Scripture can be subjectively apprehended because of the goal and purpose of the revelation, Jesus Christ. Says Luther: "Christus est punctus mathematicus Sacrae Scripturae."[28] The idea of Christ as the center point from which everything else is drawn, says W. Kooiman, is the really new element in the Reformation doctrine of Scripture in comparison to the Middle Ages:

> To place the Bible in a central position had been done by the theologians of earlier centuries. To place Christ in the centre of the Bible, as totally as Luther did, was previously unheard of. With great monotony he hammered consistently upon this single anvil.[29]

Runia has collected many quotations which demonstrate the importance of this principle for Martin Luther and, by extension, to the Reformation movement more broadly:[30]

> In the whole of Scripture there is nothing but Christ, either in plain words or in involved words.[31]

The whole of Scripture is about Christ alone everywhere, if we look to its inner meaning, although superficially it may sound different.[32]

[Christ is] the sun and truth in Scripture.[33]

Christ is the scopus of the whole Scripture [including the Old Testament].[34]

[In the Scripture] you will find the swaddling clothes and the manger in which Christ lies, and to which the angel points the shepherds (Luke 2:12). Simple and lowly are these swaddling clothes, but dear is the treasure in them.[35]

If there is a central, most important hermeneutical principle for Luther and the Reformers, it is this: the Bible is in its purpose and in its entirety a revelation of God's grace in Jesus Christ.

John Calvin

Klaas Runia says, "More than anyone else, [Calvin] influenced the development of the Reformation movement."[36] This is because while Luther was the pioneer, exuding creativity and originality, Calvin was the systematician;[37] he "amplified the new exegetical insights and put them into practice in his commentaries."[38]

A perusal of scholars of Calvin reveals how difficult it is to encapsulate his exegetical message.[39] The following points are not, therefore, exhaustive by any means. We focused on the most important ones with a view toward their employment on our passage.

One other point: Calvin had a very high regard for Scripture *in its canonical form* as the Word of God. Christ is for Calvin still very much the center of Scripture. But Scripture itself, in its entirety, is the instrument which the Spirit uses to reveal Christ.[40] This affected his view of the Old Testament. While Luther saw a significant dichotomy between the testaments, representing the dialectic of law and gospel, Calvin emphasizes a fundamental unity between the testaments. Moreover, Calvin was less inclined to discriminate between the New Testament books which best preached Christ. Perhaps it is for this reason that Calvin felt obliged to comment on this passage. For he produced commentaries on almost every book of the New Testament.[41]

sensus literalis. "Calvin," says Runia, " was still more consistent than Luther in his rejection of all *allegoresis* and his stress on the need for historical-grammatical exegesis."[42] Commenting on Paul's use of the word [*allegoroumena*] in Galatians 4:22-24 and the use of this verse to justify allegorization of Scripture broadly, Calvin wrote:

On the basis of [Paul's] writing that these things are [*allegoroumena*], Origen and very many others have seized the occasion of twisting Scripture this way and that *a genuino sensu*. They inferred from this passage that the *literalem sensum* is too lowly and mean and that beneath the rind of the letter there lie hidden deeper mysteries which can be extracted only by inventing allegories. And this continued without much opposition, for the world always has and always will prefer apparently clever speculations to sound teaching. Having such approbation, the license was increased more and more, so that this game in treating Scripture was not only permitted without censure, but was given the highest praise. For many centuries none was thought clever if he lacked the skill and daring to transform the sacred Word of God by his subtlety. This was undoubtedly a trick of Satan to diminish the authority of Scripture and to take away any real profit in reading it. God avenged this profanation with a just judgment when he suffered the pure understanding of it to be buried under false glosses. "Scripture", they say, "is fertile and thus bears more than one sense." I acknowledge that Scripture is the most rich and inexhaustible fount of all wisdom; but I deny that its fertility consists in the varied meanings which anyone may fasten to it at his pleasure. Therefore let us know *eum esse verum Scripturae sensum, qui germanus est ac simplex,* and let us embrace it and hold it resolutely. As for those pretended expositions which lead us *a literali sensu,* let us not merely neglect them as doubtful, but boldly reject them as deadly corruptions.[43]

And reject them he did. None of the allegorical suggestions so common in earlier commentaries reappear in Calvin. Origen's suggestion that "the first maid of the High Priest, who makes Christ's disciples to deny, is the synagogue of the Jews...the second is the assembly of the Gentiles...the third group...are the ministers of various heresies" gets no attention at all in Calvin's exposition. He rather offers a reasonable explanation for the supposed discrepancy between the Synoptic accounts:

> We tend to guess, from Mark's account, that it is the same maid: he certainly does not say she is a different one. There is nothing contradictory, in fact it is likely, that one girl's remark went round them all, the first point him out to many over and over again, the others going up to find out for sure and spreading the discovery further still. John says that the second questioning came not from a maid, but from a crowd of men. Obviously the report that started with the girl was picked up by the bystanders, who turned it against Peter.[44]

Regarding the crowing of the cock, Bede thinks "that by this cock must be understood some teacher who rouses us when we are asleep, and reproving our sleepiness says: 'Come to your right mind, and sin no more.'" Again, Calvin is concerned with the literal meaning:

> There is another difference between Mark and the other three. He mentions the cock crowing twice, the others say that it only crowed when Peter had denied the Lord for the third time. This problem too has an easy solution, since

Mark says nothing to contradict the report of the others. What they pass over in silence, he relates explicitly. I have no doubt when Christ said to Peter, "Before the cock crows," He meant the cock-crowing in its various repetitions. Cocks do not only crow once but repeat their calls several times, yet all the cock-crows of one night are called the cock-crowing. So Matthew, Luke and John say that Peter denied the Lord thrice before the end of cock-crowing. Mark gives the greater detail, that Peter came in quite a short space of time to his third denial, and did not repent at the first cock-crow. We do not say profane historians are in disagreement if one of them tells a thing the others leave unmentioned. Although Mark's narrative is different it is not at odds with the others.[45]

It would be difficult to think that Calvin did not know of the commentaries of both Victor and Theophylact, whose explanations are very similar to Calvin's above, in one or two places almost to the word. Hans-Joachim Kraus says that Calvin's method was, "insofar as possible, [to] hold to the work of earlier exegetes."[46] For allegories this was clearly not possible. For the interpretations of Victor and Theophylact it clearly was. However, if Calvin was using these men as resources, he does not say. At any rate, Calvin will entertain no allegorization, not even to explain an otherwise apparent contradiction. He is concerned with the natural historical meaning.

scopus Christus. For Calvin there is no need to search for a spiritual sense behind the literal, nor is the spiritual sense opposed to it. The literal sense is the historical record of God's revelatory activity in history in the Person of His Son Jesus Christ. That message *is* the spiritual message.[47] Understand the literal history of Scripture and you have understood the spiritual. It is for this reason that Calvin speaks of Scripture as having at its very center the *scope* (purpose, goal) *of Christ.*[48]

Commenting on John 5:39 Calvin said: "First, then, we ought to believe that Christ cannot be properly known in any other way than from *the Scriptures;* and if it be so, it follows that we ought to read *the Scriptures* with the express design of finding Christ in them."[49] Thus, the goal of exegesis is clearly defined: find Christ! Indeed, Calvin found Christ in our passage.

Besides the cock-crow Luke tells us there was the sight of Christ: for he had first ignored the cock's crow, as we have learned from Mark. *So he had to meet Christ's eyes to come to himself. This is the experience of each one of us.* Which of us does not neglect with deaf ear and unconcern—not only the many and various songs of birds (and yet they prompt us to glorify God)—but the actual voice of God, which in Law and Gospel clearly and distinctly resounds for our learning? And it is not for one day only that our minds are seized with this dumb stupidity, but on and on, until He grants us a sight of Himself. This alone converts the hearts of men. It is well worth noting, that it was no ordinary look (since He had already looked at Judas, who became none the better of it), but with the turning of His eyes on Peter, there went the secret power of the Spirit piercing his heart with the radiance of His grace. *Whence we learn, that as often as a man has lapsed, repentance for him only starts from the look the Lord gives* [emphasis added].[50]

Throughout the passage Calvin finds Christ preached; he says of His punishment:

...once we deprive ourselves of the assistance of the Holy Spirit, that He allows Satan to work his power on us with violence, tossing us this way and that in our utter addiction and slavery;[51]

of His providence:

...unless the Lord had regard for our weakness and held off the brunt of his rage, we should have to encounter a vast onslaught of temptation. In this respect we must glory in the Lord's mercy, that He allows no more than the bare hundredth part of our enemy's evil purpose to make way against us;[52]

of His goodness:

Christ's goodness is the more wonderful, that He healed the disciple brought forth from such a pit;[53]

Calvin's exegesis of our passage justifies the conclusion: Calvin's exegesis is thoroughly Christocentric.

Spiritus Sanctus est Verus Interpres Scripturae. Calvin, as did Luther also, realized the necessity of the work of the Holy Spirit in interpreting His Word. The Word, it is true, possesses an inner clarity and self-revelatory character. The testimony of the Word and the testimony of the Spirit are two different testimonies; even less do they conflict. But the Spirit reveals and confirms to us the truth of Scripture *through* Scripture, so that the testimony is one and the same:

By a kind of mutual bond the Lord has joined together the certainty of his Word and of his Spirit so that the perfect religion of the Word may abide in our minds when the Spirit, who causes us to contemplate God's face, shines; and that we in turn may embrace the Spirit with no fear of being deceived when we recognize him in his own image, namely, in the Word.[54]

That Scripture is God's Word is revealed by the Spirit. That the message of Scripture is for us personally and individually is also revealed by the Spirit. Calvin would have regarded all of Scripture as having been urged by the Holy Spirit and possessing a message to us. But he sometimes points this out explicitly, as he does in his commentary on our passage.

[That Peter] denied before them all...is a circumstance that aggravates the offence; Peter, in denying his Master, did not take note of the crowd of witnesses in his fear. *The Spirit precisely wishes to impress on us that the sight of men should embolden us to hold firm to our faith.* If we deny Christ in the sight of the weak, they may be shocked and cast down by our example, and thereby we destroy all the souls we can. If, in the presence of wicked scorners of God and enemies of the Gospel, we cheat Christ of His due testimony, we expose His sacred name to the ridicule of all...The higher a man stands the more he should take care to himself, for he cannot fall from his rank without doing greater damage...Take this point; as soon as one departs from a simple and sincere profession of Christ, one robs Him of His rightful witness.[55]

Scriptura scripturae interpres. This, as has been asserted earlier, is not a completely different principle from the previous one of the Spirit's interpreting Scripture. But a separate treatment of it will allow us to explore a couple of nuances. Scripture possesses a fundamental unity and utility for addressing our need for Christ. It proclaims Him as the Church's salvation. One of Calvin's principles, therefore, says Wallace, is that the "true meaning of a passage will be found only as its relevance is found for the constantly urgent situation of the Church in the world."[56] It was by this principle of Scripture's self-interpretation to the Church that Calvin could say of the account of Peter's denial:

> Peter's fall, here described, brilliantly mirrors our own infirmity. His repentance in turn is a memorable demonstration for us of God's goodness and mercy. *The story told of one man contains teaching of general, and indeed prime, benefit for the whole Church;* it teaches those who stand to take care and caution; it encourages the fallen to trust in pardon [emphasis added].[57]

It was this propensity of Calvin to interpret pastorally and with such freshness that so sets him apart from the efforts of the fathers. Of Peter's weeping, says Calvin:

> The example teaches us that however lame our repentance, yet we may have good hope. As long as it is sincere, God scorns not even feeble repentance. Peter's secret tears testified in the Face of God and of the angels that his sorrow was true. Hidden from the eyes of men he puts before him God and the angels: from the inmost feelings of his heart flow those tears. We should note this, since we see many in floods of tears, as long as there is someone to watch, eyes are dry as soon as they are by themselves. No doubt tears that are not forced from us by God's judgments, spring from self-seeking and hypocrisy. It is asked whether true penitence requires weeping. I answer that the faithful often sigh unto God with dry eyes, and confess their fault, to obtain pardon: but in the graver sins it is too stupid and unfeeling not to be wounded with grief and sorrow to the point of shedding tears. *Scripture, after convicting men of their crimes, urges them to sackcloth and ashes* [emphasis added].[58]

Cornelius à Lapide

Cornelius à Lapide (1567-1637), a Belgian exegete who entered the Jesuit order in 1592, earned a reputation as a scholar with profound spiritual insight.

> His works have owed their enduring popularity, esp. among preachers, to their clarity, deep spirituality, and allegorical and mystical exegesis, buttressed by a wide erudition which enabled the author to draw extensively on the Fathers and on medieval theologians.[59]

The "Introduction" to his *Commentary on Mark* alone would justify such an assessment of his work. Although many of his conclusions would be liable to correction by modern scholarship and his discussion is almost "pietistic," yet his knowledge and critical evaluation of the Fathers and the traditions about Markan authorship rivals modern critical introductions. "[N]o one ought to be a teacher and doctor," he says, "until he has spent long time in studying as a disciple of the doctors."[60] His commentaries on the Gospels reflect this mature study.

From a thorough discussion of the traditions he concludes that the Mark who authored the Gospel was not John Mark, the companion of Paul, but rather another, a companion of Peter in Rome while John Mark was with Paul in Greece. He wrote in Greek, not Latin, as many of the Fathers thought. He demonstrates in an impressive manner that the Latin texts of Mark are translations of the Greek text, especially in his treatment of Mark 2:2; 4:10; 7:17, 18, 20. Following Eusebius, he believes the Gospel to have been written in Rome in A.D. 45, the third year of Claudius, from where he went to Alexandria where he founded both a thriving church and school.

Exegesis of Mark 14:54, 66-72. Lapide is familiar with Augustine's judgment that Mark was an "abbreviator" of Matthew,

> not because he made a compendium of his Gospel, as some say, but because he often relates more briefly, as he had received them from S. Peter, the things which Matthew records at greater length. I said "often," for occasionally Mark relates events in the life of Christ more fully than Matthew does, as is plain from the account of Peter's denial. Some things also he unfolds with greater clearness than Matthew. Mark is fuller in narrative than Matthew, but has less of Christ's doctrine. Mark's, therefore, is an independent Gospel.[61]

It was this "fuller narrative" which in part necessitated a commentary on Mark, "because most have been spoken of in S. Matthew. There the reader will find them annotated. Here, therefore," he asks permission to "be brief."[62]

Discrepancies. "The discrepancies of the Evangelists," proclaims Lapide, "are the greatest possible testimony to their truthfulness."[63] Citing the argument from Chrysostom in his Preface to Saint Matthew, he concludes that perfect agreement would rightly invite the criticism that the Evangelists "had framed the Gospels by human understanding." On the other hand, if one of the Gospels contained absolutely everything, the others would be superfluous; likewise if any of them contained material which could not be validated at all from the others, the discrepancies would be genuine contradictions. In his own words, therefore, he says:

> These four so appropriately wrote the words and deeds of Christ, that they seem to make a kind of musical harmony of four chords; for what each one writes is different in style from the others, but agrees with them in meaning and in facts. What one is silent about, another supplies: what one gives concisely, another relates more at large: what one obscurely hints at, another gives at length.[64]

The perfect example of this is Mark's mention of a cock crow after Peter's first denial. Lapide follows Chrysostom here at precisely the same point Victor of Antioch quoted him, especially to note that

> Mark only has written thus, most accurately detailing the gracious care of the Master for His disciple, and Peter's weakness. Wherefore we ought especially to admire him, because he not only did not hide his master's fault, but wrote the account of it in greater detail than the others, for this very reason that he was Peter's disciple.[65]

That which had troubled so many for so long thus became a source of comfort to Lapide for at least two reasons: (1) This "discrepancy" is proof that the account of the event is trustworthy, for it adds another, yet distinctly different testimony; (2) The more detailed narrative at this point implies that Mark had more detailed knowledge, namely from Peter himself. Moreover, rather than protect his mentor from embarrassment or ridicule, he expounded "the account of it in greater detail than the others." It was part of the proof that the author really did know Peter! Hence, Mark is uniquely qualified to relate that "neither by the crow of the cock was he led to remember, nor did it keep him from denial."[66]

Exegetical Sources. Much of the strength of Lapide's commentary, and that which consequently earned him a reputation as such a thorough scholar, is his breadth of sources. In addition to direct appeal to the Greek text, he was familiar with various textual traditions and texts in other languages. In particular he appeals to the Arabic version for clarification of v. 70, "For thou art also a Galilean," which of course implies, "[because] thy speech is similar to their speech."[67]

Of the possible translations of the troublesome Greek *epibalon eklaie* in v. 72, which he translates literally as "adding he was weeping," he prefers Theophylact's interpretive translation. His rendition of Theophylact's Greek is, "he began to weep very violently."

Peter did this "not in the court before the Jews," says Lapide, "that he might not betray himself to them, but when he was alone, having gone out of it as appears from S. Matt. xxvi. 75."[68]

Pasquier Quesnel

Quesnel was born in Paris in 1634. He entered the Congregation of the Fathers of the Oratorium in 1657 and became a priest in 1659. When he was approximately twenty-eight, he became the director of the Paris Institute, the seminary of his order. It was here that he began the work which drew such enmity from the Jesuits, *Reflexions morales sur le Nouveau Testament*. It was perceived by them as "Jansenistic." The Order to which he belonged was already involved in the Jansenistic controversies, and Quesnel's life and work were almost totally defined by this controversy.[69]

Jansenism takes its name from Cornelius Jansen (1585-1638), a French priest whose attraction to and exposition of Augustine were the cause of much dissension. Under other circumstances or in a different age it would perhaps have been otherwise. However, since an Augustinian understanding of Paul became the determining characteristic of both Luther and Calvin, the Counter-Reformation was itself frequently characterized by a sometimes hostile reaction to Augustine. Indeed, as the chasm between the Reformed churches and Rome widened, semi-Pelagianism assumed an ever greater dimension within Catholicism. A revival of Augustinianism within the Church by Jansen and Quesnel was especially objectionable to the Jesuits.[70]

Moreover, the entire issue was complicated manifold by a political factor, Gallicanism—a view supporting greater religious independence from Rome by virtue of a stronger affinity with respective States, especially in seventeenth and eighteenth century France. Because the Jesuits enjoyed the ear of the papacy, they also favored strong centralized control over the Church, which would in turn afford more control over dissident views like Jansenism. Many in the Church, the Jansenists in particular, defended the liberties of the Gallican Church which meant liberty from the censorship of the Jesuits. Slightly different ideological and political views strengthened one another and became so entrenched as to force open conflict. It is against this ideological and political background that Jansen's and Quesnel's interests in Augustine and his influence on their theology must be placed.[71]

Moral Reflections and the Bull *Unigenitus*. At a time when Jansenism had just quieted as an issue, the political and ideological forces collided once again.[72] Long after the death of Jansen, Quesnel published a defense of the Gallican Church in 1675 which gained the ire of the Roman Church, especially the then archbishop of Paris. Thus began a sort of exile through France lasting several years and ultimately leading Quesnel to Brussels.

In the meantime, Louis XIV found himself in opposition to the Jansenists who were not inclined to overlook his many sins. Thus, when Quesnel's *Reflections* appeared in a new and complete edition in 1693, Louis XIV took the opportunity to attack the Jansenists by asking Pope Clement XI to denounce the work. The Pope willingly seized the unusual opportunity to assert authority over the Gallican Church. The controversy lumbered on for twenty years and, says Neale, "the very name of

Jansenism nearly gave way to that of Quesnelism."[73] Finally, in 1713 the pope issued the bull *Unigenitus,* in which a hundred and one propositions of Quesnel's work were extracted and condemned as heretical.[74]

How complicated and politically charged the whole issue became is clear on hindsight, and hard for moderners to imagine. Acceptance or rejection of the bull came easily for some, owing to their previously declared positions. For others compliance was more difficult. As the comparison of some of the propositions with Quesnel's exposition of our passage below indicates, among the propositions "were not only some which may be found almost literally in Holy Scripture and in Augustine, but even some substantially identical with the decrees of the Council of Trent."[75] Numerous bishops begged to be allowed to make the distinction between the fact of heresy and opinion in human knowledge. The controversy continued into the end of the eighteenth century.[76]

The audacity of the bull *Unigenitus* is perhaps exceeded by the reception of Quesnel's work at the hands of the Protestants. In the Preface to the American edition, the revisor decries the bull for censoring the one hundred and one propositions which are "for the most part of an eminently scriptural and evangelical character,"[77] only to introduce his edition as having been edited of its "Romish errors":

> A large portion of the obnoxious passages were *omitted* in the English edition of the work; but a careful revision has brought to light a considerable number which had been overlooked. These have been expunged. To this point, indeed, the editor's task has been chiefly restricted—the cancelling of Romish errors —which must have impeded the circulation of the volumes and limited their usefulness.[78]

The material "expunged," though different in content, is about the same in quantity as that of the bull. Thus, a work which earned such high praise from those of both the Roman (there is one story that the pope who issued the bull had earlier read and praised the *Reflections*)[79] and Protestant churches, suffered no end to its censorship of expression.[80]

Methodology of Adoration. At first glance Quesnel's method makes it even more surprising that his work should have occasioned so much suspicion and animosity. It was not a strictly exegetical work but rather a practical reflection on the moral implications of the New Testament. Its first edition was published before 1670, while he was still director of the Paris Institute, and was intended for the practical use and meditation of his order. This methodology was not without a doctrinal basis, however.

In his preface to the *Reflections,* Quesnel declares that the gospel "is not 'the power of God unto salvation,' except only when the finger of God, that is, his Spirit, vouchsafes to write in our hearts the faith or belief of the eternal truths and mysteries of Christ." Indeed, "without this quickening Spirit, the letter, even of the gospel, is a letter which killeth."[81] This may be fairly compared with several of the propositions contained and condemned in the bull *Unigenitus:*

> #1. In vain, O Lord, thou commandest, if thou thyself dost not give that which thou commandest.[82]

> #5. When God does not soften the heart by the inner unction of his grace, exhortations and external graces avail only to harden it the more.[83]

> #41. No knowledge of God, even natural, even among pagan philosophers, can come except from God; and without grace it produces only presumption, vanity, and opposition to God himself instead of the feelings of adoration, gratitude, and love.

From this theological insight of the work of the Holy Spirit in imparting knowledge and spiritual understanding, Quesnel deduces his chief exegetical principle:

> From whence it is easy to infer, that in order to read it with advantage, it is necessary to join to this holy exercise such fervent prayer as may draw down upon us his Spirit and his benediction. Our own sanctification, as well as the sanctity of his word, requires that *our reading should have more in it of adoration than of study.* And since even the food of our body ought to be received with prayer and thanksgiving, how much more ought this spiritual food to be so, which is not at all beneficial to the soul, but only so far as the heart is open to receive it, and the eternal truth speaks to the heart?[85]

The nature of Quesnel's immediate spiritual insight is evidenced in several remarks found on Peter's denial of Jesus. Of Jesus' prediction of Peter's fall, Quesnel remarks:

> Christ knows even the least motion of our heart: let us, therefore, beseech him to impart some of his knowledge to us, that we may know it ourselves, and to our own advantage.[86]

When the text records that Peter followed Jesus into the palace of the high priest, Quesnel offers a maxim:

> Peter has rashly boasted of his courage, his honour is at stake, he will by no means go back, and nothing is wanting on his part to his destruction. But it is much better for a man to retreat and humble himself for his fault, than thus blindly to pursue it to the last.[87]

Of Peter's cursings and denials, Quesnel warns:

> What knowledge, what faith, what zeal soever a man has, he my lose it all in a moment, and become like Peter. Presumption was the cause of his fall: let humility support us, and conserve in us the gifts of God.[88]

Jansenism: Grace and Election. The theological basis of Quesnel's *Reflections* is, of course, Jansenism, whose centerpiece is the doctrine of grace. Jansenism has been compared with French Calvinism, and with good reason.[89] The following propositions from the *Unigenitus* are illustrative:

> #10. Grace is the operation of the hand of almighty God, which nothing can hinder or retard.[90]

Moreover,

> #2. The grace of Jesus Christ is necessary for all good works; without it nothing (truly good) can be done.[91]

Thus,

> #38. The sinner is not free except to evil without the grace of the Savior.[92]

In regards to Peter's denial, therefore, Quesnel is only exemplifying a consistency in his theological position. For Antoine Arnauld, the leader of the Jansenist party after the death of Jansen and who had handed the reins of leadership to Quesnel, had in 1654 published a work in which he had said of Peter:

> The grace of God, without which we can not do anything good, had left Peter at the time when he denied the Lord.[93]

Naturally Quesnel would concur:

> In vain does the cock crow to the ears of Peter; in vain do all preachers cry aloud to awaken the sinner, unless the grace of Christ open his understanding, his memory, and his heart and draw from thence the tears of repentance.[94]

Repentance. In Quesnel's theology,

> #28. The first grace which God grants the sinner is forgiveness of sins.[95]

And the proper response to this grace is silent love:

> #54. Charity is the only thing that talks with God; that alone does God hear.[96]

According to Quesnel, this grace was extended to Peter, and this was evident by his response.

> Peter's tongue utters not a word, but his heart speaks by his eyes. A true penitent ought to begin by silence, especially if his tongue has been the instrument of his sin. *Such a person should speak to God by his love,* and to men by his tears. It is to his heart that God speaks, when it is touched with a sense of his sins; and it is his heart which must speak to God, if it desires to be cured.[97]

Pastoral Concern and Praxis. As earlier indicated, a pastoral concern and a desire for practical morality are the most distinguishing characteristics of Quesnel's *Reflections*. Thus the admonition found in the *Unigenitus*,

#70. God never afflicts the innocent; and afflictions always serve either to punish sin or to purify the sinner,[98]

is borne out in Quesnel's comment about Peter:

...pride has drawn a veil over his heart, and his fall is necessary, to convince him that he is capable of falling. Pride is obstinate in the presumption which it has of its own strength. This is a very contagious distemper. One of the chief of the pastors was more sick of it than the rest, and even infected the others therewith. God permitted this, to the end that his example, being the more remarkable, might make the deeper impression, and raise a greater apprehension of falling into it. God punishes those more severely who are the first in giving a bad example, and become thereby the source of sin in a community.[99]

Scripture. Quesnel's view of the study of Scripture was more egalitarian than the Roman practice at that time. The following excerpts from the *Unigenitus* indicate the viewpoint which was a source of contention:

#79. It is useful and necessary at every time, in every place, and for every class of persons to study and to know the spirit, piety, and mysteries of sacred Scripture.

#80. The reading of sacred Scripture is for all.

#81. The sacred obscurity of the word of God is no reason for the laity to dispense themselves from its reading.

#82. The Lord's Day ought to be sanctified by Christians by readings of piety, and above all of the sacred Scriptures; it is wrong to wish to restrain the Christian from this reading.[100]

Thus, according to Quesnel, both the events recorded in Scripture and "readings of piety" (of which one assumes the *Reflections* could be included) are for the edification of the elect and to the saving of their souls. Even the tragic account of Peter's denial is such. Says Quesnel:

He falls, both for himself and for us: let us profit by his fall, as he did.[101]

John Albert Bengel

Born in 1687 in the small town of Winnenden in Würtemberg, Bengel took his theological training primarily at Tübingen beginning 1703. After a few brief pastoral and teaching posts, he was appointed to the theological gymnasium at Denkendorf where he spent twenty-eight years of his life ministering as a preacher, teacher and scholar. It was here that the *Gnomon* was written.[102]

If Quesnel represents a reaction to the general trend within Catholicism, Albert Bengel represents a reaction to the general trend in Protestantism. Bengel has been called "the most celebrated exegete that German Pietism produced."[103] He was strongly influenced by Spener via J. Böhme and J. Arndt, but in Bengel's day that "pietism had lost its original power."[104] Bengel, therefore, represents a distinct beginning. His work is not only distinct from the "historico-critical school, which handles Biblical dogmatics as a testimony to primitive Christianity in a historical interest,"[105] but also from Protestant theology in general which, although deriving salvific principles from Scripture, had nevertheless "made the principle of the subjective way of salvation the theological centre-point of Christian doctrine."[106] Herein lies one of the chief contributions for which Bengel is remembered, namely, that Scripture was not merely the basis of truth, nor even the criterion by which truth is judged, but rather was the source of truth.[107]

His Exegesis of Mark 14:54, 66-72. Although Bengel˚published over thirty original works and translated or edited many more, he is remembered for three chiefly, and these three indicate the three areas of chief academic contribution: (1) Being perplexed over the myriad of textual variants, he purposed to ascertain as nearly as possible the correct text of the New Testament. His *Apparatus Criticus* won international fame and earned him the title of "the father of textual criticism."[108] (2) The work of procuring the correct text led naturally to commenting on the text as he lectured. These lecture notes underwent several editions but finally appeared as the celebrated *Gnomon Novi Testamenti* in 1742.[109] (3) Lastly, he won fame as a specialist in prophecy and biblical chronology. This was not always positive, however, owing to some of the excesses in speculation. Sympathetic scholars of Bengel play this down. The most renowned work in this area was *Ordo Temporum* in 1741.[110]

His methodology was driven by his objective, and his objective is succinctly expressed in the preface to the *Gnomon*, namely, to recreate for his reader a context which was as nearly like that of the first reader as possible.

> Writings and commentaries are chiefly available for the following purposes: to preserve, restore, or defend the purity of the *text;* to exhibit the exact *force of the language* employed by any sacred writer; to explain the *circumstances* under which any passage was uttered or written, or to which it refers; to remove *errors* or abuses which have arisen in later times.—The first hearers required none of these things. Now, however, it is the office of commentaries to effect and supply them in some measure, so that *the hearer of to-day, when furnished with their aid, may be in a condition similar to that of the hearer in primeval times who made use of no such assistance.*[111]

Textual Criticism. The following three principles will indicate to what extent Bengel influenced the modern science of textual criticism: (i) Bengel was the first to arrange the manuscripts of the Greek New Testament into families, two chiefly: Asiatic and African. He thought the African was in general the more reliable. By recognition of families of manuscripts, he successfully discredited the notion that the majority opinion was for that reason the correct reading.[112] (ii) The criterion that the harder reading is generally to be preferred to the easier is Bengel's.[113] (iii) That the consistent application of multiple criteria (of which he enumerated at least twenty-seven) would allow the critic to ascertain the relative certainty of a variant; he "denoted these degrees by the Greek letters, *a* (i.e., alpha), *b* (i.e., beta), *c* (i.e., gamma), *d* (i.e., delta), *e* (i.e., epsilon),"[114] a method identical to the evaluative method in modern apparatuses.[115]

Exegetical Method. Bengel's exegetical method is best indicated by the title of his work, *Gnomon.*

> I have long since given the name of GNOMON, a modest, and, as I think, appropriate, title, to these *Exegetical Annotations*, which perform only the office of an *Index;* and, I should have chosen the term *Index*, as the title of my work, but for the misconception which would have arisen, in the minds of most persons, from the ordinary and technical use of that term [i.e., a *Registery or Table of Contents*]. It is, in short, my intention, briefly to *point out,* or *indicate,* the full force of words and sentences, in the New Testament, which, though really and inherently belonging to them, is not always observed by all at first sight, so that the reader, being introduced by the straight road, into the text, may find as rich pasture there as possible. The Gnomon points the way with sufficient clearness. If you are wise, the text teaches you all things.[116]

Because the work is result of lecture notes which assumed an active role on the part of the student, so also the *Gnomon* has this characteristic. It presumes on the reader a working knowledge of the biblical language, Christian thought, and an active interaction with the text. He was frequently criticized by his friends for a brevity of which Bengel himself was proud. "Let me beg of you," wrote Marthius of Presburg, "not to give your critical annotations too concisely, under the idea that your readers will take the trouble to *think out* all the meaning which you intend to convey in some two or three words."[117]

This criticism was more justified than realized even at the time. For not only was Bengel assuming too much of the reader of his day, namely that he would "think out" all the implications. He apparently did not foresee that it is quite difficult even for a reflective reader of a different historical context to put himself into the context which Bengel presumed. It is amazing, therefore, that Bengel's work has so endeared itself to following generations. The comments are pithy, frequently in incomplete sentences, the character of the comment on one verse differing from the following. This was, once again, by design:

> ...all these things are laid before the reader in such a manner, as to give him the opportunity and inducement to pursue the train of thought further himself. At each separate annotation the GNOMON must be supposed to say *"The Text runs thus,* not otherwise. *This,* and no other, is the noun; *this,* the verb; *this,* the particle; *this,* the case; *this,* the tense; *this* is the arrangement of the words; *this* is the repetition or interchange or words; *this,* the succession of arguments; *this,* the emotion of the minds, etc."[118]

The enduring vitality of the *Gnomon* resides not in its system, which is predictable only in its unevenness, but rather in its spiritual insight. As a true pietist, Bengel was able not only to explain the letter but also to capture the spirit of the writer. For him there could be no true exegesis apart from a prayerful and consecrated heart. His first hermeneutical principle, therefore, was

> Apply yourself wholly to the text;
> Apply the text wholly to yourself.[119]

That gift for insight is evident in our text, though the comments are characteristically brief and jumpy.

> 14:54. *With the attendants)* Often a fall is incurred more easily in the presence of such as servants, who are less feared, than among their masters.—*warming himself)* Often under care for the body the soul is neglected—*the light)* Appropriately *light* is the expression used instead of *fire*: Peter was recognized by the *light,* when under other circumstances he might have been safer: comp. ver. 67.

> 14:66. *Beneath)* There seem to have been a flight of steps there.

> 14:69. *The maid)* That same maid: or else a second one, so that the *again* may be connected with the participle alone, *having seen* him.—*to them that stood by)* She said it then in the spirit of joking, not with the intent to hurt him—*of them)* The expression, *of them,* shows, that speaking against Jesus and His disciples was most common and frequent.

> 14:72. *he betook himself)* To weeping, or, as Stapulensis interprets it, *He broke forth into weeping.* The French happily express it, *il se mit á pleurer.* Theophr. charact., *peri logopoiias; euthus erotesai—kai epibalon erotan:* as to which see Casaubon.[120]

Bengel's comments on our passage bear out Goltz' description of Bengel's method as "grammatico-historical exposition." Almost the totality of the *Gnomon* can be categorized as grammatical, historical, philological, or the spiritual principles to be derived from the use of them. It was his attempt to "put nothing into the

Scriptures but draw everything from them, and suffer nothing to remain hidden, that is really in them."[121]

Student of Prophecy. At least two assumptions motivated Bengel in his prophetic studies: (i) That nothing in the Bible was of mean consequence; (ii) That "Divine Economy" had so ordered creation that everything was "measured... connected," and symmetrical, especially history. Sympathetic scholars usually underscore his motive while downplaying his results. While he was successful at impressing other theologians to develop eschatologies, he himself was conspicuously in error in attempts to identify the beast of Revelation and his prediction that the world would end in 1837.[122]

Summary

The Reformation and its effects on Biblical scholarship afterwards mark a shift in methodological approaches. The scholastic approach as represented by the *Glossa* and the Orthodox scholars such as Theophylact looks much closer to works a millennium older when compared to the freshness of the works of Calvin, Lapide, and Bengel. In contrast, the nineteenth century appears to mark much more a shift in presuppositional framework than methodological procedure. The seeds for the modern Biblical hermeneutic were planted in the sixteenth century.

But it is also interesting to note that it was the Roman Church of the West, which had adopted so thoroughly the allegorical method of Alexandria, which experienced an eruption in the sixteenth century. And although the dispute was not over the allegorical method per se, the resulting exegetical efforts by the Reformers were a rejection of the spiritualizing tendencies of their precursors, almost, it seems, in favor of the Antiochene approach of the East.

However, one must add immediately that a rejection of allegorization was not motivated by unconcern for the spiritual sense of the text, nor did it result in a dry lifeless exegesis. On the contrary, a reading of the text by the Reformers and Post-Reformers yielded profound theological and pastoral implications, and even set the agenda for half of Christendom. And one cannot help but notice that this propensity impacted Catholicism as well, as the exegeses of Lapide and Quesnel indicate. It would be the nineteenth century before Biblical studies in general and Markan studies in particular experienced such a radical transformation.

Endnotes for Chapter Four

[1]Klaas Runia, "The Hermeneutics of the Reformers," *CTJ* 19 (1984) 122; This fourfold interpretation was called the *quadriga*. On this point cf. our conclusions in chapter four below: A.1.

[2]Thomas Aquinas, *Summa Theologica*, 1, 1, 10, ad 3. Cf. Beryl Smalley, *The Study of the Bible in the Middle Ages* (New York: Philosophical Library, 1952) 299.

[3]Runia, "Hermeneutics," 122; T. H. L. Parker, *Calvin's New Testament Commentaries* (Grand Rapids: Wm. B. Eerdmans, 1971) 61.

[4]Runia, "Hermeneutics," 122.

[5]Ronald S. Wallace, "Calvin the Expositor," *CT* 8 (May 22, 1964) 9.

[6]J. Michael Reu, *Luther and the Scriptures* (Columbus: Wartburg Press, 1944) 24.

[7]Runia, "Hermeneutics," 123.

[8]*Ibid.*; Wallace, "Calvin," 9.

[9]*Ibid.*, 123-4.

[10]Martin Luther, *Works*, ed. Jaroslav Pelikan, et. al. (St. Louis: Concordia) 35:361-2.

[11]*Ibid.*, 35:362.

[12]A perusal of Kealy (*Mark's Gospel: A History of Its Interpretation* [New York: Paulist Press, 1982] 44-51) will indicate that the scholars of the era almost always treated Mark only partially, as part of a harmony, or in conjunction with at least one of the other Gospels.

[13]Martin Luther, "On the Bondage of the Will," in Ernst Gordon Rupp and Philip S. Watson, tr., *Luther and Erasmus: Free Will and Salvation*, Library of Christian Classics, vol. 17 (Philadelphia: Westminster Press, 1959) 221.

[14]Martin Luther, *Werke*, Kritische Gesammtausgabe (Weimar: Herman Böhlau, 1883-1982) 5:27; Robert M. Grant, *A Short History of the Interpretation of the Bible* (Philadelphia: Fortress, 1984) 94.

[15]Wallace, "Calvin," 9.

[16]This passage from the *Institutes* is cited in Wallace, "Calvin," 10.

[17]*Corpus Reformatorum*, 38:405, cited in Hans-Joachim Kraus, "Calvin's Exegetical Principles," *Int* 31 (1977) 10-11.

[18]Grant, *History,* 95.

[19]From Luther's *Exposition of the 37th (36th) Psalm*; quoted by J. Mackinnon, *Luther and the Reformation* (London-New York, 1930) 4:294.

[20]Luther, "Bondage," 112.

[21]*Ibid.*, 159.

[22]*Ibid.*, 112.

[23]Cited by K. Fullerton, "Luther's Doctrine and Criticism of Scripture," *BSac* 63 (1906) 18.

[24]Grant, *History,* 99.

[25]Luther, *Werke,* 10:238.

[26]This idea is already found in Origen, Jerome, and Augustine. See A. Skevington Wood, *Luther's Principles of Biblical Interpretation* (London: Tyndale, 1960) 21.

[27]*Smakcald Articles* 3:8:3, in *The Book of Concord,* ed. T. G. Tappert (Philadelphia: Muhlenberg Press, 1959) 312.

[28]Luther, *Werke,* 47:66.

[29]W. Kooiman, *Luther en de Bijbel* (Baarn: Bosch and Keuning, n.d.) 175, cited in Runia, "Hermeneutics," 129.

[30]Runia, "Hermeneutics," 129.

[31]Luther, *Werke,* 11:223.

[32]*Ibid.,* 46:414.

[33]*Ibid.,* 3:26.

[34]*Ibid.,* 24:16.

[35]Luther, *Works,* 35:236.

[36]Runia, "Hermeneutics," 140.

[37]Peter Stuhlmacher, *Vom Verstehen des Neuen Testaments: Eine Hermeneutik* (Göttingen: Vandenhoeck und Ruprecht, 1979) 98.

[38]*Ibid.,* 142.

[39]Compare, for example, the five hermeneutical principles discussed by Runia ("Hermeneutics," 140-47), the eight exegetical principles discussed by Kraus ("Principles," 12-18), and the four expository principles discussed by Wallace ("Calvin," 8-10). Even so, the gist of the discussion in these and countless others is essentially in agreement.

[40]See E. C. Blackman (*Biblical Interpretation* [Westminster Press, 1957] 125) for the view that "For Calvin the Bible itself, rather than Christ in it, is the final authority. Thus Calvin is the progenitor of Biblical literalism." And see Runia ("Hermeneutics," 146-7) for a rebuttal.

[41]Wallace, "Calvin," 8.

[42]Runia, "Hermeneutics," 143; Cf. Kraus ("Principles," 13) and Parker (*Commentaries,* 67), the latter of whom says: "In the historical books, therefore, Calvin never seeks a secondary, spiritual meaning, for the *sensus literalis* is God's own record of the outworking of his purpose in his incarnate Son and is sufficient in itself…But for Calvin the spiritual is not to be opposed to the historical, for this history is the account of God's activity within history, the account of the earthly life

of the incarnate Son of God and of his continued activity through the Church, not needing to be spiritualized."

[43]*Opera Calvini* 50:236-7, cited by Parker, *Commentaries,* 63-4.

[44]Our text (which may be found in its entirety in Appendix G) is that of D. W. and T. F. Torrance, eds., *Calvin's Commentaries: A Harmony of the Gospels: Matthew, Mark and Luke,* translated by A. W. Morrison (Grand Rapids: Wm. B. Eerdmans, 1972) III:171.

[45]*Ibid.*

[46]Kraus, "Principles," 11.

[47]Parker, *Commentaries,* 67.

[48]Runia, "Hermeneutics," 142; Kraus, "Principles," 17.

[49]*Ibid.,* 145.

[50]Morrison, III:173.

[51]*Ibid.,* III:172.

[52]*Ibid.*

[53]*Ibid.*

[54]Calvin, *Institutes,* 1:9:3, cited in Runia, "Hermeneutics," 146.

[55]Morrison, III:170-1.

[56]Wallace, "Calvin," 10.

[57]Morrison, III:169-70.

[58]*Ibid.,* III:173.

[59]Cross, *ODCC,* s.v. "CORNELIUS À LAPIDE," 348.

[60]Cornelius à Lapide, *The Great Commentary of Cornelius à Lapide,* tr. by Thomas W. Mossman (Edinburgh: John Grant, 1908) Vol. 1, xxxi.

[61]*Ibid.,* Vol. 3, 358.

[62]*Ibid.,* 365.

[63]*Ibid.,* Vol. 1, xxvii.

[64]*Ibid.*

[65]*Ibid.,* Vol. 3, 438.

[66]*Ibid.*

[67]*Ibid.*

[68]*Ibid.,* 439.

[69]Charles Hodge, ed., "Quesnel and the Jansenists," *BRPR* 28 (1856) 132-56; K. R. Hagenbach, *History of the Church in the Eighteenth and Nineteenth Centuries,* 2 Vols. (New York: Charles Scribner & Co., 1869) 2:425; Pasquier Quesnel, *The Gospels: with Moral Reflections on Each Verse* (Philadelphia: Parry & McMillan,

1855), "Introductory Essay" by Daniel Wilson, vii-xxvi; J. M. Neale, *A History of the So-Called Jansenist Church of Holland; with A Sketch of its Earlier Annals, and Some Account of the Brothers of the Common Life* (Oxford: John Henry and James Parker, 1858; AMS Edition, 1970) 33-5; C. Pfender, s.v. "Quesnel, Pasquier," *S-HRE* 9:374.

[70]Paul Tschackert, s.v. "Jansen, Cornelius, Jansenism," *S-HRE* 6:95-8,

[71]J. F. von Schulte, s.v. "Gallicanism," *S-HRE* 4:424-6.

[72]Neale, *History,* 33.

[73]*Ibid.*

[74]S.v. "Unigenitus," *S-HRE* 12:65. The full text of this bul can be found in the second volume of the American edition of Quesnel cited above, 631-42.

[75]*S-HRE* 6:97.

[76]*Ibid.,* 6:98.

[77]H. A. Boardman, "Preface," to Quesnel, *Reflections,* v.

[78]*Ibid.*

[79]Quesnel, *Reflections,* xiii; *CBTEL,* 8:841.

[80]There is one story that abbe Renaudot visited Pope Clement XI and found him reading the *Reflections.* "This," he said, "is an extraordinary performance; we have no one at Rome capable of writing in this manner. I wish I could have the author by me" (Wilson, "Introduction," to Quesnel, *Reflections,* xiii). The story, even if embellished, is believable in light of Voltaire's remark that "thirty pages of this book, properly qualified and softened, would have prevented much of the disturbance which Jansenism created in France" (s.v. "Quesnel," *CBTEL* 8:841).

[81]Quesnel, *Reflections,* xxxviii.

[82]Quesnel," 140.

[83]*S-HRE* 12:65.

[84]*Ibid.*

[85]Quesnel, *Reflections,* xxxviii.

[86]*Ibid.,* 524.

[87]*Ibid.,* 531.

[88]*Ibid.,* 535-6.

[89]*S-HRE* 6:95.

[90]*S-HRE* 12:65.

[91]*S-HRE* 6:97.

[92]*S-HRE* 12:65.

[93]*S-HRE* 6:97.

[94]Quesnel, *Reflections,* 536.

[95]*S-HRE* 12:65.

[96]*Ibid.*

[97]Quesnel, *Reflections,* 536.

[98]*S-HRE* 12:65.

[99]Quesnel, *Reflections,* 524-5.

[100]*S-HRE* 12:65.

[101]Quesnel, *Reflections,* 526.

[102]John Albert Bengel, *Gnomon of the New Testament,* 5 Vols., (Edinburgh: T. & T. Clark, 1859), esp. "Sketch of the Life and Writings of J. A. Bengel," by A. R. Fausset, vol. 5, vii-xxxii; J. F. von der Goltz, "The Theological Significance of Bengel and his School," *BFER* 11 (1862) 304-42; Charles T. Fritsch, "Bengel, the Student of Scripture," *Int* 5 (1951) 203-15; J. C. F. Burk, *A Memoir of the Life and Writings of John Albert Bengel* (London: William Ball, 1837).

[103]Fritsch, "Bengel," 203.

[104]Goltz, "Theological Significance," 307; C. J. Weborg, "Pietism: A Question of Meaning and Vocation," *CovQ* 41/3 (1983) 59-71.

[105]*Ibid.,* 304.

[106]*Ibid.,* 305.

[107]*Ibid.,* 309.

[108]C. J. Weborg, "The Eschatological Ethics of Johann Albrecht Bengel," *CovQ* 36/2 (1978) 31. o62

[109]In addition to the edition above in note 206, see W. L. Blackley, ed., *The Critical English Testament: Being an adaptation of Bengel's Gnomon, with Numerous Notes, showing the Precise Results of Modern Criticism and Exegesis* (London: Daldy, Isbister & Co., 1876).

[110]*Ordo temporum á principio per peridos oeconomioe divinoe,* etc. (Stuttgart, 1753).

[111]Bengel, *Gnomon,* 1:7.

[112]E. F. Hills, s.v. "Bengel, John Albert," *EC* 1:630.

[113]Fausset, "Sketch," in *Gnomon,* 5:xv.

[114]Bengel, *Gnomon,* 1:20.

[115]See for example the textual apparatus of *The New Testament Greek* edited by Kurt Aland, Matthew Black, Carlo M. Martini, et. al. (New York: United Bible Societies, 1968).

[116]Bengel, *Gnomon,* 1:9.

[117]Fausset, "Sketch," in *Gnomon,* 5:xxix.

[118]Bengel, *Gnomon,* 1:50-1; see also pp. 64-5.

[119]*Te totum applica ad textum, et totum textum applica ad te*; Fritsch, "Bengel," 210; Goltz, "Theological Significance," 311.

[120]Bengel, *Gnomon,* 1:567-8.

[121]Fritsch, "Bengel," 212.

[122]*Ibid.,* 213.

Chapter 5

The Nineteenth and Early Twentieth Centuries

Victor of Antioch decried the total lack of attention paid to Mark in his day. Chapters two through four demonstrate that the situation hardly improved until the early nineteenth century. This neglect was probably due to the widespread conviction best articulated by Augustine that Mark was the lackey and abbreviator of Matthew. There seems to be a direct correlation between this conviction and interest in Mark. Until this view began to be called into question, Mark's importance for historical and critical purposes remained undiscovered.

Vincent Taylor notes that at the beginning of the nineteenth century there were three main theories about the origins of the Gospels. J. G. Eichorn's "Original-Gospel Hypothesis" proposed the existence of a brief written historical overview of Jesus' life which each Gospel writer used independently as the foundation for his work. F. D. Schleiermacher's "Fragment-Hypothesis" argued for the circulation of Gospel tradition on multiple tablets or leaves of papyrus which eventually became the chief source of the Evangelists. But the most popular theory, and one which is influential even today, was J. L. Gieseler's "Tradition-Hypothesis" which proposed the transmission of tradition chiefly in oral form under the oversight of the Apostles until it attained written form.[1]

In this environment, Mark continued to be neglected. It was the growing conviction that *the Gospels were related literarily rather than merely sharing a common oral or written source* that began a reinvestigation into the relation of the Gospels to one another.

The Markan Hypothesis

The Gospel of Mark essentially entered onto the stage of relevance for biblical scholars about 150 years ago. Until that time Mark was relegated to the wings because of the commonly accepted opinion that it was "merely" a compendium of the Gospel of Matthew. Augustine is usually regarded as the father of the opinion that "Mark follows [Matthew] closely, and looks like his attendant and epitomizer."[2]

That opinion began to change, however, when in 1835 Karl Lachmann published an article analyzing the order of events recorded in the synoptics.[3] He demonstrated that Matthew and Luke share a common order with material that is also found in Mark. But for material not found in Mark, no such common order could be detected. His conclusion was that Mark was not merely an abstract of Matthew and/or Luke but rather that all three Gospels used a more original source. Moreover, Mark was most faithful to that original source.

Lachmann's studies inspired scholars to look at Mark differently. In particular, Lachmann's conclusions gave impetus to C. H. Weisse's research. He concluded that Mark was both the earliest Gospel and one source on which Matthew and Luke depended for their information.[4] This thesis was further solidified by H. J. Holtzmann[5] and became known as the "Markan hypothesis." Although it has not gone unchallenged, it had become for the most part the common consensus of biblical scholarship of the late nineteenth century. Moreover, its assertion of Markan priority is still persuasive to many today, so that Dibelius' judgment a half century ago is still valid: the Two Source Hypothesis "is still the sure foundation of the criticism of the Synoptics."[6]

The Effect of the Mark Hypothesis on the Interpretation of Mark 14:54, 66-72

Mark's Account Prior to Matthew's and Luke's. As a test case, Mark's version of Peter's Denial is an important example of how scholars came to view Mark's Gospel as the chief source for Matthew and Luke. John C. Hawkins' now classic *Horae Synopticae: Contributions to the Study of the Synoptic Problem* (1899) made careful calculation and comparison of the three synoptics including, for example, a section listing Mark's "rude, harsh, obscure or unusual words or expressions, which may therefore have been omitted or replaced by others."[7] Mark's word describing the "forecourt," *proaulion*, in 14:68 is used "here only in the N.T. and not in the LXX. Its place is supplied by [*pulon*] in Mt xxvi. 71, and Luke has no parallel."[8] Moreover, Mark's use of *epibalon* in 14:72 is "a strange and obscure word as used here"[9] and is changed by both Matthew and Luke. When Hawkins compared those words peculiar to each of the evangelists with the Septuagint, he found Mark's "on the whole much less accordant."[10] Matthew and Luke may justly be said to "improve" Mark.

> It thus appears that there was a certain unusualness in Mark's vocabulary which would render it probable *a priori* that those who used his memoirs would, intentionally or unconsciously or both, modify the language of them by substituting more familiar or more conventionally sacred expressions.[11]

There is the further example of "duplicate expressions" (one could perhaps say redundant) in Mark of which Matthew and Luke almost invariably substitute only one of the words (or its equivalent) for the two. For example, Mark's "I neither know nor understand what you mean" (14:68) is reduced in Matthew 26:70 to "I do not know what you mean" and in Luke 22:57 to "I do not know him." The overall force of these and many other "statistics" is that Matthew and Luke used and modified Mark rather than vice versa.[12]

Mark's Account the Most Historically Accurate. A concomitant conclusion of the Markan hypothesis was that since Mark was the earliest Gospel, it was therefore also likely the most reliable record of the historical Jesus. This led to numerous attempts to reconstruct the "Life of Jesus" from the data of the documents and, almost without exception, Mark was considered the best.

A. B. Bruce's commentary on Mark (1897) in the celebrated *Expositor's Greek Testament* reflects this tradition. "The realism of Mark makes for its historicity," says Bruce. "It is a guarantee of first-hand reports, such as one might expect from Peter."[13] In Mark's Gospel "we get nearest to the true human personality of Jesus in all its originality and power, and as coloured by the time and the place."[14] Naturally he finds evidence of this in Mark's account of Peter's denial.

Bruce's commentary is terse and logical with a penchant for reconstructing the actual events. For example, Mark says the same maid recognized Peter a second time; Matthew says another maid. Mark's account is to be favored since "two able to recognize Peter is more unlikely than one."[15] Moreover, in Matthew's account the bystanders seem to have a knowledge of Peter apart from the remarks of the servant girl. In Mark's account they take their cue from her. Says Bruce, "On the whole, Mk., as was to be expected, gives the clearer picture of the scene."[16]

1900–1914

Markan Priority Survives: The Impact of the Markan Hypothesis. By the turn of the century it was an accepted fact of Biblical scholarship that Mark was the earliest of the Gospels and was one of the twin foundations of the "Two Document Hypothesis."[17] The few dissenters[18] were unpersuasive in light of the refinement of the hypothesis by B. H. Streeter. His "Four Document Hypothesis" extended and elaborated the basic viewpoint that Mark was the earliest of the Gospels and the main source of information for Matthew and Luke.[19]

One of the few cogent arguments against Markan priority is the rare occurrence of agreements between Matthew and Luke against Mark, which would seem to suggest a common source other than Mark. In our passage there are three such instances:

Mark	Matthew	Luke
14:70	26:73	22:58
Alethos ex auton ei	Alethos [*kai su*] ex auton ei	...*kai su* ex auton ei

14:72	26:75	22:61
anemnesthe...to	emnesthe...*ou*	upemnesthe*tou*
rema	rema*tos*	rema*tos*

14:72	26:75	22:62
epibalon eklaien	*exelthon exo*	[*exelthon* exo
	ek*lausen pikros*	ek*lausen pikros*]

Streeter argued that the agreements of Matthew and Luke against Mark in the first and third examples above are not real. Those words in brackets in Matthew 26:73 in the first example and Luke 22:62 in the third example are due to textual assimilation rather than documentary dependence. According to Streeter, if the more accurate text is used in each instance, these agreements cease to exist. Of the second example, says Streeter, the agreement is not due to a common source. On the contrary, "verbs of remembering in Greek normally take the genitive; the case alteration is then one that would inevitably occur to two editors independently."[20]

Thus, the examples which occur in our passage are illustrative of Streeter's argument "that the only valid objection to the theory that the document used by Matthew and Luke was our Mark—that, namely, based on the existence of the minor agreements of these Gospels against Mark—is completely baseless."[21] This was the culmination of the opinion begun early in the nineteenth century. It remains persuasive to most even today.

Markan Historicity Collapses: The Impact of Wilhelm Wrede's The Messianic Secret. A concomitant conclusion of the Markan hypothesis was that since Mark was the earliest Gospel, it was therefore also likely the most reliable record of the historical Jesus. Unlike the assertion of Markan priority, scholars came to doubt this claim about the turn of the century, and the beginning of this scrutiny is usually associated with the name Wilhelm Wrede.[22] Wrede explored the so-called "messianic secret" in Mark's Gospel, those moments at which Jesus enjoins those around him to secrecy about his miraculous deeds and his Person. Because these injunctions occurred at such inappropriate and arbitrary places, Wrede concluded that they constituted a Markan literary construction.

According to Wrede, no one thought of Jesus as the Messiah before the resurrection chiefly because Jesus "actually did not represent himself as Messiah."[23] Belief in Jesus as the Messiah occurred after the resurrection. But the church faced the difficulty of a paucity of references to or declarations of messiahship. The church met this absence of messianic claims with the explanation that Jesus withheld his identity to all but the closest disciples, who themselves misunderstood Jesus and his ministry. Mark took this idea and gave it full expression in his Gospel.

The result was that the church was able to live with the incongruity of the evidence, and Mark's Gospel, far from being the reliable guarantor of history as was previously thought, "must be recognized as a bold attempt to give a messianic interpretation to the non-messianic character of Jesus' earthly ministry."[24] Wrede's legacy for biblical scholarship of the twentieth century, explains H. C. Kee, was that "the ground was already laid by the turn of the century for a view of Mark as interpreter rather than as archivist or neutral reporter."[25]

Karl Ludwig Schmidt and the Emergence of *Formgeschichte*

If Kee is correct that the ground for a view of Mark as interpreter was laid by Wrede, the cultivation of that ground fell to form criticism. First developed and applied to the Old Testament by Hermann Gunkel, one of his students Martin Dibelius then applied the method to early Christian traditions about John the Baptist.[26] Dibelius and Rudolf Bultmann are the premier figures in the development of the form critical approach to the New Testament.[27] But the most significant name for Markan studies directly is perhaps Karl Ludwig Schmidt.[28]

In keeping with form critical concerns, Schmidt focused on the individual stories which comprise the Gospel. He concluded that the times, places, and order of events did not depend on any earlier tradition based on historical memory, which had been the contention of those in the nineteenth century who were attempting to construct a "life of Jesus" from Mark's Gospel. What order could be detected, argued Schmidt, was due far more to the Evangelist's attempt to serve the liturgical and missionary needs of his community. Schmidt was programmatic for Markan studies for decades with his suggestion that Mark's narrative is *not* a "string of pearls" whose order was historically important, but rather a "heap" of pearls; only rarely could one be detected as related to another.

> Im Bilde könnte man das so veranschaulichen: die Mk-Darstellung ist nicht eine Perlenkette von lose aneinandergereihten Perlen, zwischen denen man andere bald hier, bald da einschieben kann, sondern ein Haufe von nicht aufgereihten Perlen, wenn auch ab und zu mal einige Perlen zusammengehören.[29]

Schmidt's conclusion, literally the last sentence of his book, is that there is "kein Leben Jesu im Sinne einer sich entwickelnden Lebensgeschichte, keinen chronologischen Aufriß der Geschichte Jesu, sondern nur Einzelgeschichten, Perikopen, die in ein Rahmenwerk gestellt sind."[30] Scholars of the early twentieth century had become convinced that the "historical Jesus" was the concern, even product, of the nineteenth-century church. The early church had concerned herself with the kerygmatic Christ! The "life of Jesus" approach was passè.

The Effect of Form Criticism on the Interpretation of Mark 14:54, 66-72

Martin Dibelius. The Passion story, unlike the rest of the Gospel material, seems to have come together as a unit rather early. Dibelius thinks this due to the likelihood that it formed so important a part of the typical sermon.[31] But this also indicates that the interest of the church in the story was primarily soteriological, and not historical. This is especially the case with the denial of Peter, since there is "no express reference" to an eyewitness in the Markan account.[32] "It was narrated in the Church from the standpoint that it shared in the fate of Peter," says Dibelius. But also "the Church's interest in Peter's fall could be explained if the event were felt in some way to be the pre-supposition [sic] of the Easter appearances."[33] Jesus promised an appearance to the disciples and Peter especially, and the prophecy denial was remembered in connection with it. "But if the denial was prophesied it has to be described."[34]

Dibelius holds out the possibility of some element of historicity in the account in connection with the witness of John's unnamed disciple of 18:15f. Even so, the story evolved into an "artistic" composition:

> This holds in regard to the individualization of the three acts, but especially of the cock-crow. Perhaps originally at the bottom there was a proverbial use of cock-crow, or even the second cock-crow, as an indication of time (Mark xiii, 35), and this was then developed dramatically.[35]

Rudolf Bultmann. Bultmann draws a similar conclusion. Mark's prediction of the denial in 14:27-31 "has to be classed as an historical account with legendary traits."[36] However, "the story of Peter is itself legendary and literary."[37] It was not originally part of the Passion Narrative[38] and is itself awkwardly divided by the account of the trial of Jesus.[39] Bultmann claims to have discovered another oral tradition behind Luke 22:31ff which knows nothing of a denial by Peter.[40] It was exactly these suggestions that fueled an ongoing debate among German scholars, Günther Klein in particular.[41]

Maurice Goguel. The suggestions of Dibelius and Bultmann were further developed by Goguel.[42] Several pieces of evidence contradict the historicity of the account and thus arises the need to account for the story having been created. First, Mark's account, which is the oldest, contains certain obscurities and incoherencies which indicate that it is not an integrated whole. How, for example, could Peter be found in the hall for a second denial when the text says clearly that he exited after the first denial? According to Goguel, Mark has joined together two separate traditions.

Secondly, the story is not integrated well in its context, but merely inserted. Third, it contradicts directly what is said about the flight of the disciples (14:50). If all the disciples did indeed flee, then Peter could not have followed Jesus. Fourth, there is no evidence in all of the history of the primitive Church that Peter's denial was used against him as one might expect, for example, from Paul during the Antioch incident (Galatians 2:11f).

On the other hand, there are no difficulties in supposing that Jesus predicted Peter's weakness and that that prediction came to be regarded as prophecy. Nor is it reasonable to assume that the denial was created *ex nihilo*. Thus, concludes Goguel, "what Jesus had foretold had necessarily to become a fact. To pass from the belief that

Peter had denied the Lord to the complete narrative of such a denial was an easy step."[43]

Günther Klein. The interests introduced by the form critical methodology were pursued beyond the introduction of redaction criticism in the 1950s. Seldom is one methodology completely abandoned in favor of a newer one. Thus, Günther Klein advanced the argument he saw in Bultmann and others. The story as it appears in Mark, says Klein, is artificial. "Die oft geäusserte Vermutung, dass hier marcinisches Interesse an einprägsamer Konfrontation des bekennenden Jesus mit dem verleugnenden Petrus die Komposition bestimmt habe, leuchtet ohne weiteres ein."[44] Not only is there no specific relation to the story of Jesus' trial before the sanhedrin, neither is there any general connection to the larger Passion story; "es sich hier nich um eines der primären Elemente der Passionsüberlieferung handeln kann."[45]

The pericope can be isolated without doing harm to either the story or its context; in fact, the context is improved thereby, and the pericope can then be seen for the inconsistent account it is. How could Peter have remained within such a circle of enemies for such a long time once his identity was questioned? Is not the very number three indicative of its literary nature? The nature of Peter's first denial is so vague as to question what he was even denying. There is the indication from Luke's account (22:31–32a) that Peter did not fail Jesus but in fact was preserved by Jesus' prayer.

> Ziehen wir das Fazit! Sämtliche Beobachtungen an der Verleugnungstradition—ihre Isolierbarkeit; synthetische, nicht eliminierbare Einzelzüge; die Existenz alter Konkurrenztradition führen zu dem Schluss: Die Überlieferung von der Verleugnung des Petrus ist unhistorisch.[46]

Klein offers an alternative explanation of the origin of the tradition based on a reconstruction of early Christian leadership. The institution of the Twelve was a short-lived group of which Peter was the head. The Apostolate was yet another group who rose to power and of which Peter was a leader. Eventually this group was replaced by the "pillars" at Jerusalem. Peter was only of secondary importance within this group. Lastly, Peter is seen as a lone missionary.

> Blicken wir nunmehr zurück, so stellt sich uns Petrus als die einzige Persönlichkeit unter den urchristlichen Autoritäten dar, von der wir mit einer auch der schärfsten Kritik standhaltenden Sicherheit wissen, dass sie nacheinander Mitglied des Zwölferkreises, der Apostelgruppe, des "Säulen" kollegiums und schiesslich ein hervorragender Einzelgänger war.[47]

According to Klein, Peter's threefold denial is nothing more than his abdication of three positions of authority in the early church read back into the story of Jesus.

> In der Tat scheint die Tradition von der Verleugnung des Petrus nichts anderes als ein legendarischer Reflex dieses dreimaligen Positionswechsels zu sein; wie so mancher Tatbestand der urchristlichen Geschichte zurückprojiziert ins Leben Jesu.[48]

Endnotes for Chapter Five

[1]Vincent Taylor, *The Gospel According to St. Mark* (London: Macmillan, 1952) 9-11; Cf. J. G. Eichhorn, *Einleitung in das Neue Testament* (1804); F. D. Schleiermacher, *Über die Schriften des Lukas. Ein kritischer Versuch* (1817); J. L. Gieseler, *Historisch-kritischer Versuch über die Entstehung und die frühesten Schichsale der schriftlichen Evangelien* (1818).

[2]Augustine, "The Harmony of the Gospels," 1, 2 (4); of Mark he says further that "in his narrative he gives nothing in concert with John apart from the others: by himself separately, he has little to record; in conjunction with Luke, as distinguished from the rest, he has still less; but in concord with Matthew, he has a very large number of passages. Much, too, he narrates in words almost numerically and identically the same as those used by Matthew, where the agreement is either with that evangelist alone, or with him in connection with the rest." But M. B. Riddle (Philip Schaff, ed., *Saint Augustine,* NPNF 6 [Grand Rapids: Eerdmans, (1886) 1979] 78) in an annotation to this edition notes: "This opinion is not only unwarranted, since Mark shows greater signs of originality, but it has been prejudicial to the correct appreciation of the Gospel of Mark. The verbal identity of Matthew and Mark in parallel passages is far less than commonly supposed."

[3]K. Lachmann, "De Ordine narrationum in evangeliis synopticis," *TSK* VIII (1835) 570ff.

[4]C. H. Weisse, *Die evangelische Geschichte kritisch und philosophisch bearbeitet* (2 vols. Leipzig: Breitkopf & Härtel, 1838).

[5]H. J. Holtzmann, *Die synoptischen Evangelium: Ihr Ursprung und geschichtlicher Charakter* (Leipzig: Breitkopf & Härtel, 1863).

[6]Martin Dibelius, *From Tradition to Gospel* (Cambridge & London: James Clarke, 1971) 9.

[7]John C. Hawkins, *Horae Synopticae: Contributions to the Study of the Synoptic Problem* (Grand Rapids: Baker, [1899] 1968) 131.

[8]*Ibid.*, 134.

[9]*Ibid.*

[10]*Ibid.*, 135.

[11]*Ibid.*

[12]See also Francis Crawford Burkitt, *The Gospel History and its Transmission* (Edinburgh: T. & T. Clark, 1911) 51.

[13]W. Robertson Nicoll, gen. ed., *The Expositor's Greek Testament*, 5 vols. (Grand Rapids: Eerdmans, [1897] 1976), vol. 1: *The Synoptic Gospels,* by Alexander Balmain Bruce, 33.

[14]*Ibid.*

[15]*Ibid.*, 444.

[16]*Ibid.*

[17]V. H. Stanton, *The Gospels as Historical Documents*, 3 vols. (Cambridge, 1903-20); W. Sanday, ed., *Studies in the Synoptic Problem* (Oxford, 1911); J. Moffatt, *Introduction to the Literature of the New Testament* (Edinburgh, 1918); A. Loisy, *Les Evangiles synoptiques,* 2 vols. (Paris, 1907); idem, *L'Evangile selon Marc* (Paris, 1912); C. S. Patton, *Sources of the Synoptic Gospels* (New York, 1915).

[18]E.g., H. G. Jameson, *Origin of the Synoptic Gospels* (1932).

[19]Burnett Hillman Streeter, *The Four Gospels: A Study of Origins* (London: Macmillan, 1964).

[20]*Ibid.*, 322.

[21]*Ibid.*, 331.

[22]W. Wrede, *Das Messiasgeheimnis in den Evangelien* (Göttingen: Vandenhoeck & Ruprecht, 1901; 1963); Eng. tr. by J. C. G. Greig, *The Messianic Secret* (London: James Clarke, 1971). Paginations in this dissertation refer to the English edition.

[23]*Ibid.*, 77.

[24]W. L. Lane, "From Historian to Theologian: Milestones in Markan Scholarship," *RevExp* 75 (1978) 604.

[25]H. C. Kee, "Mark's Gospel in Recent Research," *Int* 32 (1978) 353.

[26]M. Dibelius, *Die urchristliche Überlieferung von Johannes dem Täuer* (Tübingen: J. C. B. Mohr, 1911); idem, *Die Formgeschichte des Evangeliums* (Tübingen: J. C. B. Mohr, 1919); English tr. by B. L. Woolf, *From Tradition to Gospel* (New York: Charles Scribner's Sons, 1934).

[27]R. Bultmann, *The History of the Synoptic Tradition* (Oxford: Basil Blackwell, 1963); J. D. Kingsbury, "The Gospel of Mark in Current Research," *RelSRev* 5 (1979) 101-7.

[28]K. L. Schmidt, *Der Rahmen der Geschichte Jesu* (Berlin: Trowitzsch, 1919; 1964).

[29]*Ibid.*, 281.

[30]*Ibid.*, 317.

[31]Dibelius, *Tradition*, 178-9.

[32]*Ibid.*, 183.

[33]*Ibid.*, 215.

[34]*Ibid.*, 183.

[35]*Ibid.*, 216.

[36]Rudolf Bultmann, *The History of the Synoptic Tradition* (New York: Harper & Row, 1976) 267.

98   MARK'S ACCOUNT OF PETER'S DENIAL OF JESUS

[37]*Ibid.*, 269.
[38]*Ibid.*, 278.
[39]*Ibid.*, 269.
[40]*Ibid.*, 266-7.
[41]See discussion below at point d.
[42]Maurice Goguel, "Did Peter Deny His Lord?" *HThR* 25 (1932) 1-27.
[43]*Ibid.*, 27.
[44]Günther Klein, "Die Verleugnung des Petrus. Eine traditionsgeschichte Untersuchung," *ZTK* 58 (1961) 295. See also idem, "Die Berufung des Petrus," *ZNW* 58 (1967) 1-44.
[45]*Ibid.*
[46]*Ibid.*, 311.
[47]*Ibid.*, 323-4.
[48]*Ibid.*, 324.

Chapter 6

Post World War II

Willi Marxsen and the Emergence of *Redaktionsgeschichte*

On hindsight one could suggest that the appearance of the redaction critical method was "natural," even predictable. Scholars first abandoned the view of Mark as "history," then affirmed the hand of the Evangelist in producing a "theological" document. Not only was redaction criticism not predicted, but it was viewed as a radically different approach to the Gospels. And, "ironically," notes W. L. Lane, "it was the interruption in literary publications during the second World War which made possible the asking of new questions and the re-thinking of accepted positions in Synoptic studies."[1] Appearing virtually simultaneously and independently were Günther Bornkamm's work on Matthew,[2] Hans Conzelmann's work on Luke,[3] and Willi Marxsen's work on Mark.[4]

Marxsen reaffirmed the nineteenth century conviction of Mark as the first Gospel, and he built upon the results of form criticism in order to discern the traditions the Evangelist received from his own work. But Marxsen was in reality charting new territory. First, Mark was, in his view, neither an historian nor a mere *Sammler* of Jesus traditions. Rather, he was a creative "theologian" producing a unified literary work. To use Schmidt's imagery of the string and pearls, the very "string" with which Schmidt was so wont to dispose was to Marxsen the nerve center of Mark's message. Every word of the evangelist, whether connecting phrases, alterations in wording, or summaries, provided a larger framework. And the "pearls" of which the form critics were so fond were only intelligible "within the context of Mark's point of view as gleaned from his scenic framework and programme."[5]

Secondly, Marxsen distinguished three levels of activity, or *Sitze im Leben*, in the history of the early church. The first level is the life and ministry of Jesus, those events the nineteenth century "life of Jesus" scholars thought could be so readily detected in Mark's order. The second level is that of the church from the time of Jesus until the writing of the Gospels; it was here that stories of Jesus were transmitted in oral "forms" which the form critics thought could be so readily detected in Mark's collection. The third level identifies that of the community which produced the written Gospel. Marxsen focused almost all of his attention here because, in his view, "a literary work or fragment of tradition is a primary source for the historical situation out of which it arose, and is only a secondary source for the historical details concerning which it gives information."[6]

Thirdly, Mark's concern was neither to "historicize" nor "collect" Jesus traditions, but rather to "present" Jesus to his community in such a manner that he became the "present" risen Lord. Mark is a sermon![7] In conclusion, since a document's primary witness is to its own context, and since Mark's primary objective was also that same context, Marxsen "defined the essential question [for the redaction critic] as the determination of the life situation out of which a particular Gospel emerged... [and] to the specific interest and basic conceptions of the evangelist himself."[8]

Marxsen's impact has been so great and so recent that it is too soon to tell if anyone or anything since has quite measured up to him.[9] That will require the perspective of more time. Moreover, it is not individuals so much as methodologies and issues which have commanded the attention of Markan scholars. Of the methodologies representative of the present trends are genre analysis, historical-sociological investigations, structuralism, and literary criticism.[10] The most obvious shared characteristic is their interdisciplinary nature. Almost all biblical methods of the last twenty years integrate two or more fields.

Dominant Markan Issues

Of the issues dominating Markan studies since Marxsen, perhaps three stand out: christology, discipleship, and pursuit of the Gospel's *Sitz im Leben,* in that order. They are, of course, intricately related. But the questions of discipleship and the historical situation initially followed christology. Neither is it the case that Mark's christology, discipleship motif, and *Sitz im Leben* were not of concern before or contemporaneously with Marxsen. But, as J. D. Kingsbury notes, there was a remarkable shift in emphasis from the time Marxsen's monograph appeared in 1956 until 1970.

At that time Norman Perrin could write that scholars were in "general agreement" that "...a major aspect of the Markan purpose is christological: he is concerned with correcting a false Christology and its consequences for Christian discipleship."[11] There is no indication in Marxsen's evaluation of Mark of a christological debate. "What, then," asks Kingsbury, "took place between 1956 and 1970 that caused scholars to alter so radically their estimate of Marcan christology?" His answer is perspicacious:

What happened is that in certain circles scholars became convinced that the interpretive key to Mark lies in understanding this Gospel as in some sense overcoming an erroneous *theios-aner* ("divine man") christology of Hellenistic stripe which pictured Jesus as one who had been gloriously powerful in word and deed but had had no truck with suffering and death. This *theios-aner* christology is variously thought of as associated with the tradition Mark received or as being espoused by members of his community.[12]

This fascination with a *theios-aner* christology in Mark seems to have been influenced by Dieter Georgi's contention that such a false, *theios-aner* christology characterized the opponents of Paul in Corinth.[13] "The effect of Georgi's contention on Marcan scholarship," says Kingsbury, "was that it held out the prospect that a similar situation might well have existed in the Marcan community."[14] But more was made of that prospect than was justified, especially since for the Gospels this is almost totally conjectural. But this brings us to a brief survey of literature related to discipleship which will of necessity touch on the two issues of christology and the historical situation.

The Effect of Redaction Criticism on the Interpretation of Mark 14:54, 66-72

The Focus on "Discipleship Failure" in Mark. The line of investigation which has probably received the most attention (both positively and negatively) is that which discerns in Mark's presentation of the disciples a polemic against a theology espoused by an alternative tradition within the community. A history of this development would focus on three figures: Alfred Kuby, Joseph B. Tyson, Theodore J. Weeden, and the development and dependence of ideas to be detected with them.[15]

Alfred Kuby. In our opinion the first scholar to note the "ignorance" of the disciples in the spirit of the modern discussion (i.e., in a manner akin to the technically argued theory of Weeden) was Alfred Kuby. Kuby's objectives were modest. By demonstrating that the three predictions of Jesus' passion and the disciples' consistent misunderstanding of them (8:31ff; 9:31ff; 10:33ff) were introduced by the story of the healing of the blind man in Bethsaida (8:22-26), he established this block of material to be a carefully constructed whole.

His conclusions were two. First, this healing pericope was a turning point in the flow of the story. From 1:16-8:21 the disciples fail to understand who Jesus is; from 8:22-14:72 they refuse to accept the fact that the Messiah must suffer. "Die Erkenntis dieser Gliederung und der Stellung der Einzelerzählungen in ihr, besonders der Titelerzählungen im zweiten Hauptteil, ist wesentlich für deren Verständnis und Auslegung im Sinne des Markus-Evangelisten."[16]

Moreover, Peter's denial brings the entire design to a punctuated conclusion: "Die Erzälung von der Verleugnung Petri setzt den Schlusspunkt unter den grossen

Abschnitt vom enlichen und doch—in seiner Art—von Anfang an vergeblichen Messiasglauben der Jünger."[17]

The second objective was more modest still: "Es erscheint auch angebracht, im NT Graece von Nestle die große Zäsur nicht mehr hinter Mc 8:26, sondern hinter Mc 8:21 zu setzen."[18]

In one brief essay Kuby anticipated two important developments in Markan discipleship: the redaction critical method[19] and the focus of attention on the negative portrayal of the disciples. "Diese Tragik der Jünger ist von Markus meisterhaft herausgearbeitet. Es verwundert, daß die Kommentatoren dies so wenig bemerkt haben."[20]

Almost simultaneous to Kuby's publication, Mark's "masterful redaction" was thoroughly explored by Marxsen whose conclusion Kuby recognized as similar to his own. "Markus baut in seiner Predigt die Apokalyptik um zur Eschatologie, er gestaltet seinen Stoff nach einer klaren Konzeption."[21] Kuby expressed a desire for his thesis to be considered a voice in the discussion of the new view of Mark as a redactor,[22] but his voice is seldom heard. His insight was noticed by Tyson in his article "The Blindness of the Disciples in Mark's Gospel."

Joseph B. Tyson. Before Tyson's article had appeared, the "blindness" of the disciples was usually either overlooked or attributed to Wrede's Messianic Secret.[23] Tyson challenged this "neglect." Focusing especially on the three predictions of the passion (8:31ff; 9:31ff; 10:33ff) Tyson suggests the author was not weaving a pattern of secrecy but of incorrigible blindness: "Mark is not here saying that the disciples understood that Jesus was Messiah and were commanded not to broadcast it; rather he is saying that they completely misunderstood the nature of Jesus' Messiahship, not understanding it as suffering Messiahship but as a royal Messiahship which would issue in benefits for themselves."[24]

With a motivation to ascertain "exactly what Mark would seem to be driving at," Tyson concludes that "Mark seems to be trying to indicate that the disciples really misunderstood the position of Jesus...Mark is aware of a significant difference between his own point of view and that of the disciples."[25]

Tyson attempts to reconstruct this point of view. If the attitudes of the disciples in the text reflect the view of the historical disciples as the author perceives them, then their position entails: (1) A deprecation of the soteriological significance of the death of Jesus in favor of a resurrection theology; (2) An emphasis on "royal" Messiahship which entertains little of the necessity of suffering and much about the question of rank and prestige. Tyson judged the conflict between Jesus and the disciples in the text to correspond to opposing Christian viewpoints in the first century. In sharp criticism of the theology of Jerusalem Christianity ("which probably included most of the original disciples, [and] took the form of a mildly modified Judaism"),[26] Mark emphasizes the death on the cross over the resurrection, overshadows the Son of David christology with a Galilean Son of Man, and corrects a desire for a nationalistic identity with a global missionary appeal. Although a position such as Mark espouses could have originated in a Pauline community or Galilee, Tyson feels it is more likely that Mark is "writing from and representing the point of view of the church which is soon to become the leading church of Christendom" (i.e., Rome).[27]

Tyson advanced the idea begun by Kuby on three fronts: (1) The tension within the text represents a polemic against another point of view within Christian circles; (2) The disciples are not only representative figures of this group but are attacked historically as well; (3) The ending of the Gospel was intended to undercut further a possible claim to legitimacy on the part of the historical disciples.[28] These points are picked up and honed by Weeden.

Theodore J. Weeden. Weeden is given credit for having "brought the discipleship phenomenon in Mark into focus."[29] Weeden pointed to two recent developments in Markan research which he felt were related: A Markan polemic against the disciples and an apparent identification of two opposing christologies with the Gospel. Their occurrence together was to Weeden more than coincidental. Weeden's assessment of the disciples' lack of understanding was the most pointed to date.

> This evolution in the disciples' relationship to Jesus from imperceptivity (1:16-8:26) to misconception (8:27-14:9) to rejection (14:10-72) is no accidental development, nor is it intended to be an objective presentation of the actual historical relationship which existed between Jesus and his disciples.[30]

Weeden concludes that the evangelist "is assiduously involved in a vendetta against the disciples. He is intent on totally discrediting them."[31] Naturally one wonders why.

Weeden employs a hermeneutic which centers on characterization as a clue to discovering authorial intent and the historical *Sitz im Leben*. Judging from the disciples' understanding of Jesus which culminates in Peter's confession (8:27-33), and based on the wonders of Jesus presented prior to it, Weeden feels "Mark intends the reader to draw the only conclusion possible: Peter makes a confession to a [*theios aner*] Christ."[32] Moreover, "the corollary must follow: their orientation toward discipleship must also be [*theios aner*]-directed."[33] Mark highlights this tension in the second half of the Gospel where Jesus' teaching that the Messiah must suffer and his steadfast journey to Jerusalem contrasts with the disciples who, in Weeden's estimation, are constantly seeking power, approval, and prestige.

This dispute is not rooted in history and so must reflect a dispute within Mark's own community. Mark's opponents were proclaiming that an authentic Christian existence is a glorious *theios aner* existence. This, says Weeden, would be especially troubling to a community suffering from persecution and disillusionment over the delay of the parousia (cp. Ch. 13). Mark answered this dilemma by telling a story of Jesus in which he projects the position of his opponents onto the historical disciples.

This was necessary because the opponents invoked apostolic legitimacy. His own view is articulated through Jesus. To anyone who would insist on a *theologia gloriae* after reading his Gospel, Marks says to him (through Jesus): you are of Satan, for you prefer the things of men to the things of God (8:32).

In light of this understanding of Mark's story of Jesus, the denial pericope serves the purpose of punctuating the difference between Jesus and the disciples. Although Jesus is betrayed by Judas (14:43-52) and the rest of the disciples forsake him (14:50),

> it is the denial of Peter that underscores the complete and utter rejection of Jesus and his messiahship by the disciples. Upon the condemnation of the Sanhedrin, Peter completely renounces Jesus, adamantly denying that he ever knew him (14:66-72). The type of messiahship to which Jesus committed himself has now been totally rejected by the disciples.[34]

The Perrinschule *and Kim Dewey.* Although Kuby, Tyson and Weeden can be credited with the development of the theme of "discipleship failure" in Mark's Gospel, this approach could also be identified with the so-called *Perrinschule*, since many of the leading exponents were students of or worked closely with the New Testament scholar Norman Perrin who himself argued for such an interpretation.[35] There is some justification for such a designation, especially with the publication of a collection of essays by these men who are essentially in agreement that "with the disciples there is an element of disintegration in the Gospel story, and the readers are alerted to the fact that to follow the twelve, or Peter, is to court disaster."[36] This collection of essays includes a treatment of the denial pericope in Mark by Kim E. Dewey. It may be the best example of a redaction critic uncovering the "anti-Petrinism" of the author of Mark within the denial pericope.

Dewey's stated objective is to separate tradition from redaction with the result that "we not only gain insight into the nature and function of the traditional material but also bring into sharper focus those concerns of Mk for which the story has been adapted and redactionally expanded."[37] According to Dewey, "by observing the confluence" of Mark's recognized characteristics such as vocabulary, style, themes, and compositional techniques, one can detect Mark's source and the extent to which he embellished it. Mark's source consisted of a simple one-stage denial (although it cannot be known whether this was oral or written, historically accurate, or circulated independently or as part of a larger story).

> Jesus is led to the High Priest (14:53a), Peter follows (14:54) and is confronted by a servant (14:66b) who accuses him of having been with Jesus (14:67b); this he denies, saying that he neither knows nor understands what she is saying. He flees from the courtyard (14:68) and then, remembering Jesus' prediction, weeps (14:72b, d and par.).[38]

This is what Mark received. He is himself responsible for reintroducing the denial story when it would have been more natural to omit it, since the narrative already records the flight of all the disciples. And he added a second and third denial, each stronger than the previous one, ending in Peter's cursing. The ambiguity of the object of the curse, says Dewey, is intentional and

> ...creates the highly ironic situation in which Peter either directly curses himself or indirectly does so by cursing Jesus, and by attempting to save himself in this situation in reality loses himself and is placed in even greater jeopardy. Peter, in denying Jesus, denies his own identity and becomes subject to the curse spoken by Jesus (8:38). In effect then Jesus and Peter have cursed each other.[39]

Mark's redaction of the story of the denial reveals clearly his concerns. He has taken a simple story of a single denial and embellished it into a three-fold denial. He has Peter disavow his own Galilean identity and Jesus *as Nazarene,* each of which implies his disassociation from everything the author considers positive. Thus, the author deliberately creates an image of Peter as a negative role model in the extreme: "A weak Peter is transformed into a hostile Peter, an opponent";[40] and "Peter, more than the betrayer, is the chief antagonist."[41] According to Dewey, Mark is thereby sending a message to his readers regarding contemporary power structures: "Those who attach themselves to Peter or to his view will suffer the same fate."[42]

The Most Recent Development: Biblical Literary Criticism

While redaction criticism is concerned with the hand of the author in the production of a story, literary criticism focuses more specifically still on the final product, the story itself apart from the hand which produced it. It is thus almost a "natural" development of redaction criticism.

Redaction criticism concerns itself with the meaning the author intended to give his story, and is therefore interested in the historical development of the text. Literary criticism, on the other hand, is concerned with the meaning of the text as a final product. The text is said to possess a meaning regardless of the ability to detect the hand of the author. Literary critics, for example, frequently distinguish between the "real author" (in this case, the historical Mark himself) and the "implied author" (i.e., "the literary version of Mark as discerned from the text").[43] In brief, what distinguishes literary criticism from previous approaches to the Biblical texts is its steadfast attempt "to maintain the methodological distinction between looking *through* the text [for something else such as the history of transmission or the work of the author] and looking *at* the text [for the final meaning conveyed]."[44]

As Augustine Stock describes the task,

> Literary criticism moves away from bondage to the distinction between tradition and redaction as the only gateway to Markan theology. It regards

Mark in its final form as the product of one creative mind. Questions of tradition and redaction are comparatively unimportant: what matters is the function of the text concerned in the gospel as a whole.[45]

Hence there is introduced entirely new concerns and objectives. The Gospel story is analyzed for the role of the author (both "real" and "implied"), narrator, themes and counter-themes, settings and plot, character development, and overall impact on the "implied" reader (i.e., "the imaginary person who responds appropriately to each of the narrator's strategies").[46]

The "author" with whom the literary critic has to do is not the historical personage who penned the Gospel but rather the literary role this personage gave himself in the production of his work. In this capacity the "implied author," sometimes called the narrator, of Mark is described as omniscient, omnicompetent, and omnipresent. He *knows* everything necessary to the "story world" without explaining the source of his knowledge. And he usually lets his readers in on this knowledge at crucial moments. As a creator of a story he has the *power* to control every aspect of it, including the arrangement of events, their prediction and fulfillment, and the response of the characters. He can be *everywhere* it is necessary to be to advance the story, is bound by the location of none of his characters, and therefore introduces his reader to different places and times at will.

Literary critics concentrate on the "story world" by emphasizing the unity of the text. Comparisons of events in the story with events which may have occurred in history are usually considered inappropriate. The events in the story have their primary significance from within the story, and more specifically the effect upon the "implied reader," i.e., the imaginary reader who responds appropriately to the narrator's strategies. The most important way to read the text, say literary critics, is to ascertain what expectations, hopes, fears, emotions, and conclusions the author intends to convey.[47]

By the nature of the method it is difficult to treat individual pericopae in isolation. We have found no such treatment on Peter's Denial. Rather, individual pericopae are commented on within the context of a larger consideration of the Markan narrative.

David Rhoads and Donald Michie

One of the best examples of a literary reading of Mark is that of David Rhoads and Donald Michie. Rhoads, a professor of New Testament, and Michie, a professor of English,[48] combine their areas of expertise to "read" the Markan story.

Mark as *Story*. Their conclusion is that the story world of the Gospel of Mark is fraught with reversals, ironies, riddles and hidden meanings. What may appear at first to be a simple collection of moralizations turns out to be an engaging statement on the great issues of life: "life and death, good and evil, human triumph and human failure."[49] The chief characteristics of the story are "irony and paradox: to be most important, one must be least; to enter the rule of God, one must become like a little child; nothing is hidden except to become known; whoever wants to save one's life must lose it."[50]

The characters themselves are caught in the reversals and paradoxes: "the disciples follow Jesus expecting glory and recognition only to find servitude and death confronting them; the authorities kill Jesus in order to preserve their traditions and authority, but they doom themselves by their action; the women come to anoint the dead Jesus, but discover he is among the living."[51]

But the main objective of the author is to tell a story which challenges the reader, to "lead the reader to see the hidden rule of God in Jesus and to follow him."[52] By introducing the many characters who are (in varying degrees) blind to what the writer has already made the reader privy, the reader is challenged to know and understand even more fully. The author leads the reader to identify (again in varying degrees) with the many characters who attempt to understand and follow Jesus, but especially to respond "in sympathetic tension with the uncomprehending disciples."[53] Ultimately the irony and paradox are turned on the reader as the story ends with the women who visited the (now empty) tomb flee in silence. It demands a witness, a "resolution" to the story, which only the reader can supply.

Peter's Denial. It would be uncharacteristic of literary criticism to treat a pericope, or "episode," *apart* from the larger story; it rather has meaning *as part* of the larger story.

Rhetoric. The way in which a story is told to create certain effects on the reader is called rhetoric. And such characteristics as narrator, style, and narrative patterns are known as rhetorical devices. The narrator, for example, is not the author, but rather a rhetorical device an author uses to tell his story. A narrator may be a character in the story and thus tell the story from his perspective in the first person. Mark uses a narrator who is not part of the story and who is, so far as the story is concerned, omniscient and can introduce the reader to any information prior to the story world, or perhaps something which will occur later than the time of the story world.

Nor is the narrator limited by space as a first person narrator might be. "The narrator depicts *mostly* scenes in which Jesus is present," note Rhodes and Michie, "but can also shift to other settings instantaneously to depict the high priests plotting against Jesus, or Peter denying Jesus."[54]

In this particular instance the author uses a narrative device called "framing." "After Peter sits down with soldiers in the courtyard of the High Priest, Jesus' trial begins before we learn what happens to Peter."[55] The result is to create suspense for the reader, encouraging him to remember that at this point in the narrative several events are transpiring simultaneously. One experiences one event in anticipation of the resolution of another which has been thereby suspended.

But this device also allows the author to provide commentary. One story is suspended to tell another, thus allowing the two stories to be compared or contrasted:

"Peter's denial of Jesus illuminates, by contrast, Jesus' courageous confession at his trial."[56]

Characterization. "Characters," say Rhoads and Michie, "are a central element of the story world."[57] They are integrally related to the development of plot and the resolution of conflicts. But they assume yet larger roles, for the reader tends to remember them apart from the rest of the story. Jesus as the protagonist is, of course, the most dominant character. But the disciples are important, too. They are "round" characters (as opposed to "flat" characters) because they have conflicting traits. They have many positive characteristics, including a significant degree of loyalty and courage, sacrifice and determination to follow Jesus. On the other hand, they seldom live up to their own expectations or those of Jesus. This development of their characters serves the larger purpose of the story.

> In fact, their failures constitute the primary literary device by which the narrator reveals Jesus' standards for discipleship, for much of his teaching comes in the course of correcting their behavior and attitudes. Their contrast with Jesus is sharpest when, by use of the framing device, the narrator places Jesus' trial and Peter's denial side by side."[58]

Jesus gives some of his disciples nicknames. James and John, for example, are the "Sons of Thunder." Simon is "Peter," or "Rock." Names are almost always significant in stories. The reader is challenged to discover the significance of "Peter." Is he strong and stable like a rock? Or does the name portend "rocky soil" as in the parable? Peter attempts to live up to the strength his name implies which makes it especially disappointing when Jesus reverts to "Simon" in his chastisement of Peter in Gethsemane. Perhaps he is unable to support the growth of the seed of the Kingdom of God. Indeed, Peter does react under persecution in this manner, unable to give deep root and stumbling "when oppression or persecution comes because of the word."

The reader thus learns early on that Peter is an unpredictable character, but he is unable to reject and condemn him because Jesus does not reject and condemn him. Because Jesus cares what happens to Peter and holds out hope for him, so must the reader. "The scene of Peter's denial is especially poignant," say Rhoads and Michie, "eliciting great disappointment as well as empathy from the reader."[59]

Plot. The plot of a story involves the manner in which an author arranges individual episodes to create tension, suspense, and struggle, and then resolves that tension and struggle. "In Mark's gospel, the establishment of God's rule provides the larger background for the story."[60] The foreground of the story consists of the conflicts and interactions of the protagonist Jesus with other characters of the story over the larger issue of God's kingdom. Jesus battles spiritual powers and nature, and argues with the authorities. But his conflict with the disciples is of a different nature. Jesus expects much from the disciples in terms of understanding and performance.

The disciples, on the other hand, are incapable of meeting his expectations and thus cause him much frustration. In particular they are incapable of accepting his teaching about the necessity to go to Jerusalem for the purpose of suffering and dying. "The final depiction of Peter, sobbing after his third denial of Jesus, is a stark portrayal of how much the disciples want to succeed and how utterly, at the end of the gospel, they fail."[61]

The resolution of the conflict with the disciples, suggest Rhoads and Michie, lies in the imaginary future of the story world. As the story ends, the disciples and Jesus are not "reconciled," and this leaves the reader wondering about the resolution. The disciples promised never to forsake Him, of course, but clearly they did. Although Jesus warned them of their impending flight, they would not or could not heed it. He has attempted to make them faithful disciples, but at the point at which the story ends he has not been successful. He predicts a reunion in Galilee, but that reunion is not narrated.

> The indeterminate resolution leads the reader to review the story for clues about the fate of the disciples in the future of the story world. These clues include the prophecies Jesus makes about the disciples, the conditional warnings he addresses to them, and the admonitions.[62]

Since the protagonist Jesus accurately predicts Peter's denial and many other things which have come true, the reader assumes his prediction of reconciliation will transpire as well. At the close of the story the young man clothed in white, a character whom the reader assumes to be a reliable commentator, proclaims to the women: "Go tell his disciples, even Peter, 'He's going ahead of you to Galilee. There you will behold him just as he told you'" (16:7).

Everything about this statement suggests the possibility of restoration. Simon is again called Peter, his discipleship name (Jesus addressed him as Simon at Gethsemane!). Jesus is still "going ahead" of them and they are to follow. Furthermore, the instruction to go to Galilee points to the possibility of a new start, a movement from rejection in Jerusalem toward proclaiming the good news to gentiles. There is, therefore, a pointer at the end suggesting that the disciples will go back to Galilee and there behold Jesus.[63]

> The net result of the story of Peter's denial within the larger Markan framework, therefore, is to depict a character with whom the reader could identify and empathize, but whose actions he should not emulate. His reconciliation with Jesus is strongly implied but not actualized. This is because *the action of the reader* in the future of the story world becomes more important than the action of any one character, including Peter.

Augustine Stock

Augustine Stock also approaches Mark as a literary critic who attempts to allow the text to speak for itself without concern to separate tradition from redaction in order to seek the interpretive key to the text from some source outside the Gospel, e.g., a hypothetical reconstruction of earliest Christianity.[64] Taking his cue from the literary theories of Plato and Aristotle, and also from the prevalence of Greek drama in the first century, Stock concludes that Mark shaped the gospel traditions that had come to him according to a kind of tragedy especially written for oral presentation.[65] He concurs with Gilbert Bilezikian that the genre of Greek tragedy was "the most influential and enduring aesthetic form designed by men to portray the great dilemmas of existence, and the torments brought upon mortals by their mysterious passions."[66] With this foundation Stock addresses the issue of the incomprehension of the disciples.

According to Stock, the author of the Gospel intends the story to operate on two levels: that of the characters and that of the reader. Within the narrative the two major roles are the *eiron* (ironical man or protagonist) and the *alazon* (impostor—a boastful, foolish pretender).[67] The protagonist and the narrator share the powers of omniscience. The reader is also given some knowledge which is hidden from the other characters who, because of this, are viewed as making ridiculously false judgments. Stock also discerns a parabolic quality to Mark. "Indeed, Jesus is not said to *speak* in parables to outsiders, rather that everything *is* or *occurs* in *riddles* to the outsiders."[68] When one realizes that this parabolic quality permeates the entire Gospel, its effects move beyond the characters to the reader himself.

> The disciples' behavior comes to be characterized by incomprehension, and a tension is set up, a tension internal to the narrative between Jesus and the disciples. But this tension raises in the reader's mind the possibility of another tension, an external tension, between his own behavior and Jesus' truth and goodness. After identifying with the disciples early in the gospel, the negative turn in the disciples' story leads the reader to reexamine his own discipleship. The purpose of the author of Mark was not merely to present certain ideas about Jesus but to lead his readers through a particular story in which they could discover themselves and thereby change.[69]

"The story of Peter's denial," says Stock, "illustrates two characteristics of Mark's gospel: two levels of meaning, and irony."[70] The irony is clearly evident in the framing of Jesus' trial with Peter's "trial." After setting the courtyard scene with Peter warming himself by the fire, the author relates the story of Jesus which ends with the soldiers buffeting him and demanding that he "prophesy!" "While Jesus is mocked as a false prophet one of his prophecies is being fulfilled in the courtyard. While Jesus openly acknowledges the truth about himself even though it means death, Peter, to escape death, denies that he knows Jesus—even invoking a curse upon himself."[71]

Irony is the chief transmitter of the deeper level of meaning.[72] The characters of the story operate only on the level of bare sensory perception and face value. They do not see or understand the irony or the meaning it implies. It is the reader who is led into this realm: While Jesus is convicted of being a false prophet, one of his prophecies is coming to pass at that moment. Those who condemn Jesus end up thereby condemning themselves, while Jesus the condemned is vindicated and exalted. While Jesus is being tried by the high priest, Peter is being tried by the high priest's servant girl. Peter's cursing is intended to extricate him from participation in Jesus' condemnation, but instead he "is in grave danger of making himself fully one with Satan, until the cock's crow brings him to his sense."[73]

> The story of Peter's denial operates on two levels. There is the level of bare sensory perception of the events that take place, the level to which both reader and characters, alike, have access. There is also the level of the deeper meaning of the events to which only the reader has access. And for Mark it is the meaning at this level that moves him to tell the story. At the deeper level of the story the reader sees that quite often things are not what they seem.[74]

Endnotes for Chapter Six

[1]W. L. Lane, "From Historian to Theologian: Milestones in Markan Scholarship," *RevExp* 75 (1978) 611.

[2]G. Bornkamm, G. Barth, H. J. Held, *Tradition and Interpretation in Matthew* (Philadelphia: Westminster, 1963); translated by Percy Scott from *Überliefereng und Auslegung im Matthäusevangelium.*

[3]H. Conzelmann, *The Theology of St. Luke* (New York: Harper & Row, 1960); translated by Geoffery Buswell from *Die Mitte der Zeit* (Tübingen: J. C. B. Mohr, 1953).

[4]W. Marxsen, *Der Evangelist Markus—Studien zur Redaktionsgeschichte des Evangelium* (Göttingen: Vandenhoeck & Ruprecht, 1956); Eng. tr. by R. A. Harrisville, *Mark the Evangelist: Studies on the Redaction History of the Gospel* (Nashville: Abingdon, 1969). This work was Marxsen's *Habilitationsschrift,* which is the equivalent to a second dissertation, and is required for any German who desires to hold a professorial chair at a university. Paginations in this dissertation are taken from the English edition.

[5]*Ibid.*

[6]*Ibid.*, 24, cited by Marxsen from Bultmann, "The New Approach to the Synoptic Problem," *JR* 6 (1926) 341.

[7]*Ibid.*, 94, 146-9.

[8]Lane, "Milestones," 612.

[9]For critical analyses of Marxsen's contribution see R. Mohrlang, "Redaction Criticism and the Gospel of Mark: An Evaluation of the Work of Willi Marxsen," *Studia Biblica et Theologica* 6 (1976) 18-33; W. L. Lane, "*Redaktionsgeschichte* and the Dehistoricizing of the New Testament Gospel," *Bulletin of the Evangelical Theological Society* 11 (1968) 27-33; F. J. Matera, "Interpreting Mark—Some Recent Theories of Redaction Criticism," *LS* 2 (1968) 113-31; J. Rhode, *Rediscovering the Teaching of the Evangelists* (Philadelphia: Westminster Press, 1968) 113-40; R. H. Stein, "What is *Redaktionsgeschichte?*" *JBL* 88 (1969) 45-66.

[10]Lane, "The Gospel of Mark in Current Study," 20-1; Kingsbury, "The Gospel of Mark in Current Research," 105-6.

[11]N. Perrin, *A Modern Pilgrimage in New Testament Christology* (Philadelphia: Fortress Press, 1974) 8-9, 110.

[12]Kingsbury, "The Gospel of Mark in Current Research," 102. On the issue of *theios-aner* see Lane, "*Theios Aner* Christology and the Gospel of Mark," in *New Dimensions in New Testament Study*, eds., R. N. Longenecker and M. C. Tenney (Grand Rapids: Zondervan, 1974) 144-61; O. Betz, "The Concept of the So-called 'Divine Man' in Mark's Christology," in *Studies in the New Testament and Early Christian Literature: Essays in Honor of Allen P. Wikgren*, ed., D. E. Aune (Leiden:

Brill, 1972) 229-40; H. D. Betz, "Jesus as Divine Man," in *Jesus and the Historian*, ed., F. F. Trotter (Philadelphia: Westminster Press, 1968) 114-33; D. L. Tiede, *The Charismatic Figure as Miracle Worker*, SBLDS 1 (Missoula, MT: Scholars Press, 1972); C. H. Holladay, *Theios Aner in Hellenistic-Judaism: A Critique of the Use of This Category in New Testament Christology*, SBLDS 40 (Missoula, MT: Scholars Press, 1977); J. D. Kingsbury, "The 'Divine Man' as the Key to Mark's Christology —The End of an Era?" *Int* 35 (1981) 243-257.

[13]D. Georgi, *Die Gegner des Paulus im 2. Korintherbrief,* WMANT 11 (Neukirchen-Vluyn: Neukirchener Verlag, 1964).

[14]Kingsbury, "The Gospel of Mark in Current Research," 103.

[15]A. Kuby, "Zur Konzeption des Markus-Evangeliums," *ZNW* 49 (1958) 52-64; See J. B. Tyson ("The Blindness of the Disciples in Mark," *JBL* 80 [1961] 261-8, esp. 263 n 6) for his acknowledged indebtedness to Kuby; T. J. Weeden (*Mark— Traditions in Conflict* [Philadelphia: Fortress, 1971] 25) in turn credits Tyson with having "performed an invaluable service for Markan scholarship by...opening up a fresh, new way to view the Markan treatment of the disciples." W. Kelber (*The Kingdom in Mark. A New Place and A New Time* [Philadelphia: Fortress, 1974] xi) credits Weeden with having "brought the discipleship phenomenon in Mark into focus." Thus the beginning of this line of reasoning, so far as I can tell, is traceable to Kuby. For additional studies of this type see T. J. Weeden, "The Heresy that Necessitated Mark's Gospel," *ZNW* 59 (1968) 145-58; W. Kelber, "Mark 14:32-42: Gethsemane. Passion Christology and Discipleship Failure," *ZNW* 63 (1972) 166-87; idem, *The Oral and the Written Gospel. The Hermeneutics of Speaking and Writing in the Synoptic Tradition, Mark, Paul, and Q* (Philadelphia: Fortress, 1983).

[16]Kuby, "Konzeption," 64.

[17]*Ibid.*, 62-3.

[18]*Ibid.*, 64.

[19]It is true that Marxsen's work was first published in 1956, two years prior to the date of Kuby's article in 1958. However, Kuby's work was apparently done independently of Marxsen's and had actually been accepted by *ZNW* for publication before Marxsen's work appeared in print; so says Kuby in his "Nachwort: Nach Fertigstellung dieser Arbeit Ende 1955 ist 1956 in Göttingen das Buch von Willi Marxsen *Der Evangelist Markus: Studien zur Redaktionsgeschichte des Evangeliums* ershienen" (64). It is on this basis that we say Kuby "anticipated" the redaction critical method. The appearance of Bornkamm's, Conzelmann's, Marxsen's, and Kuby's works in such a short period of time, each apparently independently of the others, is an interesting phenomenon deserving the attention of scholarly investigation.

[20]Kuby, "Konzeption," 59.

[21]*Ibid.*, 64.

[22]*Ibid.*

[23]Tyson, "Blindness," 261.

[24]*Ibid.*, 262.

[25]*Ibid.*, 263.

[26]*Ibid.*, 265.

[27]*Ibid.*, 268.

[28]*Ibid. o*62

[29]Kelber, *Kingdom in Mark,* xi.

[30]Weeden, "Heresy," 147.

[31]Weeden, *Mark,* 50.

[32]Weeden, "Heresy," 148.

[33]*Ibid.*, 149.

[34]Weeden, *Mark,* 38-9.

[35]References to a "Chicago School" or a "Perrin School" can be found in several sources: R. E. Brown, review of *The Passion in Mark,* ed. by W. Kelber, in *CBQ* 39 (1977) 283; W. Schenk, review of *Are You the Christ?,* by J. R. Donahue, in *TLZ* 100 (1975) 839; R. Fortna, "Jesus and Peter at the High Priest's House: A Test Case for the Question of the Relation Between Mark's and John's Gospels," *NTS* 24 (1977-78) 382; D. M. Smith, "John and the Synoptics: Some Dimensions of the Problem," *NTS* 26 (1979-80) 426; W. O. Seal, Jr., ("Norman Perrin and His 'School': Retracing A Pilgrimage," *JSNT* 20 [1984] 89) argues that "interdependence in effort, interaction of ideas, and consensus in position indicate that the term 'school' is quite appropriate" in reference to Perrin and the works of his students and some colleagues.

[36]W. Kelber, "Conclusions: From Passion Narrative to Gospel," *The Passion in Mark,* ed. W. Kelber (Philadelphia: Fortress, 1976) 174.

[37]Kim E. Dewey, "Peter's Curse and Cursed Peter," in *Passion* ed. by Kelber, 97.

[38]*Ibid.,* 104.

[39]*Ibid.,* 101.

[40]*Ibid.,* 108.

[41]*Ibid.,* 110.

[42]*Ibid.,* 111.

[43]Scot McKnight, *Interpreting the Synoptic Gospels* (Grand Rapids: Baker, 1988) 124.

[44]*Ibid.,* 123. The metaphor of looking *through* a text versus looking *at* a text derives from the distinction of viewing a text as a window or a mirror. These metaphors of window and mirror come from the literary critic Murray Krieger, *A Window to Criticism* (Princeton: University Press, 1964) 3-4.

[45]Augustine Stock, *Call to Discipleship: A Literary Study of Mark's Gospel* (Wilmington, DL: Michael Glazier, 1982) 12.

[46]McKnight, 126.

[47]See R. M. Fowler, "Who Is the 'Reader' of Mark's Gospel?," *SBLSP* (1983) 31-54; J. L. Resseguie, "Reader-Response Criticism and the Synoptic Gospels," *JAAR* 52 (1984) 307-24.

[48]David Rhoads and Donald Michie, *Mark as Story* (Philadelphia: Fortress Press, 1982).

[49]*Ibid.*, 1.

[50]*Ibid.*

[51]*Ibid.*

[52]*Ibid.*, 137.

[53]*Ibid.*, 138.

[54]*Ibid.*, 37.

[55]*Ibid.*, 51.

[56]*Ibid.*

[57]*Ibid.*, 101.

[58]*Ibid.*, 123.

[59]*Ibid.*, 129.

[60]*Ibid.*, 103.

[61]*Ibid.*, 93.

[62]*Ibid.*, 97.

[63]*Ibid.*

[64]Stock, *Discipleship*, 12-3; idem, "Literary Criticism and Mark's Mystery Play," *Bible Today* 100 (1979) 1909-15.

[65]Stock, *Discipleship*, 73.

[66]*Ibid*, 27, citing G. Bilezikian, *The Liberated Gospel: A Comparison of the Gospel of Mark and Greek Tragedy* (Grand Rapids: Baker, 1977) 34.

[67]*Ibid.*, 23.

[68]*Ibid.*, 99.

[69]*Ibid.*, 207.

[70]*Ibid.*, 43.

[71]*Ibid.*, 44..

[72]According to Northrop Freye (*Anatomy of Criticism* [Princeton: University Press] 40) irony "indicates a technique of appearing to be less than one is, which in literature becomes most commonly a technique of saying as little and meaning as

much as possible, or, in a more general way, a pattern of words that turn away from direct statement, or its own obvious meaning."

[73]Stock, *Discipleship,* 190.

[74]*Ibid.,* 43.

Chapter 7

Premodern and Modern Methodologies and Interpretations Compared

There are inherent tendencies in producing a history of interpretation of a single passage of a text. One is for the work to evolve into a history of interpretation of the whole book from which the passage is taken. And indeed, the dissertation has occasionally addressed the interpretation of Mark's Gospel as a whole and its place in history. The second tendency is for the study to evolve even further into a history of Biblical interpretation *per se;* i.e., a history of hermeneutics, with the passage being nothing more than a test case which could easily be replaced and almost as easily discarded.

The present work is meant to be neither of these. Our evaluation of the methodologies below, therefore, will be in light of their application to our single passage. And the objective will be to refine our understanding of this passage in light of a representative history of interpretation.

The Spiritual Sense versus the Literal Sense

Our study of the interpretation of Mark 14:54, 66-72 has borne out one obvious fact, namely that premodern exegetes inclined toward the spiritual sense of the text. Everything had potential significance: Peter's following from afar (Bede), the courtyard (*Glossa ordinaria,* Jerome), the light of the fire by which he warmed himself (Bede, *Glossa ordinaria,* Jerome), the being warmed (Theophylact), the accusers (Bede, *Glossa ordinaria,* Jerome), the accusations, the denials (Bede), the crowing of the cock (Bede, Jerome), the tears (Bede, Jerome), the late night hour and the coming of dawn (Bede, *Glossa ordinaria*).

117

But it has also borne out something not quite as obvious until the fathers are read closely, namely, that the elaborate theories of interpretation are not followed assiduously. We turn our attention now to this proposition: namely, that one can speak of a "multiple method" in theory, but probably not in practice. And although the inclination toward the spiritual sense eclipsed the concern for the literal sense, it did not obviate it.

The Spiritual Senses in Theory and in Practice. Several theories existed. The prevalence of the multiple method should probably be traced to Alexandrian philosophy and theology. There the attempt to reconcile Christianity and Platonism gave rise to allegory as the key to understanding. Jewish haggadic exegesis had pursued this allegorical reading of the Old Testament even before Philo. Philo influenced Origen, of course. And Origen moved from a two-fold meaning of Scripture (*sensus historicus* or *literalis, and sensus spiritualis*) to a trichotomous scheme: the literal, spiritual, and the moral.[1] Augustine had a four-fold sense, though it differed from the quadruple system of the Middle Ages.[2]

The four-fold sense which dominated much of Church History is sometimes attributed to Eucherius of Lyons (d. ca. 449), sometimes to Cassian,[3] but it almost certainly preceded both.[4] This hermeneutical theory was summarized in a little poem made famous by Nicholas of Lyra:

> *Littera gesta docet, quid credas allegoria,*
> *Moralis quid agas, quo tendas anagogia.*[5]

Such systems became ever more refined. Angelom of Luxeuil of the ninth century proffered a seven-fold scheme, and Martin Marrier, seventeenth century editor of Odo of Cluny, proffered eight senses of interpretation.[6] Note has already been made of Bede's elaborate system.[7] In theory he functioned with seventeen "schemes" (figures of speech) and thirteen "tropes" (figures of thought). Allegory was a species of trope which in turn had seven subspecies: irony, antiphrasis, enigma, charientismus, parhoemia, sarcasm, and asteismus.

But the point is that almost none of these elaborate theories were employed very vigorously. The most common one, the four-fold sense of interpretation, was in practice usually employed as a two-fold sense, literal and spiritual, with the second subsuming the three senses corresponding to the theological virtues.[8] The allegorical sense expounded what the church should believe and therefore corresponded to the virtue of faith. The tropological sense exhorted the individual in behavior and therefore corresponded to the virtue of love. The anagogical sense, because it anticipated the future, corresponded to the virtue of hope. These latter three senses were blurred and frequently overlapped, and this was recognized by many of the fathers.[9]

This multiplicity of meaning was defended and justified by St. Thomas Aquinas. It was due not to ambiguity and equivocation, he claimed, but rather to the recognition that while words signify things, things in turn signify other things. Says Aquinas:

> The multiplicity of these interpretations does not cause ambiguity or any sort of equivocation, since these interpretations are not multiplied because one word signifies several things; but because the things signified by the words can themselves be types of other things.[10]

To offer a positive explanation, the Fathers' attempt to elucidate the different levels of meaning of Scripture was a profession that the Bible could not be interpreted either literally or rigidly: "their methods of interpretation were intended to free the faithful readers from inherited claims of reason by attributing cogency to shifting points of view."[11] Probably any system, including an allegorical system, were it followed rigidly, would undermine the legitimacy of this shifting point of view.

Bede turns out not to have been an exception at all, but a dependable rule. It would be difficult to sort out to what extent he merely mirrored his age or was programmatic for it and generations to follow. But it remains the case that although elaborate exegetical schemes were worked out in theory, at least so far as they were applied to our passage (Mark 14:54, 66-72) it seemed to boil down to the fact that Scripture had more than a literal meaning which could be detected and expounded upon and given any number of names.

The Literal Sense in the Shadows. The second point is that not even the literal or historical meaning was abandoned altogether;[12] even if it was eclipsed by the spiritual, it was always in the shadows. Indeed, the spiritual sense was defined in contrast to the literal. Thus, says Gregory the Great, in describing his tripartite method:

> First we lay the foundations in history; then by following a symbolical sense, we erect an intellectual edifice to be a stronghold of faith; and lastly, by the grace of moral instruction, we as it were paint the fabric in fair colors.[13]

As examples, the discrepancies of the cock crows and the identification of Peter's accusers were perennial problems for premodern exegetes, underscoring their concern for the literal-historical understanding of the text. The significance of the discrepancies was sometimes dismissed, as Victor dismissed the discrepancy of the identification of the maids between Matthew's and Mark's accounts: "it was not necessary for saving faith"; after all, "it agrees with what has been previously stated, that Peter denied a second time with an oath not to have known the man."[14]

But the Fathers frequently demonstrate a genuine astuteness in grappling with the historicity of the text. One example is the exposition of the second cock crow by Theophylact. The "roosters were accustomed, according to one school of thought," says Theophylact, "to crow several times, thereupon to fall into a kind of sleep, and again after some time to begin another 'crowing.' Therefore Matthew says, 'Before the cock crows,' by which he means '[Before] the completion of the cock-crow, you will deny me thrice.'"[15]

Theophylact's understanding of the customs and behavior of the animal life is only slightly less sophisticated than explanations by modern scholars. One modern study of the crowing of roosters in Palestine confirms that there is indeed such a pattern of three crowings occurring approximately one hour apart and each lasting approximately five minutes.[16] Whether this solves the problem of a discrepancy either between the Synoptic accounts or within Mark's own account is beside the point. Theophylact's source on this point is well informed, and he addressed the problem responsibly.

One can speak of a propensity or inclination to read the spiritual sense over the literal-historical, but not to its exclusion. For there is ample evidence that the fathers knew how to grapple with the historical question, even if their view of the problem and solutions is unacceptable to us.[17]

Looking *At* the Text versus Looking *Through* the Text

It is also the case that both our presuppositions and our base of knowledge have so drastically altered our approach and world view that even the literal-historical interpretations of the premodern exegetes ring peculiar in our ears. In this regard, the recent contribution of literary criticism's voice to the debate has awakened us to another, perhaps better, way of categorizing and contrasting the premodern with the historical-critical method.

Modern Literary Criticism: Looking *At* the Text. Biblical historians have for over a century now been concerned to uncover some meaning or intent *behind* the text. For the historians of the nineteenth century, this was the historical Jesus. For the form critics of the early twentieth century it was the earliest form of an oral tradition and/or the accretions which witnessed to the concerns of the community which shaped it. For the redaction critics it was the editorial work of the evangelist and/or the evidence for the theological position of the community which produced the Gospel. In one sense, therefore, the premodern method may have something in common with the literary approach in biblical criticism, for they both seemed inclined to derive the primary meaning of the text directly from the text.

The inclination of the historical critical method to look through the text (at the historical event it purports to portray, or the theological position which might have produced it) is partly explained by the paradigm with which it works. According to Norman Petersen, the historical-critical paradigm is a concern for "the value of biblical texts as evidence for reconstructing the history to which they refer or of which they are documents."[18] In this operation historical criticism is propelled by two principles. According to Petersen:

> (1) every text is first and foremost evidence for the circumstances in and for which it was composed, and in this respect texts serve as documentary *evidence for the time of writing;* (2) seek the earliest and best *evidence for the events referred to in the text.*[19]

Source and form critics readily focused on the written or oral sources of the Gospels on the assumption that they provided the earliest and best evidence for the events referred to in the text. In the case of the form critics, this was the *Sitz im Leben* of the community which transmitted, shaped, and/or created the oral traditions. Thus, the first principle was neglected in favor of the second.

Redaction criticism, says Petersen, attempted to return to the first principle and ask once again after the evidential value of the texts for the time of writing rather than as evidence of the events to which they referred. A form of this first principle can be traced to Willi Marxsen and ultimately to Rudolf Bultmann, namely, that "a literary work is a primary source for the historical situation out of which it arose, and is only a secondary source for the historical details concerning which it gives information."[20]

However, in the attempt to look at the text holistically, redaction criticism found its concern focused not on the text itself, but rather on the author of the text, his theology and motive for writing. Redaction critics so defined their task that they were forced to look *through* the text at the relation of the author to his sources, and thereby neglected to look *at* the text in order to see how all the sources and authorial contribution meshed into a whole. In Petersen's words:

> In its quest for the earliest and best evidence for the events referred to in biblical narrative, historical criticism defaulted on its own first principle, which holds that a text is first and foremost evidence for the time of writing. Redaction criticism sought to remedy this situation and in its failure showed that *literary issues are bound up with the first principle: The text itself must be comprehended in its own terms before we can ask of what it is evidence, whether in relation to the time of writing or in relation to the events referred to in it* [emphasis added].[21]

I have understood Petersen and other biblical literary critics to be saying that the evolutionary model of historical criticism demands a certain logical order in its questions. Historical events are remembered and carried in oral traditions which are collected in various ways and eventually written down. Before one can ask after these events, one must ascertain the earliest and best oral tradition. Before one can ask after the earliest and best oral tradition, one must know how it was shaped by the author in a written text. Before one asks about the theology of the author and his creative contribution, one must comprehend the text *as it is in its totality.*[22]

From this we will deduce a "tentative working" hermeneutical principle and apply it below to our passage, namely, that nothing can confidently be attributed to the redactor which cannot be supported from the story world of the text. In other words, what the text says is logically prior to how and why it was said, or its historicity. Says Petersen, "Literary criticism would thus be either a fundamental stage of historical criticism or a stage which in this respect must precede historical criticism."[23]

This, it seems, would greatly explain why so much of premodern exegesis resembles the results of literary criticism. They, much as modern biblical literary critics, looked *at* the text to derive meaning from it, rather than at something or someone *behind* the text. This is true even if much of the meaning derived was intuited, lacking the more sophisticated techniques and safeguards of literary criticism.

It is also true that this simultaneously describes to a large extent their difference with modernity. Because they lacked the "multi-dimensional, critical" view of modern historians, premodern exegetes tended to view their text one dimensionally. The story world was equated with the real world it purported to portray.[24] This, says Grant, is why it is important to remember that "literalism is different from historical criticism."[25] They neglected the complicated context and process by which the story came to be told.

Premodern Hermeneutics: Looking *At* the Text. By focusing on the text directly, the Fathers were frequently if unwittingly capable of discerning with remarkable insight the text's message. This is not at all to suggest that the Fathers were as sophisticated as modern literary critics, nor that they were inerrant in their judgments. But they had one advantage of which they were unaware, and which is too often overlooked by us, namely, their willingness to accept the meaning of the text at face value.

Negative Typology. They were able, for example, to accept the fact that Mark's account of Peter's denial seemed somehow the harshest. But Victor's assessment of this is not much less sophisticated than some modern Biblical literary critics. Mark's account is fuller and harsher because, he says, "he had learned these things from his teacher. For he was a disciple of Peter."[26] If he displays little understanding of the historical problems of the Gospel's authorship, he has nevertheless grasped correctly what appears to be a significant motive of the Gospel's author: Peter "did not miss the mark, for he had remained, indeed was, a genuine disciple. He won the hope of pardon. Indeed, we say that because we learn of the failures of the saints through the Scriptures, in order that we should be imitators of their repentance."[27]

The literary critics, of course, usually use terminology like "negative types" and a *theologia crucis.*[28] But the gist of their interpretations is the same. Peter provides a negative example by spurning Jesus' road to shame and death. Victor and many others of the Fathers already knew this.

Setting. Another example would be the recent recognition by Biblical literary critics of the importance of setting in the Gospel of Mark. According to Rhoads and Michie:

> The settings of a story provide the context for the conflicts and for the actions of the characters. That context is often quite integral to the story, for settings can serve many functions essential to plot: generating atmosphere, determining conflict, revealing traits in the characters who must deal with problems or

threats caused by the settings, offering commentary (sometimes ironic) on the action, and evoking associations and nuances of meaning present in the culture of the readers. Settings may even provide structure to a story, in addition to conveying important themes. Settings can be no less significant for a story than stage sets are for theater drama...

As a dimension of setting, the "time" is also highly charged.[29]

This seems to us very close to Bede's hermeneutical principle of *Circumstantiae:*

Scripture is accustomed to point out the mystery of causes by the circumstances of the times. Hence Peter, who made his denial in the middle of the night, repented at cock crow. He also, after the Lord's resurrection, at daylight professed three times equally that he loved him, whom he denied three times, because undoubtedly what he erred through forgetfulness in the darkness he both corrected by recalling the hoped-for light and in the presence of this same true light he completely strengthened that in which he had wavered. I think that by this cock must be understood some teacher who rouses us when we are asleep, and reproving our sleepiness says: "Come to your right mind, and sin no more."

Granted that Bede is guided by a theological view of Scripture and the modern critic by explanation of literary phenomena, the result is nevertheless much the same. They have neither one created this insight. Rather, each of them has recognized and explained a reality actually there as best he could given his world view and schema.

Spatialization. The Fathers intuited the importance of setting throughout their works, and if they erred in its application, it was on the side of overimagination. The Fathers could readily assent to Rhoads' and Michie's claim that "major settings in Mark's story are seldom neutral."[30] In fact, it is even possible that Mark has *spatialized* his story to indicate the sacred and profane and to symbolize the characters' orientation to each.[31] At least recent redaction critics have claimed that Mark made use of such a distinction to indicate loyalties. Mark, it has been claimed, uses a topological scheme to define the true family of God in chapter 3, for example, in terms of "insiders and outsiders."[32] Something very similar to this motivates the commentary of both Bede and the *Glossa ordinaria.* Says Bede:

Rightly was he following him at a distance who was already close to denying him. For he would not have been able to deny him, if he had remained close to Christ.

And,

Peter himself among the faithless denied that he knew the man whom he had confessed to be the Son of God among his fellow disciples! But he could not be penitent while detained in the court of Caiaphas. He goes outside, as the other Evangelists narrate, so that being removed from the council of the impious he might wash away the filth of a timorous denial by unrestrained weeping.

Adds the *Glossa ordinaria:*

> The courtyard is a worldly (profane) surrounding. [The] Servants are demons. Fire is carnal desire, he who remains with which has not the strength to lament his sins.

The "Spirit" of the Text. The irony of this is that the premodern inclination to look *at* the text yielded most readily not the literal-historical understanding of the text, but rather the "spirit" of the text—that is, not just the bare fact but the theological and pastoral implications of the fact for the reader. The premodern approach demonstrated an intuition that the text could and would speak to later readers. The "spirit" of the text was ever alive.[33]

Premodern exegetes worked with the assumption that a text possesses not only an original "literal" meaning of the author (which had theological and pastoral implications in and of itself) but other meanings as well.[34] They took their cue from the words of St. Paul: "The letter kills but the spirit makes alive" (2 Cor. 3:6). This was usually used to discuss the distinction between law and gospel, demand and grace. But, notes Steinmetz,

> Paul could also have in mind a distinction between what William Tyndale later called the "story-book" or narrative level of the Bible and the deeper theological meaning of spiritual significance implicit within it.[35]

This distinction is not too unlike the fundamental difference in Ethics between the letter of the law and the spirit of the law. Just as an isolated instance of telling the truth could be extrapolated into the principle of veracity, so an isolated instance of moral failure within a story could be extrapolated into a theological principle underlying it.

It is possible, of course, that an author could record an instance of moral failure in order to discredit his/her character. Several of the scholars in chapter six above have concluded that the church would preserve the story of Peter's denial, or that Mark would record it, only if they were operating with an anti-Petrine bias. Theophylact, on the other had, feels that the evangelists "made the shortcomings of the saints a matter of public record, in order that we, if we should at any time stumble, should also have their examples in mind, and should through repentance hasten to be reconciled."[36] On the whole, Theophylact seems nearer the truth, as we argue below.[37]

The Inclination to View History One-Dimensionally versus the Inclination to View History Multi-Dimensionally

The Premodern One-Dimensional View of Reality: A Weak Historical Foundation. The primary weakness of the premodern method is almost tautological:

the premodern method was precritical. Although we have argued and maintain that the Fathers were not unconcerned with historical questions, it is nevertheless the case that those concerns were overshadowed by dogmatic and pastoral matters. The premodern exegete gained some advantage in looking *at* the text in terms of understanding the flow of the narrative and the "spirit" of the text. But, to state the obvious, they were without the world view necessary to allow them to ask the questions by which the moderner is driven. Thus, looking at the text for the premodern exegete too often meant looking at the text as though it were a flat replica of the historical events it reported.

The modern exegete may employ a literary analysis of the text as a legitimate first step in the hermeneutical process (as suggested above by Petersen). One proceeds from there to ask the appropriate historical questions. For the premodern exegete the subsequent questions were too often tangential, allegorical, and spiritualizing. By equating the events and world of the text with the events and world the text purported to portray, premodern exegetes failed to grasp the "historical problem." They too often forgot the foundation on which Gregory claims the spiritual meaning was constructed. Inference gave way to unbridled imagination.

It is not just that the author of the Gospel was regarded as Mark, the disciple of Peter, for example, and therefore the author of a more exact report. Many modern scholars believe the same.[38] It is that for the Fathers, tradition rather than evidence guaranteed that tenet. Beyond an embellished account of the Papias tradition, the evidence necessary to substantiate such a claim is seldom if ever considered. After a while, even the Papias tradition is no longer recounted.

Further, our text does not provide the best example of how a meaning can be read *into* a text rather than exegeted from it. Yet even in the commentaries on Mark 14:54, 66-72 much can be found that is due more to the interpreter than to the text. How Bede (following Augustine) could confidently assert that the "fact that Peter followed the Lord at a distance as he was going to his passion signified that the Church was going to follow" the Lord as well, would seem to demand an interpretation foreign to the text.

The fire by which Peter warmed himself was sufficient for Bede to find parallel spiritual fires from the lakeside of John 21:9 to the cloven tongues of Acts 2:3. According to (Pseudo-) Jerome, the fire symbolized the attack of the high priests against Jesus. But "fire without wood goes out. And the testimony did not agree."[39]

The Modern Multi-Dimensional View of Reality: A Critical View of History. The modern approach begins where Gregory (and many of the Fathers) claimed to have begun, by laying a foundation in history. This, says Krentz, "is taken for granted; we cannot go back to a precritical age."[40] In fact, this may mark both the minimum and extent of agreement among modern exegetes: "that historical criticism, the best method of discovering the literal sense, cannot be given up."[41] The historical critical method accomplishes at least two things.

First, in focusing on the history the text purports to portray, it helps to establish parameters of thought and theology, thus guarding against the unbridled imagination of allegorism. Says Culpepper: "The historical-critical approach has been indispensable because it has served to break the hold of non-critical devotional, allegorizing, and spiritualizing exegesis."[42] Extracting theological and pastoral implications is not the same as eisegeting one's position into the text. The historical-critical method insists that the Bible is a record of historical events. But one can never assume a one-to-one correspondence between the events presented in the text and those historical events. The modern approach demands a wrestling with the historicity of the text, and the results necessarily establish certain parameters for interpretation.

Second, in focusing on the history the text purports to portray, it reminds us that the text is *con*textual. This step is so fundamental it is often overlooked and is (must be) assumed even by the literary critic. Again, Culpepper reminds us that, "in the process of attempting to recover the history behind the gospels, scholars realized that the gospels are documents written within and for specific historical settings, and therefore their meaning can be understood only as we interpret the gospels in their historical context."[43] If we have belabored the point that a text can have more than one meaning, then it requires us once more to underscore that those meanings must be oriented around the intention of the author in attempting to communicate a message to his or her readers.

Endnotes for Chapter Seven

[1]Harry Caplan, "The Four Senses of Scriptural Interpretation and the Medieval Theory of Preaching," *Speculum* 4 (1929) 285.

[2]*Ibid.*

[3]See pp. 36ff.

[4]Caplan, 286, note 12.

[5]*Ibid.*

[6]*Ibid.,* 287.

[7]See pp. 36ff.

[8]Caplan, 286.

[9]*Ibid.,* 287. According to Caplan (287, n. 3), "Gazaeus discloses this in studying the method of Jerome, *Epist. ad Hedibiam, quaest. 12, Ezech.* xvi, and *Amos* iv. See Cassian, *Collationes* xiv, 8, Migne, *Pat. Lat.,* XLIX, 962."

[10]*Ibid.* The precise reference is *Summa Theologica,* I, art. 10, Reply obj. 3.

[11]Charles W. Jones, "Some Introductory Remarks on Bede's Commentary on Genesis," *SacEr* 19 (1969-70) 135.

[12]George H. Brown, *Bede the Venerable* (Boston: Twayne, 1987) 47.

[13]Caplan, 284. The precise reference is found in F. H. Dudden, *Gregory the Great: His Place in History and Thought* (New York, 1905), I, 193, of Gregory, *Epp.* 5, 53a.

[14]Appendix A.

[15]Appendix E.

[16]See H. Kosmala, "The Times of the Cock-Crow," *ASTI* 2 (1963) 118-20; 6 (1968) 132-4.

[17]Patrick Henry (*New Directions in New Testament Study* [Philadelphia: Westminster Press, 1979] 58-9) suggests that the Biblical interpreters in the ancient and medieval church "were aware of the 'hermeneutical problem,' that is, of the difficulties of determining the meaning of ancient texts (after all, the New Testament was already an 'ancient text' to persons in the fourth and fifth centuries; and was Augustine's 'world' much less different from the world of the apostles than is ours?), and while their solutions of the problems cannot be our own, their formulations of the problem can be instructive."

[18]Norman R. Petersen, *Literary Criticism for New Testament Critics* (Philadelphia: Fortress Press, 1978) 9.

[19]*Ibid.,* 15.

[20]Rudolf Bultmann, "The New Approach to the Synoptic Problem," *JR* 6 (1926) 341, cited by Willi Marxsen, *Mark the Evangelist* (Nashville: Abingdon Press, 1969) 24.

[21]Petersen, 20.

[22]The diagram Petersen uses (on page 15) to illustrate this is reproduced below:

analytical process

Final Text
(Luke's Gospel)

One of Its Sources
(Mark as a source)

Collections of Traditions
(e.g., underlying Mark 2:1-3:6;
4:1-34; and 4:35-6:56)

Individual Traditions
(e.g., the individual traditions contained
in the above-mentioned collections)

"Events"   *evolutionary process*
(i.e., referred to in the narrative
traditions or implied by sayings traditions)

[23]*Ibid.,* 21.

[24]*Ibid.,* 20-3.

[25]Robert M. Grant, "Historical Criticism in the Ancient Church," *JR* 25 (1945) 195.

[26]Appendix A.

[27]Appendix A.

[28]For the actual term *typology per contrarium,* see D. J. Hawkin, "The Incomprehension of the Disciples in the Mark Redaction," *JBL* 91 (1972) 500. On the idea and term *theologia crucis,* see T. J. Weeden, *Mark: Traditions in Conflict* (Philadelphia: Fortress, 1971) 75.

[29]David Rhoads and Donald Michie, *Mark as Story* (Philadelphia: Fortress Press, 1982) 63-4. On the significance of settings see Seymour Chatman, *Story and Discourse: Narrative Structure in Film and Literature* (Ithaca, N.Y.: Cornell University Press, 1978) 138-45; Robert Liddell, *A Treatise on the Novel* (London: J. Cape, 1947); Wesley Kort, *Narrative Elements and Religious Meanings* (Philadelphia: Fortress Press, 1975) 20-39.

[30]*Ibid.,* 63.

[31]David J. Minnich, "Space and Place in the Gospel of Mark," an unpublished dissertation proposal, Rice University, January, 1982; R. H. Lightfoot, *Locality and*

Doctrine in the Gospels (New York: Harcourt, Brace & World, 1937); Mircea Eliade, *The Sacred and the Profane* (New York: Harcourt, Brace & World, 1959); Yi-Fu Tuan, *Space and Place: The Perspective of Experience* (Minneapolis: University of Minnesota Press, 1977).

[32]Werner Kelber (*The Oral and Written Gospel: The Hermeneutics of Speaking and Writing in the Synoptic Tradition, Mark, Paul, and Q* [Philadelphia: Fortress Press, 1983] 102), argues that "Apart from conflict with the disciples and prophets, Mark's gospel registers consistent hostility toward Jesus' own family." As evidence of this he says: "A topological scheme dramatizes the outsider-insider dichotomy. Jesus is inside the house (3:20) with a crowd sitting about him (3:32: *ekatheo peri auton ochlos*), while his mother and brothers are 'standing outside' (3:31: *exo stekontes*). In response, Jesus identifies those around him as the true family of God (3:34), thereby symbolically solidifying the outsider role of his blood relatives."

[33]Benjamin Jowett, "On the Interpretation of Scripture," *Essays and Review*, 7th ed. (London: Longman, Green, Longman and Roberts, 1861) 330-433.

[34]David C. Steinmetz, "The Superiority of Pre-Critical Exegesis," *TToday* (1980) 27.

Chapter 8

Reflections on Mark 14:54, 66-72

Tentative Working Hermeneutical Principles

According to Edgar Krentz,

> A method does not have faith or unbelief; there are only believing or un-
> believing interpreters. As little as there are sacred engineering and architec-
> ture used in the construction of a church building, so little is there a sacred
> method of interpreting a text.[1]

While we would agree with Krentz' statement that a methodology is neither
sacred nor profane, our study has indicated that methods do have inherent tendencies
which, if unchecked, could possibly lead to a misunderstanding of the text rather than
its elucidation.

The following are some general "tentative working" hermeneutical principles
which we have induced from the particular examples in our representative history of
interpretation, and which we think would further the understanding of this passage.
Together they constitute a sort of multi-methodological approach which attempts to
avoid the extremes and tunnel vision inevitable when one method is used to the
exclusion of all others. We can at least claim that they elucidate the meaning of Mark
14:54, 66-72.

What the Text Says is Prior to *How* and *Why*. We have been persuaded by the
arguments of the literary critics that ascertaining *what* the text says is logically prior
to *how* and *why* it was said, or its historical accuracy. Moreover, this seems to be
collaborated by our study of the Fathers. We argued above that the Fathers were

131

frequently if unwittingly capable of understanding the text because they looked *at* the text to discern its meaning, not at someone or something behind it. We have concluded that it follows that nothing can confidently be attributed to the redactor which cannot be supported from the story world of the text.

According to our discussion above, Petersen and other biblical literary critics are saying that the evolutionary model of historical criticism demands a certain logical order in its questions. Historical events are remembered and carried in oral traditions which are collected in various ways and eventually written down. Before one can ask after the events, one must ascertain the earliest and best oral tradition. Before one can ask after the earliest and best oral tradition, one must know how they were shaped by the author in a written text. Before one asks about the theology of the author and his creative contribution, one must comprehend the text *as it is in its totality.*

It follows that nothing can confidently be attributed to the redactor which cannot be supported from the story world of the text. In other words, what the text (author) says is logically prior to how and why it was said, or its historicity. Says Petersen, "Literary criticism would thus be either a fundamental stage of historical criticism or a stage which in this respect must precede historical criticism."[2]

Detect the Hand of the Author. Redaction criticism has done Biblical criticism a valuable service. It demonstrated a fact so obvious that it too frequently went overlooked, namely, that texts are written by persons to persons for reasons. Asking after those persons and reasons is crucial to understanding the text.

Willi Marxsen, the pioneer of redaction criticism for Mark, describes his task thusly:

> Finally, we should note the circular character which redaction-historical work also shares. The form of the Gospels should help us to draw inferences as to the author's point of view and the situation of his community. On the other hand, when these two factors come more clearly into focus, they can help explain the history of the redaction leading directly to this form.[3]

That which must be safeguarded is the tendency to allow this legitimate "circular character" to become a "vicious circle," as Marxsen was careful to note.[4]

One good example of this is Dewey's explanation of Mark's account of Peter's remembering and weeping in 14:72. Dewey's concern to separate tradition from redaction leads her to overstate her case. Having detected the hand of the evangelist at one point, she allowed a tentative conclusion to misinterpret other evidence.

We will demonstrate below that Dewey has misunderstood how *hos, pikros,* and *epibalon* should be translated. But that point aside, the fallacy of Dewey's argument can be explained thusly. Mark is said to have altered his source in 14:72, ostensibly since "*pikros* gives a repentant force which Mk would perhaps downplay in Peter's case."[5] But Mark is believed not to have altered the occurrence of *hos* in his source, a word which, it turns out, might very well indicate a true remembering and repentance. A more responsible and fruitful redactional analysis of a text will allow the evidence to have priority over the critic's theory.[6]

Ask After the 'Spirit' of the Text: Pastoral and Theological Implications. Steinmetz is perhaps overly optimistic in his judgment that the "Medieval exegetes held to the sober middle way, the position that the text (any literary text, but especially the Bible) contains both letter and spirit."[7] But he is undoubtedly correct that such a sober middle way exists. The Biblical text is not all letter, i.e., with only one literal-historical meaning. The Biblical writers themselves worked with a hermeneutical presupposition of sorts; namely, that although the words of Scripture had a meaning determined by the historical context in which they were written, the meaning of Scripture is not limited to that historical context, nor even necessarily to the intention of the author.

On the other hand, points out Steinmetz, "the text cannot mean anything a later audience wants it to mean. The language of the Bible opens up a field of possible meanings."[8] Moreover, it is reasonable to assume that if Biblical writers *read* Scripture with more than one meaning in mind, they probably also *wrote* with more than one meaning in mind, or at least with the knowledge that their own text would be so read. This is perhaps the most important contribution of redaction criticism. Thus, the nature and purpose of the text help determine the parameters of meaning for itself.

It was these parameters that were so frequently exceeded by the premodern exegetes. But that excess does not justify abandoning the position that a text has a "spirit," perhaps a "spiritual," meaning. This includes most obviously the theological and pastoral implications of the text. Failure to recognize this and to pursue it actually violates the text. "The notion that Scripture has only one meaning is a fantastic idea," concludes Steinmetz, "and is certainly not advocated by the biblical writers themselves."[9]

What the Text Says

According to Weeden, Mark "is assiduously involved in a vendetta against the disciples. He is intent on totally discrediting them."[10] Moreover, the denial of Peter "underscores the complete and utter rejection of Jesus and his messiahship by the disciples."[11] According to Dewey, Mark took an almost innocuous tradition of one denial and embellished it into a damning and complex three-fold denial in which Jesus and Peter curse each other. The author deliberately created an image of Peter as a negative role model in the extreme: "A weak Peter is transformed into a hostile Peter, an opponent";[12] and "Peter, more than the betrayer, is the chief antagonist."[13] Both Weeden and Dewey believe the denial pericope marks the tragic end of Peter's role in Jesus' story. Of the three predictions made by Jesus in 14:27-30, says Dewey, "one, that Jesus will go ahead of his disciples into Galilee after he is raised (14:28), is completely ignored by Peter."[14] By 14:72 Peter drops out of the story a complete and unredeemable failure. As for Mark's abrupt ending, says Weeden, Mark intends to say that

> the disciples never received the angel's message, thus never met the resurrected Lord, and, consequently never were commissioned with apostolic rank after their apostasy...As inconceivable as this suggestion may be at first blush, it is in complete harmony with Mark's attitude toward and treatment of the disciples throughout his Gospel...As the coup de grace, Mark closes his Gospel without rehabilitating the disciples."[15]

There is not full agreement on what the text says and means. Other redaction and literary critics have offered alternative suggestions for the negative shadow the denial pericope casts on Mark's story.

Literary criticism could probably not legitimately look at just one pericope. By definition of its task it must look at the whole story. Thus, it may not be possible to do total justice to an attempt to interpret our pericope literarily without offering an interpretation of the whole book of Mark. Nevertheless, we think an attempt would have to be pursued along the following lines.

Post-textual Resolution. Recently T. E. Boomershine addressed himself to the issue of the narrative's ending.[16] He examined "in turn the interpretations of 16:8 as recommendation of holy awe, as a theological polemic, and as the conclusion of the motif of the messianic secret."[17] Boomershine concludes that the author has carefully woven both positive and negative connotations into the narrative role of the women. The explanations of Lightfoot[18] and R. H. Fuller[19] that the women's response was an appropriate "awe or dread or holy fear of God" do not account sufficiently for the negative connotations: "Mark in no way minimizes the wrongness of their actions."[20] The explanations which see in the narrative's ending the appropriate climax of a theological polemic[21] fail to account for the author's attempt to construct "sympathetic distance" from the women: "Mark's negative norms are directed against the women's *response* of flight and silence rather than against the women themselves."[22] The theories of Willi Marxsen[23] and Reginald Fuller[24] develop the idea of a Markan redaction at 16:7 for the purpose of defining the Church's mission which is in contrast to the silence of the women in 16:8. But "neither has provided a detailed account of the meaning of 16:8. Their proposal can be tested, therefore, by an analysis of the narrative structure of the ending and of the meaning of 16:8 within that structure."[25]

According to Boomershine, the author has prepared the reader for this ending by bringing to a close previous reports within the story in a similar manner, including the story of Peter's denial (14:50-52, 66-72; 15:47): "In each case, the narrator reports responses of Jesus' followers which call for negative judgments while at the same time appealing for the maintenance of sympathetic distance in relation to the characters."[26] The purpose of the blunt ending is to prompt the reader to respond, not as the women, but correctly, i.e., to proclaim the gospel.[27]

Boomershine has correctly identified the major options with regard to interpreting the narrative's ending and their relative strengths and weaknesses. Moreover, we think his interpretation correct. But what of Mark's judgment of the disciples and especially Peter? One could judge the women's actions to be an appropriate "holy awe" or conclude that the author wants to prompt the reader to action and still not answer the question of the position of the disciples in the author's judgment. The polemical interpretation is still, therefore, to the point. Does the author intend to preclude in the reader's mind the possibility of reconciliation with Jesus? Is Peter's denial to be read as the last chapter so far as he is concerned?

Petersen engages the theory that the author's intention is to read the ending "literally," i.e., that the women literally told no one what they had heard, that the disciples consequently never learned that Jesus had been raised from the dead, and that the reader has no justification for imagining a reconciliatory Galilean meeting. He concedes that such a reading is consistent with Weeden's view of a thoroughgoing polemic, the disciples are incorrigible to the very end.[28] "A reading of Mark's narrative predicated on a literal interpretation of its closure in 16:8 is not literarily impossible, but its results assault its own credibility."[29] The author has established Jesus' character as "reliable." What he has predicted has come to pass within the textual world. What has not come to pass within the text can be expected to come to pass post-textually. Otherwise the narrative must be judged either nonsensical or perversely cruel. Petersen's reasoning is very insightful:

> ...we expect the disciples to come to their senses because the reliable narrator led us to believe that the reliable Jesus assumed, intended and expected that they would. But when they do not the characterization of Jesus is transformed and the purpose of the narrator becomes suspect. Because the twelve disciples, who alone among men were expected to perceive things in terms of the things of God, fail to achieve the expected enlightenment, Jesus' intent, expectations, and predictions prove to have failed. All of a sudden the finality of the things of men becomes real. Once Jesus is shown to have been deluded about the disciples, the sense we have had of him throughout the narrative is rendered a delusion and the tables of meaning are overturned. The disciples really completely abandoned Jesus (Mark 14), the establishment really succeeded in their execution of a deluded troublemaker (Mark 15), and the credibility of the young man's explanation of the empty tomb is shattered by his erroneous prediction about the meeting in Galilee (Mark 16). And God made a really big mistake. The domino-effect is relentless, but one final effect is note-worthy. With the collapse of Jesus' credibility as a predictor all that he said about his parousia, and perhaps much of what he said about the events leading up to it (Mark 13), is emptied of its credibility.

By the same literal token that brings about this inversion of the characterization of Jesus, the assumed persona of the narrator becomes a devilish mask in the service of a perversely massive irony. Precisely because for a time —until 16:8—he invited us to believe Jesus and to believe in his and Jesus' imaginative world, a literal interpretation of 16:8 unmasks the narrator and discloses a very nasty ironist who has consistently misdirected our affections and expectations and offered us phony satisfactions from the very beginning. I do not believe it.[30]

Petersen prefers an "ironic" reading of 16:8 with the effect of directing the reader's attention back into the text for clues to the outcome of the story. There one finds key references such as 9:9, chapter 13, 14:27, 16:7, which indicate that "this plot is resolved not in the narrative itself but outside of it in connection with a projected postresurrection meeting between Jesus and his disciples in Galilee."[31] Petersen is thus in agreement with Tannehill's projected post-textual resolution: Mark 13 "anticipates a continuing role for the disciples beyond the disaster of Ch. 14."[32]

Future of the Story World. The literary critical method makes a distinction between the time of the story and time outside the story. Rhoads and Michie distinguish, for example, between the "story world" and the "future of the story world,"[33] and Petersen distinguishes between "story time" and "discourse time."[34] Every story reflects a "time" given it by the author. It has a beginning and an end, and the story transpires between these temporal references.

But a story can have temporal references which fall outside of the story's narrated time. This is especially true if, as in Mark's story, the narrator is omniscient or one of his characters possesses special knowledge as does Jesus.[35] References to Old Testament events or persons refer the reader to the time prior to the story. And it is universally agreed that chapter 13 is one example of a reference to events which will occur in a time after that of the story. The reader is expected to use these references to inform the story. One knows why something prior to the story world is important because its effects are narrated within the story. Likewise, the reader can legitimately draw conclusions about the future of the story world on the basis of events transpiring within the story which necessitate those future happenings.

Petersen and Tannehill were appealing to references of this nature which seemed to place the disciples in a time frame after the story. These references would seem to justify the conclusion that the author did not intend to preclude a resolution to the conflict between Jesus and the disciples with the close of the story. There are other references which do not relate specifically to the meeting in Galilee and do not function normally as keys which unlock the meaning of the story, but which nevertheless place the disciples in the future of the story world. Taken together with the futuristic function of chapter 13, 14:27, and 16:7, the reader must conclude that the author has not intended to preclude a reconciliation of the disciples with their master. Some other explanation for the ending must be sought.

When the disciples of Jesus come under attack for not fasting as the disciples of other leaders, Jesus comes to their defeñse (2:18-20). He describes his relationship to them as one of a bridegroom entertaining wedding guests: "As long as they have the bridegroom with them, they cannot fast. The days will come, when the bridegroom is taken away from them, and then they will fast in that day" (2:19-20). The story speaks of actions on the part of the disciples in the future of the story world. The taking of the bridegroom is a cryptic reference to the crucifixion. Could the author be suggesting that the disciples would fast even though unreconciled to their master, or that such an action would then have any significance? Such a view would appear to cast a negative shadow onto the passage that is not there. B. M. F. van Iersel sees this as "a concrete example" of a reference to the future of the story world.[36] It seems not to make a difference that the Twelve have not been appointed officially yet. At least five of those who will become the Twelve are present and are the object of the attack, the most important being Peter.

The potentially proud statement of Peter that "we have left everything and followed you" (10:28) is responded to by Jesus with a promise of restoration "a hundredfold" of things given up "for my sake and for the gospel" (10:29-30). The promise that persecution would accompany the restoration is no new element in Jesus' teaching. The concluding statement, "But many that are first will be last, and the last first" (10:31), does not exclude the disciples' future relationship with Jesus.[37]

The most explicit reference to the role of the disciples in the future of the story world occurs in 10:35-45. James and John selfishly ask for places of honor when Jesus comes in glory, "one at your right hand and one at your left" (10:37). Throughout the discussion James and John never understand that Jesus' "cup," his "baptism," and his "glory" are not at all what they envision. Discussions on the meaning of the passage have entertained cryptic references to the sacraments, eschatological judgment, and disputes about whether these two disciples actually experienced martyrs' deaths.[38] As van Iersel notes, "in either case it remains true that the text also mentions the martyrdom of the sons of Zebedee."[39] Jesus states flatly that these disciples will share his cup[40] and his baptism,[41] even if presently they have not understood that this entails persecution and death. The places of honor "at [his] right hand or at [his] left" are spared the impetuous disciples within the story. But the reader cannot have missed the careful play on words. The verbal identity describing the robbers in 15:27 with the earlier prediction in 10:40 reveals to the reader for whom these places were prepared.[42] That James' and John's moment of "glory" would come, however, is indisputable: "you will be baptized!" (10:39)

In each of these instances (and others could be adduced) two stories are being told simultaneously. The author is telling the story of Jesus (as a past event), and Jesus in turn is telling a story (as a future event). In the stories within the story, the author envisions a different "setting" and a different "time." When we compare these minor instances above with the more centrally important chapter 13 discussed by Petersen and Tannehill, we see an important common ground: "The disciples are the only characters that the stories have in common, but whereas in Mark's story they were among Jesus' antagonists because they were without understanding, in Jesus' story they...assume the role of collective protagonist."[43]

If the author intended the reader to conclude that the disciples experienced no reconciliation with Jesus and thus no continuing ministry, then Petersen's judgment above about the author's being "a very nasty ironist" is actually optimistic. More nearly correct is that the author is clumsy and has produced an illogical story.[44] It would thus be inappropriate to apply logical literary categories to it.[45]

We do not think Mark either clumsy or illogical. Rather we think him an artful story teller who desired to elicit a response from his reader. The tension between Jesus and his disciples in general and Peter in particular is part of his design.

Detecting the Hand of the Author

hos. It is important to Dewey's theory that Peter's remembering of Jesus' prophecy be as innocuous as possible:

> ...of the three predictions made by Jesus in this complex (14:27, 28, 30), one, that Jesus will go ahead of his disciples into Galilee after he is raised (14:28), is completely ignored by Peter and the disciples. They respond to the predictions of flight and denial but not that of resurrection and parousia. This is no surprise since the disciples have opposed, ignored, or misunderstood Jesus' earlier predictions of death and resurrection as well (8:32; 9:10; 9:32; 10:33-45). Prediction of eschatological return falls on deaf ears, and, within the dynamic of the scene, it is again Peter who has deflected attention away from Jesus' future and toward his own fate in the present.[46]

In the phrase, "and Peter remembered the word which Jesus said to him," the relative pronoun "which" actually translates the Greek word *hos,* which is adverbial in force: "Peter remembered *how* Jesus said the word to him..." Translated thusly it would appear to confront Dewey's theory. Some explanation would have to be found. Therefore, it is suggested that "normally Mk would use *hote* or *hotan,*"[47] or perhaps a relative pronoun. The use of *hos,* therefore, "appears to be from Mk's source."[48]

Upon reflection it is clear why this occurrence of *hos* should be attributed by Dewey to Mark's source rather than to Mark himself, or at least to his intentional retention of the word. Its position and implications underscore the author's concerns about the character Peter. What has been referred to as awkward by Taylor,[49] or more often simply ignored by others, has been called by Birdsall an important "subtle idiom." "Since Luke left it uncorrected, it may seem a little harsh to judge it without further considerations as simply a Marcan awkwardness. Indeed it has recently been argued that the very awkwardness of Mark—down to the last unrepentant [*gar*]—can be of considerable significance."[50]

Birdsall marshals evidence from classical Greek of instances in which *hos* was used where one might normally expect a relative pronoun.[51] The purpose would be to emphasize "more than the mere existence of the antecedent," but rather an entire context, not only *what* was said, but *how* and *why* it was said.[52] Birdsall concluded that Mark 14:72 does not refer to

> a simple recollection on Peter's part of the words of a prediction by Jesus so shortly before, but the flooding back into his mind at the cockcrow, of the whole situation described for us in Mk. xiv. 17-31—the startling coexistence of Jesus' intended sacrifice "as a ransom for many" and the predicted treachery and desertion; the hasty and exaggerated assertions of faithfulness "unto death" and the calm though sorrowful prophetic words of the Master. Not the mere word came back to Peter—but the whole situation, as the setting or accompaniment or "correlative" of the predicted and fulfilled word. Doubtless any exegete might suggest this even if [*ho*] stood in the place of [*hos*]; but it is the contention of this note that Mark explicitly displays his intention that the situation should be so understood, by his unusual but not unidiomatic employment of [*hos*] at this point and in this way.[53]

In support of Birdsall's point one may say the following. One of the reasons Mark portrays Peter throughout the narrative as one who has not, indeed cannot, fully grasp Jesus' Person and message is because of Mark's christology. Donahue, Senior and others have pointed out that the Jesus of Mark's story is the "Suffering Just One," the righteous man of the Psalmic tradition who is forsaken by friends and surrounded by accusers, but who remains faithful to God.[54] The parallels between this Psalmic prototype and the author's use of scriptural citations seem to confirm the correctness of this conclusion. Notes Donahue: "Such a process fits in well with the needs of the nascent Church to affirm two things: that the death of Jesus was according to scriptures (I Cor 15:3), and that, though dying a criminal's death, Jesus was still innocent."[55]

This motif also bears directly on Peter and his denial in at least two ways. First, in the Gospel of Mark, Peter fulfills the role of Jesus' companion and friend (Ps. 55:12-14) who becomes one source of Jesus' bitter agony. This is most obvious when the author uses the exact words from Ps. 38:11 to describe precisely the part Peter plays: "My friends and companions stand aloof from my plague, and my kinsmen stand afar off."

Second, one can hardly conclude that "a weak Peter is transformed into a hostile Peter, an opponent."[56] It is true that Peter seems to be characterized as one who is simultaneously responsible for his actions and yet is fated to commit them. It is a paradox one finds often in Scripture. But, as Rhoads and Michie note, the disciples "are not against Jesus. They fail at being *for* him. And, in a sense, those closest to Jesus fail the most."[57] This describes exactly the secondary role of Peter and his abhorrent action of denial to the primary role of Jesus' faithfulness to God. One has only to remember that Jesus *must* be rejected, not only by Peter but also by God on the cross (15:34)! "The agony caused by the disciples' desertion is exceeded still by God's abandonment."[58] It is this moment to which the story is driven: "the darkness with which the outsiders were threatened in 4:10-12 fell on Jesus, making him an outsider, causing outsiders to now live in the light of the new age."[59]

Peter's role and his denial must take account of this perspective. In Mark's theology Peter could not possibly have come to an understanding of Jesus' Person and his message without thwarting God's plan for Jesus to die forsaken by his kinsmen. Although we agree with the majority of scholars that the cross is indeed the climax of Markan themes and the supreme revelation of Jesus, we cannot concede that only the centurion and a few "little people"[60] recognize Jesus before this point. This full recognition comes to Peter at precisely that moment in the text in which he fulfills the role of forsaking Jesus, when he can no longer thwart divinely laid plans by *not* forsaking Jesus!

Joel Marcus has said, "Peter, following Jesus' arrest, has become, by his own admission, one who neither knows nor understands."[61] With such a conclusion one misses one of the most startling and ironic scenes in the story: Peter, first among the Twelve, the second most important character in the story, finally comes to a full knowledge and understanding of the events transpiring before his eyes and his own gory participation in them. He is now witnessing these events from the "outside," owing to his three denials; for this, too, is part of his revelation. Says Lane: "It was like awakening from an evil dream that had begun with the failure to stay awake in Gethsemane."[62] The author indulges the reader in the only appropriate response: Peter broke down and wept.

pikros. But even this response can be made to support a theory rather than inform one. Matthew (26:75) and Luke (22:62) appear to agree against Mark: "And he went out and wept bitterly." According to Dewey, this is evidence that Matthew and Luke have retained the traditional material, and that Mark has altered the tradition. Why? Because *"pikros* gives a repentant force which Mk would perhaps downplay in Peter's case."[63]

Streeter long ago demonstrated that the apparent agreement between Matthew 26:75 and Luke 22:62 was due to textual assimilation in Luke's text rather than dependence on a common tradition. If the more accurate text is used, this agreement ceases to exist.[64]

Moreover, Dewey's interpretation of *pikros* is highly doubtful. The precise meaning and correct translation of *epibalon* is uncertain, to be sure. "Among commentators," remarks Taylor, "the utmost variety of opinion prevails."[65] If anything can be concluded from this variety, however, it is that the author is portraying boldly the overwhelming sorrow which the full revelation has brought upon Peter. In any case, the text cannot be intended, as Dewey suggests, to avoid "a repentant force which Mk would perhaps downplay in Peter's case."[66]

If Dewey is correct in this contention that Peter is Jesus' enemy, then the author was highly incompetent to include a scene such as this, and his redaction of it even more incompetent. Much more likely is the suggestion of Moulton that the phrase "expresses with peculiar vividness both the initial paroxysm and its long continuance, which the easier but tamer word of the other evangelists [i.e., *pikros*] fails to do."[67]

How and Why

Why would the author want to tell such a story, and how has he done it?

Context of Persecution. Of all the various approaches and interpretations of Mark's story, there is wide agreement that the narrative reflects a context of persecution. "To be sure, it is by no means a martyrology in the complete sense of the type, and it had other purposes than the martyrological. But as one, perhaps as chief, of its purposes may be cited that of control in persecution."[68]

It is of course possible for an author to utilize material relating to persecutions even though neither he nor his potential readers have faced nor are expecting to face them. B. M. F. van Iersel addressed himself to this possibility in Mark and concluded that "the overall textual coherence of these signals and passage [is] such that, taken in their totality, they continue to produce an added semantic value when read in a situation of persecutions."[69] van Iersel's argument is very persuasive. How does Peter's character figure in this theme of persecution, martyrdom, and apostasy?[70]

Archetype for Apostates. The possibilities for seeing parallels between Peter and the Christian apostate are very numerous. We note here only the most obvious.

Peter "denied" his Lord as the apostate would. "*Deny,* that hateful term of the martyrologies!"[71] In the New Testament it was already a *terminus technicus* for a description of persecution and apostasy (Matt. 10:33; Luke 12:9; Acts 13:13-14; 7:35). It continues to be a painfully descriptive term in Christian literature into the following centuries. Denial was part and parcel of any religious experience. Thus, Christians were said by Lucian to have denied their Hellenistic gods to worship Christ, their crucified sophist.[72] Says Lampe, "Peter's act of 'denial' therefore makes him an archetype of the Christian who disowns his Lord under persecution."[73]

Peter "cursed" his Lord as the apostate would. Cursing Jesus was an absolutely unconscionable action for any Christian.[74] This was a common understanding and could only have had the strongest impact on readers. Of the many actions one had to perform before the official Pliny in order to clear oneself of the charge of being a Christian, one of them was to curse Christ, "things which (it is said) those who are really Christians cannot be made to do."[75]

The number and kind of questions put to Peter were those the potential apostate would expect. Lampe argues that there is no good evidence that the disciples were in any danger for their lives during the events of the Passion. The repeated accusation that Peter was "one of them," therefore, might be a construction of the evangelist and "could not but remind a persecuted Church of that recurring moment of glory and shame" when they, too, could be asked: "Are you a Christian?"[76]

Even more striking is the recurrence of the accusatory question three times. It is true that it is a Markan literary device to repeat or otherwise underscore an action or statement three times. But the thrice repeated questioning here would have special significance for believers facing possible arrest. Again reference can be made to the very early testimony of Pliny who placed such questions to Christians "a second and third time with threat of punishment."[77] Although Pliny postdates our text, "it is unlikely that he invented this procedure and that it had not previously been employed elsewhere."[78]

Peter fulfills in many ways the author's carefully drawn portrait of a man who "would save his life" (8:34-38).[79] Nor is there a better example of seed sown on "rocky ground" (4:16). The word for rocky ground is directly related to the name given Simon by Jesus: Peter (3:13). Peter is indeed not firm like a rock, but reminds the reader of the parable of the sower. A reader of the story would read this a second time with an enlightenment which can only be crudely rendered in English: "Peterish-soil." "Peter tries to live up to the heroic possibilities of the name Jesus has given him but is unable to do so."[80]

This much seems clear: the character of Peter symbolizes to a large degree failed discipleship. It may thus seem presumptuous to conclude that the author intended the reader to identify *with* Peter. Jesus is the exemplary model of submission to the will of God. "The kind of testings he undergoes at Gethsemane may be the very one Christians are exposed to in the Mkan setting," says Kelber. "As they are tempted to shortcut the way to Kingdom by avoiding the cup, so is Jesus at Gethsemane."[81] A reader might very well find in the character of Jesus the strength to endure to the end (13:13).[82] But what of those in the community who had recanted? "Such persecution produced courageous martyrs but also led to apostasy and desertion as many Christians sagged under the torment and pressures brought to bear on the community."[83] Would they discern in the narrative a message of hope or a message of doom? Would Peter's experience, especially his denial, confirm them in their dreary outsider position?[84]

Pastoral and Theological Implications

Theology of Reconciliation. If the author had desired to discredit Peter and the disciples, in what manner could he have done it that would not have violated the logic of his work? He provides himself with this possibility but does not use it. The story of Peter's denial has close affinities with Jesus' description of true discipleship and eschatological judgment in 8:34-38. Peter meets the description of the man who "would save his life." Peter had been ashamed of Jesus and his words "in this adulterous and sinful generation." Here is the author's grounds for repudiating the apostate had he wanted to: *Jesus* repudiates the apostate. But the author carefully phrases his position: of such a one "will the Son of man also be ashamed, *when he comes in the glory of his Father with the holy angels*" (8:38).

Undoubtedly we are now at the heart of the narrative's theology of reconciliation. Final separation from the Son of man and his Father is an eschatological act, for before the eschaton "all sins will be forgiven the sons of men, and whatever blasphemies they utter!" (3:28)[85] Repudiation is the prerogative of Jesus. But it is clear that Jesus does not reject the disciples. He bids them come, *"even* Peter" (16:7; my translation).[86] The author thus precludes total rejection of Peter and the disciples in two ways: 1) His major character, who possesses the power to repudiate, refrains from doing so; 2) His most reliable character places Peter (and the disciples) in the future of the story world. And yet the reconciliation is not narrated.

A Gospel of Hope. We now return to the possibility put forward by Boomershine. The most plausible reason for the text's open ending is that the author does not want the reader to feel satisfied. This "provides a closure most congruent with the narrator's storytelling art."[87] There is wide support for the conclusion that Mark's narrative is designed to persuade "the reader to do certain things."[88] Boomershine feels "the story appeals for the proclamation of the resurrection regardless of fear."[89] Likewise Rhoads and Michie: "This abrupt ending, which aborts the hope that someone will proclaim the good news, cries out for the reader to provide the resolution in the story."[90]

In keeping with our focus on Peter we find another strong message to the narrative's end, one which is not incongruent with proclamation of the good news but rather underscores the good news which the text proclaims in its own right. This good news is that *"even* Peter" (16:7; my translation) can be reconciled. The author invites the reader to repent. The effect of this appeal on a church that was undoubtedly suffering persecution and had almost as certainly to answer the question of reconciliation for its apostates needs to be restated. "Mark's stories would have a potent effect on a community context such as this."[91] The author answered this question with the character of Peter. If the possibility exists for him, it exists for all *before the parousia.*[92]

This is certainly also one of the reasons the work has enjoyed such prestige in the history of the church. Its survival might be a matter of curiosity otherwise, since its contents were essentially to be found in Matthew and Luke. Its survival is nothing short of miraculous if it were anti-apostolic.[93] Surely much of its strange appeal is to those who identified most closely with the failure of Peter, to those who had abjured, or who lived with the fear that they might abjure, their Lord. Notes Petersen, "The text ends, but the readerly work, and perhaps even the literary work itself lives on. The end of the text is not the end of the work when the narrator leaves unfinished business for the reader to complete, thoughtfully and imaginatively, not textually."[94] Indeed, it is not difficult to imagine a reader "seeing" in the darkest corner of the text, this story of the denial, a welcome ray of light; "hearing" through Peter's weeping the words of the messenger at the tomb: "tell the disciples, *even* Peter" (16:7; my translation).

—— *mutato nomine de te fabula narratur* ——

Endnotes for Chapter Eight

[1]Edgar Krentz, *The Historical-Critical Method* (Philadelphia: Fortress Press, 1975) 68.

[2]Norman E. Petersen, *Literary Criticism for New Testament Critics* (Philadelphia: Fortress Press, 1978) 21.

[3]W. Marxsen, *Mark th Evangelist* (Nashville: Abingdon, 1969) 25.

[4]*Ibid.*, 25, note 33.

[5]Kim E. Dewey, "Peter's Curse and Cursed Peter," in *The Passion in Mark*, ed. by Werner Kelber (Philadelphia: Fortress Press, 1976) 103.

[6]Raymond E. Brown, Karl P. Donfried, John Reumann, eds., *Peter in the New Testament* (Minneapolis: Augsburg, 1973) 63.

[7]David C. Steinmetz, "The Superiority of Pre-Critical Exegesis," *TToday* (1980) 37.

[8]*Ibid.*, 32.

[9]*Ibid.*

[10]Theodore J. Weeden, *Mark: Traditions in Conflict* (Philadelphia: Fortress Press, 1971) 50.

[11]*Ibid.*, 149.

[12]Dewey, 108.

[13]*Ibid.*, 110.

[14]*Ibid.*, 111.

[15]*Ibid.*, 50-1.

[16]T. E. Boomershine, "Mark 16:8 and the Apostolic Commission," *JBL* 100 (1981) 225-39; Also, T. E. Boomershine and G. L. Bartholomew, "The Narrative Technique of Mark 16:8," *JBL* 100 (1981) 213-23.

[17]*Ibid.*, 226.

[18]R. H. Lightfoot, *The Gospel Message of St. Mark* (London: Oxford, 1962).

[19]R. H. Fuller, *The Formation of The Resurrection Narratives* (New York: Macmillan, 1971).

[20]Boomershine, "Mark 16:8," 229.

[21]Boomershine is in dialogue particularly with J. D. Crossan. See his contribution to the collection of essays in Kelber, *Passion,* "Empty Tomb and Absent Lord," 135-52. Also, "Mark and the Relatives of Jesus," *NovT* 15 (1973) 81-113; "Redaction and Citation in Mark 11:9-10 and 11:17," *BR* 17 (1972) 33-50.

[22]Boomershine, "Mark 16:8," 233.

[23]Marxsen, *Mark,* 91, 111-16.

[24]Fuller, *Resurrection,* 66-7.

[25]Boomershine, "Mark 16:8," 234.

[26]*Ibid.,* 235.

[27]*Ibid.,* 237.

[28]Petersen, "When is the End not the End? Literary Reflections on the Ending of Mark's Narrative," *Int* 34 (1980) 159f.

[29]*Ibid.,* 62.

[30]*Ibid.,* 161-2.

[31]Petersen, *Literary Criticism,* 79.

[32]Robert C. Tannehill, "The Disciples in Mark: The Function of a Narrative Role," *JR* 57 (1977) 402.

[33]Rhoads and Michie, 37, 100.

[34]Petersen, "End," 156-163.

[35]Rhoads and Michie, 36-42.

[36]B. M. F. van Iersel, "The Gospel According to St. Mark—Written for a Persecuted Community?" *NedTTs* 34 (1980) 16.

[37]Rhoads and Michie, 97.

[38]J. H. Bernard ("A Study of Mark x, 38, 39," *JTS* 28 [1927] 262-70) sees an emphasis on persecution, but not death. G. Delling ("BAPTISMA BAPTISTHENAI," *NovT* 2 [1957-58] 92-115) thinks the passage implies eschatological judgment. G. Braumann ("Leidenskelch und Todestaufe," *ZNW* 56 [1965] 178-183) thinks the tradition was remembered in a context of sacramental liturgy. A. Feuillet ("La Coupe et le Baptême de la Passion," *RB* 74 [1967] 356-91) sees a distinction being made between the kind of suffering Jesus must endure and the kind his followers must endure. van Iersel ("Persecuted Community," 21, note 11) is correct, however: Although this passage can have many connotations depending on the context and stage of the tradition, in this story "the main emphasis is on the correspondences, and the passage refers to martyrdom, irrespective of the historical difficulties with respect to the martyrdom of precisely these two disciples."

[39]van Iersel, 21.

[40]Kelber, *Passion,* 51, note 21.

[41]W. L. Lane (*Mark,* 380-1) argues that "the image of baptism is parallel to that of the cup. In popular Greek usage the vocabulary of baptism was used to speak of being overwhelmed by disaster or danger, and a similar metaphorical use of submersion is present in Scripture." Since Jesus identifies the "baptism" specifically ("The baptism with which I am baptized, you will be baptized," 10:39), the conclusion is obvious: "the brothers will participate in the suffering of Jesus." This prophecy would have to find its fulfillment in the future of the story world.

[42]Donald Senior, *The Passion of Jesus in the Gospel According to Mark* (Wilmington, Delaware: Michael Glazier, 1984) 118, note 84; Rhoads and Michie, 97; D. W. Riddle, "The Martyr Motif in the Gospel according to Mark," *JR* 4 (1924) 406.

[43]Petersen, "End," 164.

[44]A "logical" text does not preclude parabolic qualities. A parable reverses expectations and challenges the reader's norms for judging, but it does not logically contradict itself.

[45]Raymond E. Brown, review of *Passion,* ed. by Kelber, in *CBQ* 39 (1977) 285.

[46]Dewey, 111.

[47]*Ibid.,* 102.

[48]*Ibid.*

[49]Vincent Taylor, *The Gospel According to St. Mark: The Greek Text with Introduction, Notes, and Indexes,* 2nd ed. (Grand Rapids: Baker Book House, 1981) 576.

[50]J. N. Birdsall, "*To rhema hos eipen auto ho Iesous:* Mark xiv. 72," *NovT* 2 (1958) 272.

[51]*Ibid.* See page 273 for examples from the *Iliad,* Aristophanes of Byzantium, and page 274 for examples from a Homeric hymn and Thucydides.

[52]*Ibid.,* 274.

[53]*Ibid.,* 274-5.

[54]John R. Donahue (*Are You The Christ?* [Missoula: SBLDS #10, 1973]) and Senior (*Passion*) are dependent on L. Ruppert (*Jesus als der leidende Gerechte? Der Weg Jesu im Lichte eines alt- und zwischen-testamentlichen Motivs* [Stuttgarter Bibelstudien 59; Stuttgart: KBW, 1972]) and R. Pesch (*Das Markusevangelium* [Herder Theologischer Kommentar zum Neuen Testament; Freiburg/Basel/Wien: Herder, 1980 2vols.]).

[55]Donahue, "Temple, Trial, and Royal Christology," in *Passion,* ed. Kelber, 66.

[56]Dewey, 108.

[57]Rhoads and Michie, 128. So also Martin Hengel (*Studies in the Gospel of Mark* [London: SCM Press, 1985] 35): "It is this *universal* disobedience which necessitates Jesus' course towards a representative expiatory death."

[58]Kelber, "The Hour of the Son of Man and the Temptation of the Disciples," in *Passion,* ed. Kelber, 53.

[59]Joel Marcus, "Mk 4:10-12 and Marcan Epistemology," *JBL* 103 (1984) 573.

[60]On the role of "little people" see Rhoads and Michie, 129-36. o62

[61]Marcus, 570.

[62]Lane, *Mark,* 543. See also Tannehill ("Narrative Role," 403) for the opinion that "The construction of the denial narrative itself encourages both sympathetic aware-

ness of Peter's plight, as he struggles to escape the persistent accusations, and full recognition of the horrible thing that he is doing." Refer now to A. Uleyn, "A Psychoanalytic Approach to Mark's Gospel," *Lumen Vitae* 32 (1977) 489.

[63]Dewey, 103.

[64]See pp. 91f.

[65]Taylor, 576.

[66]Dewey, 103.

[67]James H. Moulton, *A Grammar of New Testament Greek*, vol. 1 (Edinburgh: T. & T. Clark, 1967) 131f.

[68]Riddle, 401.

[69]van Iersel, 16.

[70]Norman Perrin (*What is Redaction Criticism?* [Philadelphia: Fortress Press, 1970] 52) supports our argument: "In a very real sense, therefore, this pericope is a tract for the times, and the times are those of formal persecution of Christians as Christians. We cannot now reconstruct the historical situation of the church to which Mark is addressing himself in the sense that we can name the Roman city or emperor concerned, but we can say that it is a situation in which persecution is a very real possibility and that preparation of his readers for this possibility is a very real part of the Marcan purpose."

[71]Riddle, 408.

[72]G. W. H. Lampe, "St. Peter's Denial," *BJRL* 55 (1973) 354.

[73]*Ibid.*

[74]For the possible exception of a gnosticizing element in early Christianity who cursed the fleshly Jesus, see B. A. Pearson, *The Pneumatikos-Psychikos Terminology in I Corinthians* (Missoula, Mont.: Scholars Press, 1980) 47-51.

[75]J. Stevenson, ed., *A New Eusebius: Documents illustrative of the history of the Church to A. D. 337* (London: S.P.C.K., 1968) 13-4.

[76]Lampe, 351.

[77]Stevenson, 13.

[78]Lampe, 352.

[79]van Iersel, 32-3.

[80]Rhoads and Michie, 128.

[81]Kelber, "Hour," 59.

[82]See, however, E. Best ("Discipleship in Mark: Mark 8:22-10:52," *SJT* 23 [1970] 323-37) who argues that in Mark discipleship is not primarily imitation of Christ, for only he gives his life as a ransom for many (10:45).

[83]Senior, 104; A. N. Sherwin-White, "The Early Persecutions and Roman Law Again," *JTS* 3 (1952) 199-213.

[84]Boomershine, "Mark 16:8," 237.

[85]Lampe, 357; Rhoads and Michie (99) say that the reader is to conclude that the disciples' "ultimate fate in the rule of God is conditional upon their behavior in the period from the death of Jesus to the return of the son of man."

[86]Notice the deletion of *kai to Petro* in Matt. 28:7 and Luke 24:6. Mark is underscoring the possibility for an apostate (but especially this apostate) to return to Jesus.

[87]Petersen, "End," 159.

[88]van Iersel, 34.

[89]Boomershine, "Mark 16:8," 237.

[90]Rhoads and Michie, 140.

[91]Senior, 105.

[92]Lampe, 358.

[93]Our research has determined that the interpretation of Mark as a polemic is a relatively recent development in the history of interpretation, beginning with this century, but in particular with the last thirty years. Kelber ("Mark 14:32-42: Gethsemane. Passion Christology and Discipleship Failure," *ZNW* 63 [1972] 166-87) traces this development in its relation to the demise of the Papias tradition. There are indications that Markan scholars are beginning to reconsider the integrity of the Papias tradition. Hengel (*Studies,* 47-50), for example, argues that "the dependence of the author on Peter, which plays a very important role in establishing the priority of Mark, but which today is usually completely ignored or even abruptly rejected, should be maintained: it makes a substantial contribution to our understanding of the Gospel." According to Hengel, the Papias tradition "represents the markedly *critical comments* of an author who rated oral tradition even higher than written works. The connection between Peter and Mark, which in fact goes back to the first century and is attested independently of the presbyter in 1 Peter 5:13, cannot be a later invention in order to secure 'apostolic' authority for the Gospel." Establishing Peter's connection to the Gospel and Markan authorship is beyond the scope of our work. However, both theses accord well with our reading of Mark's account of Peter's denial. Mark's record of Peter as the first apostate would have had a tremendous appeal to a community who knew he had indeed given his life for his master (cp. 14:31). This readership would know how the story ended for the "Rock," in whom the gospel seed at first found no depth in times of persecution, but who late lived up to the heroic potential of his Christ-given name. The invitation to the reader to complete the story for himself would take on increasingly dramatic dimensions.

[94]Petersen, "End," 153.

Appendix A

ΥΠΟΘΕΣΙΣ
ΕΙΣ ΤΟ ΚΑΤΑ ΜΑΡΚΟΝ ΑΓΙΟΝ
ΕΥΑΓΓΕΛΙΟΝ ΕΚ ΤΗΣ ΕΙΣ
ΑΥΤΟΝ ΕΡΜΗΝΕΙΑΣ ΤΟΥ ΕΝ
ΑΓΙΟΙΣ ΚΥΠΙΛΛΟΥ
ΑΛΕΞΑΝΔΠΕΙΑΣ.

ΠΟΛΛΩΝ εἰς τὸ κατὰ Ματθαῖον
καὶ εἰς τὸ κατὰ Ἰωάννην τὸν υἱὸν
τῆς βροντῆς, συνταξάντων
ὑπομνήματα, ὀλίγων δὲ εἰς τὸ
κατὰ Λουκᾶν, οὐδενὸς δὲ ὅλως, ὡς
οἶμαι, εἰς τὸ κατὰ Μάρκον
Εὐαγγέλιον ἐξηγησαμένου (ἐπεὶ
μηδὲ μέχρι τήμερον ἀκήκοα, καὶ
τοῦτο πολυπραγμονήσας παρὰ τῶν
σπουδὴν ποιουμένων τὰ τῶν
ἀρχαιοτέρων συνάγειν ποιήματα)
συνεῖδον τὰ κατὰ μέρος καὶ
σποράδην εἰς αὐτὸ εἰρημένα παρὰ
τῶν διδασκάλων τῆς Ἐκκλησίας,
συναγαγεῖν, καὶ σύντομον
Ἑρμήνειαν συντάξαι.

Περὶ ἀρνήσεως Πέτρου.

Πολλὴ θερμότης τοῦ Πέτρου·
οὐδὲ φεύγοντας ἰδὼν ἔφυγεν· ἀλλ'
ἔστη καὶ εἰσῆλθεν· ἦν δὲ καὶ
Ἰωάννης, ἐπειδὴ γνώριμος ἦν. καὶ
διατί ἀπήγαγον αὐτὸν ἐκεῖ, ὅπου
ἦσαν ἅπαντες συνηγμένοι; ἵνα μὲν
γνώμης πάντα ποιῶσι τῶν
ἀρχιερέων. ἐκεῖνος γὰρ ἦν τότε
ἀρχιερεύς. συνήχθησαν οὖν
ἅπαντες, καὶ συνέδριον ἦν λοιμῶν·
καὶ ἐρωτῶσιν οὐχ ἁπλῶς, ἀλλὰ
βουλόμενοι σχῆμα περιθεῖναι τῇ
ἐπιβουλῇ ταύτῃ δικαστηρίου.
οὐδὲ γὰρ ἦσαν ἴσαι αἱ μαρτυρίαι,
φησίν. οὕτω πεπλανημένων τὸ
δικαστήριον ἦν, καὶ θορύβου πάντα
ἔγεμε καὶ ταραχῆς. ἐλθόντες δὲ
ψευδομάρτυρες ἔλεγον ὅτι οὗτος
εἶπεν ὅτι ἐγὼ καταλύσω τὸ ναὸν
τοῦτον τὸ χειροποίητον, καὶ ἐν

The Commentary of the Holy
Cyril of Alexandria
on the Holy
Gospel According to Mark

Preface

Many have put together reflections on the [Gospel] according to Matthew and on the [Gospel] according to John the son of thunder, and a few on the [Gospel] according to Luke; but absolutely no one, to my knowledge, having expounded on the [Gospel] according to Mark (at least I have heard of nothing to the present, having been busily making a diligent gathering of works) I have sought the occasional and scattered sayings of the teachers of the Church, to collect them and construct a concise commentary.

Concerning Peter's Denial

Peter's fervor [was] great; not even after seeing the others fleeing did he flee; but he stood [his ground?] and entered; and John was [there], too, since he was known [to the high priest?] And why did they lead him there, where they were all assembled? In order that they might execute all things of the opinion of the chief priests. For that one was chief priest at that time. Therefore they were all gathered together, and it was a sanhedrin of pestilent men; and they interrogate [but] not sincerely, desiring rather to give an appearance of a court of justice to this conspiracy. For the testimonies were not identical, he says. Thusly, the court of justice was led astray, and all things [were] full of turmoil and commotion. But false witnesses had come and were saying,

149

"τρισὶν ἡμέραις ἄλλον ἀχειρο-
ποίητον οἰκοδομήσω." διὰ τῆς
προσθήκης τοῦ χειροποιήτου
ηὔξησαν τὴν συκοφαντίαν· οὐ γὰρ
εἶπε, λύσω, ἀλλὰ, "λύσατε τὸν
ναὸν τοῦτον·" καὶ οὐδὲ περὶ
ἐκείνου, ἀλλὰ περὶ τοῦ σώματος
τοῦ ἰδίου. τί οὖν ὁ ἀρχιερεύς;
βουλόμενος εἰς ἀπολογίαν
καταστῆσαι ἵνα ἐξ αὐτῆς αὐτὸν
ἕλῃ, φησίν, "οὐκ ἀποκρίνῃ οὐδέν;
τί οὖν οὗτοί σου καταμαρτυρ-
οῦσιν;" ὁ δὲ ἐσιώπα. ἀνόνητα γὰρ
ἦν τὰ τῆς ἀπολογίας, οὐδενὸς
ἀκούοντος. καὶ γὰρ σχῆμα τοῦ
δικαστηρίου ἦν μόνον.

διέρρηξεν αὐτοῦ τὰ ἱμάτια ὁ
ἀρχιερεύς. καί φησιν, ἠκούσατε
τῶν λεγομένων· τί ὑμῖν δοκεῖ; οὐ
φέρει τὴν ψῆφον οἴκοθεν, ἀλλὰ παρ'
ἐκείνων αἰτεῖ, ὡς ἐπὶ
ὡμολογημένων ἁμαρτημάτων καὶ
βλασφημίας δήλης, καὶ προλαμβάνει
τοὺς ἀκροατὰς λέγων, ὑμεῖς γάρ
ἠκούσατε τῆς βλασφημίας,
μονονουχὶ καταναγκάζων καὶ
βεβαιῶν κακῶς. μᾶλλον δὲ
βιαζόμενος τὴν ψῆφον ἐξενεγκεῖν
κατ' αὐτοῦ τοὺς παρόντας ὡς
βλασφημίαν εἰπόντος καὶ Θεὸν
ἑαυτὸν ποιοῦντος· καὶ φησίν,
"ἠκούσατε τῆς βλασφημίας, τί ὑμῖν
δοκεῖ;" τί οὖν ἐκεῖνοι; κατέκριναν
αὐτὸν ἔνοχον εἶναι θανάτου· αὐτοὶ
κατήγοροι καὶ δικασταὶ καὶ πάντα
γινόμενοι. πάντας γὰρ
ἐπεσπάσατο διὰ τοῦ ῥῆξαι τὸν
χιτωνίσκον. ἔθος γὰρ ἦν αὐτοῖς
τοῦτο ποιεῖν, ἡνίκα βλασφημίας
τινὸς ἤκουσαν ὡς ἐνόμιζον.

Ἠσθένησε κατὰ τὴν
πρόρρησιν ὁ μακάριος Πέτρος, καὶ
ἠρνήσατο τὸν τῶν ὅλων σωτῆρα
Κύριον, καὶ οὐχ ἅπαξ, ἀλλὰ τρὶς
καὶ ἐνώμοτον ἐποιεῖτο τὴν ἄρνησιν
διὰ ῥῆμα παιδίσκης, οὐ

"This man said 'I will destroy this temple
that is made with hands, and in three days
I will build another, not made with
hands.'" On account of the addition [of
the words?] "made with hands" the false
accusations grew. For he did not say, "I
will destroy," but rather, "Destroy this
temple;" and not about this, but rather
about his own body. Therefore, what
[did?] the high priest? Desiring to force a
defense, that by it he might trap him, he
says, "Do you answer nothing at all?
What therefore do these men testify
against you?" But he was silent. For the
[attempt?] of a defense was useless, no
one hearing. For it was only an appearance of a court of justice.

The chief priest tore his robes, and
said, "You heard the [confessions?]!
What do you think?" He does not cast the
vote himself, but demands [it] from them,
as though upon confessed sins and manifest blasphemy, and he anticipates the
hearers saying, "For you yourselves heard
the blasphemy," not only forcing and
negatively influencing, but furthermore
constraining those present to produce a
vote against him as speaking blasphemy
and making himself God; And he says,
"You have heard the blasphemy, what do
you think?" What [did] these men? They
condemned him as worthy of death,
themselves becoming accusers, judges,
and everything! He led them all on by
rending his vestments. For it was a
custom for them to do this, when they
heard something which they deemed as
blasphemies.

The blessed Peter was weak according to the prediction, and denied the
Savior and Lord of all, and not once, but
three times, and he made the denial con-
firmed by an oath on account of a word of
a servant girl, and forgetting [i.e., not re-

μνημονεύσας ὑπὸ τῆς παραχρῆμα
ταραχῆς τοῦ λόγου τοῦ Κυρίου·
"ὃς ἀρνήσεται με ἔμπροσθεν τῶν
ἀνθρωπων, ἀρνήσομαι αὐτὸν
ἔμπροσθεν τοῦ Πατρός μου." ἰδοὺ
γὰρ ἔμπροσθεν πάντων ἤρνηται καὶ
πάλιν εἴτε αὐτῆς τῆς παιδίσκης,
ὡς ὁ Μάρκος φησὶν, εἴτε ἄλλης,
ὡς ὁ Ματθαῖος φησί,
καταμηνύουσης ὡς εἴη τῶν μαθητῶν
εἷς, οὐ γὰρ ἐξηκρίβωται τοῦτο τῇ
μνήμῃ τῶν γαρψάντων, ἐπεὶ μηδὲ
συνέχον ἦν εἰς τὴν σωτήριον
πίστιν· ὁπότε ὁ Λουκᾶς οὐδὲ
παιδίσκην, ἀλλ᾽ ἄνδρα λέγει τὸν
δισχυριζόμενον, ὅτι μετὰ τοῦ
Ἰησοῦ καὶ οὗτος ἦν. τῶν δὴ
τοιούτων οὐ σφόδρα συνεχόντων
συμπεφώνηται τὸ προκείμενον, ὅτι
καὶ δεύτερον ὁ Πέτρος ἠρνήσατο
μεθ᾽ ὅρκου μηδὲ εἰδέναι τὸν
ἄνθρωπον. καὶ πάλιν ἄλλων τὰ αὐτὰ
ἐπιφερόντων σφοδροτέρως
ἀπώμνυτο. ὡς δὲ ὀλίγον ὁ φόβος
παρῆλθε, καὶ ἀνερρώσθη ὁ λογισμὸς
πρὸς τὴν μνήμην ἣν ἀπο τῆς
ταραχῆς ἀπωλωλέκει, καὶ
παραδόξως εὑρίσκει τὸν ἔλεγχον
αὐτοῦ γεγενημένον ὃν ὁ Κύριος
εἶπεν, καὶ τὸ σημεῖον δὲ τοῦ
ἀλεκτρυόνος αἰσθανόμενος τίνα
ἠρνήσατο, ἐξελθὼν ἔξω, φησὶν,
ἔκλαυσε δεινῶς, προσεσχηκότος
αὐτῷ τοῦ Χριστοῦ· ἐπιστρέψας οὖν
οὐ διημάρτηκε τοῦ σκοποῦ,
μεμένηκε γὰρ, ὅπερ ἦν, γνήσιος
μαθητής. πεπλούτηκε γὰρ τῆς
ἀφέσεως τὴν ἐλπίδα. πλὴν ἐκεῖνό
φαμεν ὅτι τῶν ἁγίων ὀλισθήματα
διὰ τῶν γραφῶν μανθάνομεν, ἵνα
καὶ τῆς αὐτῶν μετανοίας μιμηταὶ
γενώμεθα. φάρμακον γὰρ σωτηρίας
ἐπενόησεν ὁ φιλοκτίρμων Θεὸς τὴν
μετάνοιαν, ἣν ἀναιρεῖν πειρῶντια οἱ
καταροὺς ἑαυτούς εἶναι λέγοντες·
οὐκ ἐννοήσατες ὅτι παντός ἐστι
ῥύπου μεστὸν τὸ τοιαύτην ἔχειν ἐν
ἑαυτοις τὴν διάληψιν. καθαρὸς
γὰρ οὐδεὶς ἀπὸ ῥύπου, καθὼς
γέγραπται· κἀκεῖνο δὲ μὴ
ἀγνοείτωσαν· ὅτι πρὶν συλληφθῆναι

membering] by reason of all the confusion the word of the Lord: "He who denies me before men, I will deny him before my Father." For behold, he had denied before all; and again, whether this [same] servant girl, as Mark says, or whether another, as Matthew says, she discloses that he might be one of the disciples, for he did not ascertain this exactly by the recollection of Scriptures, since it was not necessary for saving faith; [especially] When Luke says that it was not a servant girl, but a man [who] emphatically asserts, that he was also with Jesus. Indeed while such [information?] is not essential [for salvation?], it agrees with what has been previously stated, that Peter denied a second time with an oath not to have known the man. And again, when others added the same, he swore violently. But as the fear subsided a little, and [his] reasoning was strengthened to the memory which was lost in the commotion, and he paradoxically finds his trial happening of which the Lord said, and perceiving the sign of the cock which he denied, having gone outside, [Cyril?] says, he wept bitterly, as Christ gave heed to him; therefore having turned he did not miss the mark, for he had remained, indeed was, a genuine disciple. He won the hope of pardon. Indeed, we say that because we learn of the failures of the saints through the Scriptures, in order that we should be imitators of their repentance. For the compassionate God has provided repentance as a medicine of salvation, which the "pure ones" endeavor to dispense with saying themselves to be pure; not considering that everyone who has such [ideas?] in himself is full of iniquity. For no one is pure from iniquity, as it is written. Furthermore, let them not be ignorant: that before Christ was seized and Peter denied, he was a partaker of the body of

Χριστὸν καὶ ἀρνήσασθαι τὸν
Πέτρον, μέτοχος ἦν τοῦ σώματος
τοῦ Χριστοῦ καὶ τοῦ τιμίου
αἵματος, καὶ οὕτως ὡλίσθησε, καὶ
τὴν ἐκ τῆς μετανοίας ἄφεσιν
ἐκομίζετο. οὐκοῦν μὴ
κατηγορείτωσαν τῆς τοῦ Θεοῦ
γαληνότητος, μεμνημένοι λέγοντος
ἐναργῶς, "ἀνομία ἀνόμου οὐ μὴ
κακώσει αὐτόν. ἐν ᾗ ἂν ἡμέρᾳ
ἀποστρέψῃ ἀπὸ τῆς ἀνομίας
αὐτοῦ." φησὶ δὲ ὁ Εὐαγγελιστὴς,
ὅτι ὅτε ἅπαξ ἠρνάσατο, ἐφώνησεν
ὁ ἀλεκτρυὼν, ὅτε δὲ τρὶς ἠρνήσατο,
τότε δεύτερον, ἀκριβέστερον
ἐξηγούμενος τοῦ μαθητοῦ τὴν
ἀσθένειαν. καὶ τὸ σφόδρα αὐτὸν
ἀποτεθνηκέναι τῷς δέει. καὶ
ταῦτα παρ' αὐτοῦ τοῦ διδσκάλου
μαθών. καὶ γὰρ φοιτητὴς ἦν
Πέτρου. σύμφωνα δὲ τὰ παρὰ τοῦ
Ματθαίου καὶ Μάρκου· εἰ καὶ δοκεῖ
ἐναντία εἶναι. ἐπειδὴ γὰρ καθ'
ἑκάστην ἀγωγήν καὶ τρίτον καὶ
τέταρτον εἴωθε φωνεῖν ὁ ἀλεκτρυὼν,
δηλοῖ ὁ Μάρκος ὅτι οὐδὲ ἡ φωνὴ
αὐτὸν ἐπέσχε καὶ εἰς μνήμην
ἤγαγε. ὥστε ἀμφότερα ἀληθῆ·
πρὶν γὰρ τὴν μίαν ἀγωγὴν
ἀπαρτίσαι τὸν ἀλεκτρυόνα, τρίτον
ἠρνήσατο· καὶ οὐδὲ ὑπὸ τοῦ Κυρίου
τῆς ἁμαρτίας ἀναμνησθεὶς κλαυσαι
ἐτόλμα φανερῶς. ἄλλος δέ φησιν
ὡς τοῦ Ματθαίου ἁπλῶς καὶ
ἀορίστως πρὶν ἀλέκτορα φωνῆσαι
λέγοντος τὸ παρειμένον προσέθηκεν
ὁ Μάρκος συνήθως λέγων τὴν
ἐπικρατέστεραν τῶν πάντων
ἀλεκτρυόνος φωνήν, ὥσπερ καὶ τὴν
ἡμέραν τὴν καταρὰν καὶ τοῖς πᾶσι
διαφνῆ. ἡρμήνευσεν οὖν φησιν ὁ
Εὐαγγελιστὴς τὸ πρὶν ἀλέκτορα
ἐκφωνῆσαι ποίαν εἶπε τὴν δευτέραν
καὶ πᾶσι καταφανῆ, οὐκ
ἐναντιούμενος τοῖς ἄλλοις

Christ and of his precious blood, and thusly fell, and obtained the forgiveness of repentance. Therefore let them not accuse the gentleness of God, [but] be reminded by the one who clearly says, "the lawlessness of the transgressor shall in no way cause him harm, in the day in which he shall turn from his lawlessness." But the Evangelist says, that when he denied once, the cock crowed, but when he denied a third time, then [the cock crowed] a second time, describing more exactly the weakness of the disciple, and [that] he was utterly dead with fear. He had learned these things from his teacher. For he was a disciple of Peter. Thus that which is in Matthew and Mark [is] in harmony; even if it appears to be contradictory. For since at each "crowing" [series of crowing; cycle] the cock was accustomed to crow both a third and fourth time, Mark makes clear that the sound neither gripped him nor led him to remembrance. So that both are true. For before the cock had completed the first crowing, he denied a third time. And not even when reminded of the sin by Christ did he dare to weep openly. But another says, "Matthew says simply and indefinitely 'before the cock crows,' [while] Mark in customary fashion added that which was omitted saying the prevailing sound of the cock [was heard by?] all, just as also the broad day [is] clear to all. Therefore, he [who?] says, the Evangelist interpreted the [words?] "before the cock-crow," specifying the second and making it clearer to all, not contradicting the others.

The above Greek text of Victor of Antioch's Commentary on the Gospel of Mark is taken from J. A. Cramer, S.T.P., *Catenae Graecorum Patrum in Novum Testamentum,* Tomus I: *Catenae in Evangelia S. Matthaei et S. Marci* (Oxford, 1840). The Preface is on pages 263-5; the commentary on the Denial of Peter is on pages 429-33. The English translation is my own.

Appendix B

Bedae Venerabilis	The Venerable Bede
In Marci Evangelium Expositio	Commentary on the Gospel of Mark
XIV, 54, 66-72	14:54, 66-72

XIV, 54

    Petrus autem a longe secutus est eum usque in atrium summi sacerdotis. Merito *a longe sequebatur* qui *iam proximus* erat *negaturo. Neque enim negare posset, si Christo proximus adhaesisset.* Verum *in hoc maxima nobis est admiratione* uenerandus *quod dominum non reliquit etiam cum timeret.* Quod enim timet *naturae est quod sequitur deuotionis quod negat obreptionis quod paenitet fidei.*
A Aliter. *Quod ad passionem euntem dominum longe sequitur Petrus significabat ecclesiam secuturam quidem, hoc est imitaturam, passiones domini sed longe differenter; ecclesia enim pro se patitur at*
V *ille pro ecclesia.*

14:54

    And Peter had followed him at a distance, right into the courtyard of the high priest. "Rightly was he following him at a distance who was already close to denying him. For he would not have been able to deny him, if he had remained close to Christ. Truly there is the greatest admiration to be revered by us in this, that he did not completely abandon the Lord even when he was afraid. For the fact that he was afraid is natural, that he followed him [a mark] of his devotion [to him], that he denied him [a mark] of his heedlessness, that he repented [a mark] of his faith." (From Ambroses's *Explanation of Luke's gospel)* Another [possibility of interpretation]. "The fact that Peter followed the Lord at a distance as he was going to his passion signified that the Church was going to follow [the Lord] indeed, that is, to imitate his sufferings, but in a far different manner; for the Church suffers on its own behalf but he [suffers] for the Church." (From Augustine's *Questions on the gospels)*

    Et sedebat cum ministris et calefaciebat se ad ignem. Est dilectionis ignis est et cupiditatis. De hoc dicitur: *Ignem ueni mittere in terram et quid uolo nisi ut ardeat;* de illo: *Omnes adulterantes uelut clibanus corda eorum;* iste super credentes in caenaculo Sion descendens uariis linguis

    And he was sitting with the guards, and warming himself at fire. There is a fire of love, [there is] also [one] of avarice. Of the former there is said: "I came to cast fire upon the earth; and would that it were already kindled!" of the latter: "They are all adulterers, their hearts like a heated oven;" the former, coming down upon those who believed in the upper room on [Mount] Zion, taught them to praise God in other eos Deum laudare docuit; ille in atrio Caiphae instinctu maligni spiritus accensus ad negandum ac blasphemandum dominum noxias perlinguas armabat. Quod enim intus in domo principis sacerdotum sinodus maligna gerebat hoc ignis in atrio foris inter frigora noctis materialiter accensus typice praemonstrabat. Quicumque ergo uitiosum noxiumque in se extinguit incendium potest dicere cum propheta domino: *Quia factus sum sicut uter in pruina iustificationes tuas non sum oblitus.* In quibuscumque autem flammam caritatis turbida uitiorum flumina obruerunt audiunt a domino: *Quoniam abundauit iniquitas refrigescit caritas multorum.* Quo frigore torpens ad horam apostolus Petrus quasi prunis ministrorum Caiphae calefieri cupiebat quia temporalis commodi solatium perfidorum societate quaerebat. Sed non mora, respectus a domino cum ignem prauorum corpore tum infidelitatem corde reliquit ac post resurrectionem domini sancto igni recreatus funditus excessum trinae negationis trina dilectionis confessione purgauit. Tunc etenim completa illa memorabili piscium captura cum ueniret ad dominum uidit cum condiscipulis sius prunas positas et piscem superpositum et panem moxque uidens sui cordis archana prunis inflammauit amoris.

tongues; the latter, kindled in the courtyard of Caiaphas by the prompting of the evil spirit, armed the culpable tongues of the unbelievers to deny and blaspheme the Lord. For the fact that the sanhedrin plotted evil deeds within the house of the chief of the priests is a type that foreshadowed the material fire that was kindled outside in the courtyard in the cold of the night. Therefore, whoever has extinguished the perverse and culpable flame within himself can say to the Lord with the prophet: "For I have become like a wineskin in the smoke (literally, the winter), yet I have not forgotten thy statutes." And in whomsoever the violent waters of culpable [sins] have overwhelmed the flame of charity, they hear from the Lord: "And because wickedness is multiplied, most men's love will grow cold." Being benumbed temporarily by this cold, the apostle Peter as it were desired to be warmed by the charcoal [fire] of the guards of Caiaphas because he sought the consolation of temporal advantage through fellowship with the unbelievers. But right away, when he was regarded by the Lord, he both abandoned the fire of the wicked bodily and the lack of faith in his heart, and after the Lord's resurrection, being restored by the holy fire, he completely cleansed the mistake of his threefold denial by a threefold confession of faith. For then indeed after that memorable catch of fish was finished and when he came to the Lord with his fellow disciples and saw the charcoal fire there and fish lying on it and bread, immediately perceiving [the meaning] in his inmost heart, he was on fire [with the flame] of love.

XIV, 66-67

Et cum esset Petrus in atrio
deorsum uenit una ex ancillis
summi sacerdotis et cum
uidisset Petrum calefacientem
se aspiciens illum ait: Et tu
cum Iesu Nazareno eras. At ille
negauit dicens: Neque scio
A *neque noui quid dicas. Quid*
sibi uult quod prima eum
prodit ancilla cum uiri utique
magis eum potuerint recogno-
scere nisi ut et iste sexus
peccasse in necem domini uid-
eretur et iste sexus redimeretur
per domini passionem? Et ideo
mulier resurrectionis accipit
prima mysterium et mandata
custodit ut ueterem praeuarica-
M *tionis aboleret errorem.*

14:66-67

And as Peter was below in the court-
yard, one of the maids of the high priest
came; and seeing Peter warming himself,
she looked at him, and said, "You also were
with the Nazarene, Jesus." But he denied it,
saying, "I neither know nor understand
what you mean." "What does it mean that
was first a maid who revealed him, when
there were doubtlessly men who could have
more easily recognized him, unless that sex
[women] would seem to have sinned in the
murder of the Lord also, and that that sex
would be redeemed by the Lord's passion?
And therefore it was a woman who was the
first to perceive the mystery of the resurrection and kept the commandments, so that
she might do away with the error of the
ancient transgression." (From Ambrose's
Explanation of Luke's gospel)

XIV, 68

Et exiit foras ante atrium,
et gallus cantauit. De hoc galli
cantu ceteri euangelistae tacent
non tamen factum esse negant
sicut et multa alia alii silentio
praetereunt quae alii narrant.

14:68

And he went out into the gateway, and a
cock crowed. The other evangelists are
silent about this crowing of the cock; yet
they do not deny that it took place, just as
some [of them] also pass over many other
matters in silence which the others relate.

XIV, 69-70

Rursus autem cum uidisset
illum ancilla coepit dicere
circumstantibus: Quia hic ex
illis est. At ille iterum negauit.
Non haec eadem quae prius
accusabat ancilla esse credenda
est. Dicit namque Matheus
apertissime: *Exeunte autem illo*
ianuam uidit eum alia et ait his
A *qui erant ibi,* et cetera. In has
autem *negatione Petri* discimus
non solum ab eo negari Chris-
tum qui dicit eum non esse

14:69-70

And the maid saw him, and began again
to say to the bystanders, "This man is one
of them," But again he denied it. (And after
a little while again the bystanders said to
Peter, "Certainly you are one of them; for
you are a Galilean.") This maid should not
be believed to be the same one who first
accused him. For Matthew says most
clearly: "And when he went out to the
porch, another maid saw him, and she said
to the bystanders," and so on. "In the denial
of Peter we learn that not only is Christ
denied by one who says that he is not the

*Christum sed ab illo etiam qui
cum sit negat se esse christia-
num. Dominus autem non ait
Petro, Discipulum meum te
negabis, sed me negabis. Negauit ergo ipsum cum se negauit*
V *eius esse discipulum.*

*Et post pusillum rursus qui
adstabant dicebant Petro: Vere
tu ex illis es nam et Galileus es.*
Non quod alia lingua Galilei
quam Hierosolimitae loquerentur
qui utrique fuerunt Hebraei *sed
quod unaquaeque prouincia et
regio suas habeat proprietates
ac uernaculum loquendi sonum
uitare non possit.* Vnde in
actibus apostolorum cum hi
quibus spiritus sanctus insederat
omnium gentium linguis loquerentur inter alios qui de diuersis
mundi plagis aduenerant etiam
illi qui habitabant Iudaeam
dixisse referuntur: *Nonne ecce
omnes isti qui loquuntur Galilei
sunt? Et quomodo nos au-
diuimus unusquisque lingua
nostra in qua nati sumus?*
Et Petrus fratribus loquens in
Hierusalem, *Et notum, inquit,
factum est omnibus habitantibus
in Hierusalem ita ut appellaretur
ager ille lingua eorum Achelde-
mac.* Quare lingua eorum nisi
quia idem nomen aliter illi, hoc
est Hierosolimitae, aliter sonabant Galilei.

Christ, but by him also who, while really a
Christian, himself denies that he is so. For
the Lord did not say to Peter, 'You shall
deny that you are my disciple,' but 'You
shall deny me.' Therefore he denied him
when he denied that he was his disciple."
(From Augustine's *Treatises on John's
gospel*)

*And after a little while again the by-
standers said to Peter, "Certainly you are
one of them; for you are a Galilean."* This
was not because the Galileans and the
inhabitants of Jerusalem spoke a different
language, for both were Hebrews, but
"because each province and region had its
peculiarities [in speaking] and could not
avoid the sound of its local dialect."
(From Jerome's *Commentary on Matthew's gospel*) Hence in the Acts of the
Apostles, when those on whom the Holy
Spirit had rested were speaking in the
tongues of all nations, among the others
who had come together from the different
regions of the world even those who dwelt
in Judea are reported as having said:
"Behold, are not all these who are speaking Galileans? And how is it that we hear,
each of us in his own native language?"
And Peter, speaking to his brethren in
Jerusalem, said: "And it became known to
all the inhabitants of Jerusalem, so that the
field was called in their language
Akeldama." Why [did he say], "in their
language," except that they, that is, the
inhabitants of Jerusalem, pronounced the
same name in one way, the Galileans in
another.

XIV,71-72

*Ille autem coepit anathema-
tizare et iurare: Quia nescio hominem istum quem dicitis. Et
statim iterum gallus cantauit.*
Solet scriptura sacramentum

14:71-72

*But he began to invoke a curse on
himself and to swear, I do not know the
man of whom you speak. And immediately
the cock crowed a second time.* Scripture
is accustomed to point out the mystery of

causarum per statum designare temporum. Vnde Petrus qui media nocte negauit ad galli cantum paenituit. Qui etiam post resurrectionem domini diurna sub luce illum quem tertio negauerat tertio aeque se amare professus est quia nimirum quod in tenebris obliuionis errauit et speratae iam lucis rememoratione correxit et eiusem uerae lucis adepta praesentia plene totum quicquid nutauerat erexit. Hunc opinor gallum aliquem doctorem intellegendum qui nos iacentes excitans et somnolentos increpans dicat: *Euigilate iusti et nolite peccare.*

Et recordatus est Petrus uerbi quod dixerat ei Iesus: Prius quam gallus cantet bis ter me negabis. Et coepit flere. Quam nociua prauorum colloquia! Petrus ipse inter infideles uel hominem se nosse negauit quem inter condiscipulos iam Dei filium fuerat confessus. Sed nec in atrio Caiphae retentus poterat agere paenitentiam? Egreditur foras ut alii narrant euangelistae quatenus ab impiorum concilio secretus sordes pauidae negationis liberis fletibus abluat.

causes by the circumstances of the times. Hence Peter, who made his denial in the middle of the night, repented at cock crow. He also, after the Lord's resurrection, at daylight professed three times equally that he loved him, whom he had denied three times, because undoubtedly what he had erred through forgetfulness in the darkness he both corrected by recalling the hoped-for light and in the presence of this same true light he completely strengthened that in which he had wavered. I think that by this cock must be understood some teacher who rouses us when we are asleep, and reproving our sleepiness says: "Come to your right mind, and sin no more."

And Peter remembered the word which Jesus had spoken to him: Before the cock crows twice you shall deny me three times. And he began to weep. How harmful are the conversations of the wicked! Peter himself among the faithless denied that he knew the man whom he had confessed to be the Son of God among his fellow disciples! But he could not be penitent while detained in the court of Caiaphas. He goes outside, as the other Evangelists narrate, so that being removed from the council of the impious he might wash away the filth of a timorous denial by unrestrained weeping.

The Latin text above is taken from D[avid] Hurst, O.S.B., ed., *Bedae Venerabilis Opera,* Pars II, 3: *In Lucae Euangelium expositio* [and] *In Marci Euangelium expositio,* Corpus Christianorum Series Latina, Vol. 120 (Turnhout, Belgium: Brepols, 1960) 620-25. Father Hurst also provided me with an English translation of this passage, for which I express my deep gratitude.

Appendix C

Walafridi Strabi
Sequitur Glossa ordinaria
Evangelii S. Marci
14:54, 66-72

Walafrid Strabo
Glossa ordinaria
The Gospel of Mark
14:54, 66-72

Vers. 54.—*A longe.* (BEDA) Quia negationi proximus, si Christo proximus fuisset non negasset: in hoc tamen admirandus est, quod Dominum non reliquit etiamsi timeat. Quod timeat naturae est, quod sequitur devotionis est: quod negat obreptionis est, quod poenitet didei est. *Atrium.* (Hier.) Atrium, saecularis circumitus est. Ministri, daemonia sunt. Ignis desiderium carnale, cum quibus qui manet, flere peccata non valet. *Et calefaciebat se.* (Beda.) Est ignis charitatis; de quo dicitur, etc. *usque ad* moxque sue cordis arcana prunis inflammavit amoris.

Vers. 54—*At a distance*...Bede: "Since he is nearest the denial, he would not have denied (him) if he had been nearest to Christ: in this nevertheless he is to be admired, for he does not abandon the Lord even though he fears him. That he fears him is of nature; that he follows him is of devotion: that he denies him is of surreptitious behavior, that he repents is of faith." *The Courtyard.* Jerome: "The courtyard is a worldly (profane) surrounding. [The] Servants are demons. Fire is carnal desire, he who remains with which has not the strength to lament his sins." *And he warmed himself.* Bede: "There is a fire of grace; about which it is said," etc., *as far as* "immediately perceiving [the meaning] in his inmost heart, he was on fire [with the flame] of love."

Vers. 68.—*At ille* etc. Nota, quod negat Christum qui se egat ijus esse discipulum. Dominus enim non dixit: Negabis te discipulum meum, sed *me negabis.* Negavit ergo eum cum se negavit ejus esse discipulum.

Vers. 68—*But he,* etc. Note that he denies Christ who denies that he is his disciple. For the Lord did not say: "You shall deny that you are my disciple," but *"you shall deny me."* Thus he denied him when he denied that he was his disciple.

Et exiit foras, etc. (Hier). Petrus sine spiritu, voci ancillae cessit, etc., *usque ad* et foras eximus extra quod fuimus.

And he went outside, etc. Jerome: "Peter, without the spirit, yielded to the voice of a maid-servant," etc. *as far as* "and we go out beyond what we were."

Vers. 70.—*Nam et Galilaeus.* (Beda). eadem lingua Galilaeis et Hierosolymitis est, sed tamen

Vers. 70—*You are also a Galilean.* Bede: "It is the same language for the Galileans and Jerusalemites, but neverthe-

158

quaecumque provincia et regio habet proprium loquendi sonum quem mutare, etc., *usque ad* quia nomen illud aliter Hierosolymitae, aliter Galilaei sonabant.

less each province and region has its own style of speaking which to change," etc. *as far as* "since the Jerusalemites pronounced that name one way and the Galileans another."

Vers. 72.—*Et recordatus est.* (Id). Petrus nocte negat, ad galli cantum poenitet. In die quem tertio negaverat, se tertio amare professus est. Quod enim, etc., *usque ad* egreditur foras (ut alii Evangelistae narrant), ut ab impiis secretus, negationis culpam liberius abluat fletibus.

Vers. 72—*And he remembered.* Idem: "Peter denies (him) at night, at the cock's crow he repents. Him whom he had denied three times, on the third day he professed to love. For since," etc., *as far as* "he passed outside (as the other Evangelists tell it), so that isolated from the impious, he might more freely wash away the guilt of his denial by his tears."

The Latin text is taken from Migne's *Patrologia Latina,* vol. 114, columns 234-235. The English translation is that of John F. Phillips, Associate Professor, Department of Philosophy and Religion, The University of Tennessee at Chattanooga. I acknowledge my gratitude to him for this service.

Appendix D

S. Eusebii Hieronymi Commentarius in Evangelium Secudum Marcum	Saint Jerome Exposition on Saint Mark 14:54, 66-72
[14:54-56] Petrus a longe sequebatur. *Vir duplex animo, inconstans est in omnibus viis suis* (*Jac.* I, 8). Timor retrahit, charitas trahit. In atrio cum ministris calefacit se ad ignem. Atrium sacerdotis, est saecularis circuitus: ministri, daemonia sunt. Ignis, desiderium carnale, cum quibus qui manet, flerepeccata non potest. Summi sacerdotes quaerebant falsum testimoium adversus Jesum, mentita est iniquitas sibi: ut regina adversus Joseph (*Gen.* xxxix, 14): et sacerdotes adversus Susannam (*Dan.* xiii, 36): sed ignis sine materia deficit. Et convenientia testimonia non erant. Quodvariatur, incertum habetur.	[14:54-56] Peter followed at a distance. *Man, twofold in his soul, is inconstant in all his faculties* (James 1:8). Fear holds (one) back, grace draws (one) forward. In the courtyard with the servants he warms himself by the fire. The courtyard of the priest is a worldly open space: the servants are demons. Fire is carnal desire, and those with whom it persists will not be able to lament their sins. The high priests sought false testimony against Jesus, they feigned injustice against themselves (by Jesus): just as the queen against Joseph (Gen. 39:14): and the priest against Susanna (Dan. 13:36): but fire without wood goes out. And the testimony did not agree. That which varies is thought to be uncertain.
[14:66-72] Petrus sine Spiritu, voci ancillae cessit: cum Spiritu, nec principibus, nic regibus cedit. Prima ancilla, titubatio est; secunda, consensio; tertius vir, actus est. Haec est trina negatio, quam abliut per fletus verbi Christi recordatio. Tunc nobis gallus cantat, quando praedicator quisque per poenitentiam conda nostra ad compuncionem excitat. Tunc incipimus flere, quando ignimur intus per scintillam scientiae: et foras eximus extra quod fuimus.	[14:66-72] Peter, without the Spirit, yielded to the voice of the maidservant: with the Spirit, he yields neither to princes nor to kings. The first maidservant is wavering, the second is consent; the third man is action. This recollection of the word of Christ washed away through weeping. Then the cock crows for us, when each praiser arouses our hearts to remorse through repentance. Then we begin to cry, when we are inflamed from within through the spark of knowledge: and we go out beyond what we were.

The Latin text is taken from Migne's *Patrologia Latina,* vol. 30, columns 657-659. The English translation is that of John F. Phillips, Associate Professor, Department of Philosophy and Religion, University of Tennessee at Chattanooga. I acknowledge my gratitude to him for this service.

Appendix E

ΘΕΟΦΥΛΑΚΤΟΥ
ΑΡΧΙΕΠΙΣΚΟΠΟΥ ΒΟΥΛΓΑΡΙΑΣ
ΕΡΜΗΝΕΙΑ ΕΙΣ ΤΟ ΚΑΤΑ
ΜΑΡΚΟΝ ΕΥΑΓΓΕΛΙΟΝ

Theophylact
Archbishop of Bulgaria
Commentary on the Gospel of Mark

Εφυγον οἱ μαθηταί. Ουχ ἦν γὰρ ψεύσασθαι τήν ἀτοαλήθειαν. οὐδε τοὺς προφήτας. Εἶς δέ τις νεανίσκος ἠκολούθησεν αὐτῷ. Οὗτος δὲ ὁ νεανίσκος εἰκὸς ὅτι ἐκ τῆς οἰκίας ἐκείνης ἦν, ἐν ᾗ ἔφαγον τὸ πάσχα. Τινὲς δέ φασι τοῦτον, Ἰακωβον εἶναι τὸν ἀδελφόθεον, τον ἐπικληθέντα Δίκαιον. Οὗτος γὰρ ἑνὶ περιβολαίῳ ἐκέχρητο πασαν τὴν αὐτοῦ ζωήν· ὃς καὶ τὸν θρόνον τῶν Ἱεροσολύμων παρὰ τῶν ἀποστόλων ἔλαβε μετὰ τὴν τοῦ Κυριόυ ἀναληψιν. Καὶ οὗτος τοίνυν καταλιπὼν τὴν σινδόνα, ἔφυγεν. Οὐδεν δὲ καινὸν εἰ τῶν κορυγαίων φυγόντων, καὶ οὗτος κατέλιπε τὸν Κύπιον. Ἀλλ' ὄγε Πέτρος ἀκολουθεῖ, θερμοτατην ἀγάπην πρὸς τὸν Διδάσκαλον ἐκδεικνύμενος. Τοῦ δὲ νόμου κελεύοντος ἕνα εἶναι ἀρχιερέα δια βιού, πολλοὶ τοτε ἦσαν, ἐξωνουμενοι καθ' ἕκαστον ενιαυτον παρὰ Πωμαίων τὰς ἀρχάς. Ἀρχιερεῖς οὖν λέγει, τούς ἤδη πεπληρωκότας τὸν ὡρισμένον καιρὸν αὐτοῖς. καὶ ἀποβαλλομένους τὴν ἀρχιερωσύναν.

Ἠσθένησεν ὁ Πέτρος, εἰ καὶ θερμότερος ἦν, καὶ ἀρνεῖται τόν Κύριον ὑπὸ τῆς δελίας διαταραχθείς· καὶ ταῦτα παιδίσκης ἐκπτοσησης αὐτόν· ποῦτο δὲ κατ'

14:50-54

The disciples fled. For he did not misrepresent his own truth (prophecy?), nor [that of] the prophets.

And one certain young man followed him. And it is probable that this young man was of his own house, in which [also] he ate the Passover. For certain ones say this one was James the brother of God, the one called Righteous.

And he was able with this one garment to cover sufficiently his entire person.

Who also received the See of Jerusalem from the Apostles after the ascension of the Lord. Now therefore this one having forsaken his night shirt also fled. Now [it is] nothing strange if after the leaders (i.e., twelve apostles?) flee, this one also forsakes the Lord.

But Peter himself followed, exhibiting a warm love for the Teacher.

Although the law required one to be high priest for life, there were many at that time who were buying the offices from the Romans each year. Therefore he says "chiefpriests," those having determined the limits of tenure for themselves, and disregarding the [legitimate] chiefpriesthood.

14:66-72

Peter was weak, even if he was also "warmer," and denied the Lord with timidity having been confounded; the things [accusations?] of a [mere] servant girl having frightened him.

161

οἰκονομίαν συνεχώρησεν αὐτὸν ὁ Θεὸς παθεῖν, ἵνα μὴ ἐπαίρηται, καὶ ἅμα ἵνα και τοῖς πταίουσι συμπαθὴς εἴη, ἀφ' ἑαυτοῦ παιδευθεὶς τὸ τῆς ἀνθρωπίνης ἀσθενείας βιαιον. Ἀδαφορον δὲ εἴτε ἡ αὐτὴ παιδίσχη ἦν, εἴτε ἄλλη, ἡ ἐλεγξασα τὸν Πετρον. Ματθαῖος μὲν γάρ ἄλλην ταύτην λεγει· Μάρκος δε την αὐτήν. Ουδέν δε ἡμῖν τοῦτο ἐμπόδιον πρὸς τήν ἀλήθειαν τοῦ Ευαγγελιου· μὴ γαρ ἐν μεγάλῳ τινὶ καὶ συνεκτικῷ τῆς σωτηρίας ἡμῶν διαφωνοῦσι; Μὴ ὁ μὲν εἶπεν, ὅτι εσταυρώθη ὁ Κύριος, ὅδε, ου; ἄπαγε. Ὁ τοίνυν Πέτρος ὑπο τῇ δειλίας διαταραχθείς, καὶ ἐπιλαθόμενος του λόγου οὐ εἶπεν ὁ Κύριος, ὅτι Τὸν ἀρνησαμενόν με ἀρνήσομαι κἀγὼ ἐνώπιον τοῦ Πατρός μου, ἡρνήσατο, ἀλλ' ἡ μετάνοια πάλιν αὐτόν ᾠκειωσε τῷ Χριστῷ, καὶ τὰ δάκρυα. Ἐπιβαλὼν γὰρ, φησὶν, ἔκλαιε, τουτεστιν, ἐπικαλυψάμενος τὴν κεγαλήν· ἢ ἀντὶ τοῦ, ἀρξάμενος μετά σφοδρότητος· ὅπερ δε εἶπεν ἀσαφῶς ὁ Ματθαῖος, ὅτι Πρὶν ἀλέυττορα φωνῆσια, ἡρμήνευσεν ὁ Μάρκος, ὅτι Πριν σωνῆσαι δίς. Εἰώθασι γαρ οἱ ἀλέυκτορες, κατὰ μίαν ἀγωγὴν πολλάκις φωνειν, εἶτα οἱον ὑπνωττειν, καὶ πάλιν μετά τινα καιρὸν, ἑτέραν ἀρχήν ποιεῖσθαι του φωνεῖν. Ὁ οὖν εἶπεν ὁ Ματθατος, τουτό ἐστιν, ὅτι Πριν ἀλέκτορα φωνῆσαι, τουτέστι, πληρῶσαι τὰς κραυγὰς τῆς πρώης ἀγωγῆς, ἀπαρνήσῃ με τρίς. Αἰσχυνέσθωσαν δὲ οἱ Ναυατιανοὶ οἱ τους μετα τὸ βαπτισμα καὶ τήν μεταληψιν των μυστηρίων ἁμαρτησαντας, μὴ δεχόμενοι. Ἰδοὺ γὰρ ὁ Πέτρος, και μετακαυων τοῦ ἀχρανιου σωματος και αιματος,

God permitted him to suffer this on account of his (Apostolic) commission, in order that he might not be puffed up, and in order that he may also be sympathetic with those who [cause to?] stumble, having learned for himself the violence which is a weakness common to man.

And whether this same servant girl or another, she gazed directly at Peter having detected him. For Matthew says it was another (girl); but Mark [says it was] the same one. But this [does] nothing to obstruct from us the truth of the Gospel; For do they not agree in the significant and essentail (thing) of our salvation? Did one say that the Lord was crucified, but another, [that he was] not? Away! Be gone!

What then, of Peter? With timidity having been confounded, and forgetting the word which the Lord said, "He who denies me, I will also deny him before my Father," he denied, but repentance reclaimed him to Christ, and tears. "For 'breaking down,'" he says, "he wept," by which he intends to say, "covering [his] head [he began to weep];" or perhaps rather, "he began [to weep] very violently."

Now Matthew says indistinctly, "Before the cock crows;" but Mark elaborates [interprets], "Before [the cock] crows twice." For the roosters were accustomed, according to one school of thought, to crow several times, thereupon to fall into a kind of sleep, and again after some time to begin another "crowing." Therefore Matthew says, "Before the cock crows," by which he means "[Before] the completion of the cock-crow, you will deny me thrice."

The Novatianists should be ashamed for refusing to receive [back into fellowship] those who sinned with the baptism and the partaking of the mysteries.

For behold Peter, having forgotten the undefiled body and blood, and having denied, was restored by repentance.

και ἀρνησαμενος, δια της
μετανοίας προσεδέχθν. Τα
γαρ ἐλττώματα τῶν ἁγίων δία
τοῦτο ἀνεγραγνσαυ, ἵνα και
ἡμεις. εἰ ποτε ἐξ ἀπροσεξιας;
ἔχωμεν ἀφοραν εἰς τα πα-
ραδείγματα, και δια μετανοιας
σπευνδωμεν διορθωθηναι.

For they (i.e., the Evangelists) made the short- comings of the saints a matter of public record, in order that we, if we should at any time stumble, should also have their examples in mind, and should through repentance hasten to be reconciled.

The Greek text above is taken from Migne's *Patrologia Graeca,* vol. 123, columns 487-682. The English translation is my own.

Appendix F

EUTHYMII ZIGABENI
TO KATA MAPKON
EYAΓΓEΛION.

Euthymius Zigabenos
Commentary on the Gospel of Mark

KEΦ. MΣ'. Περὶ τῆς
παραδόσεως προφητεία.

Chapter 46:
"Concerning the Prophecy of the Betrayer"

Καὶ ἀπήγαγον – πρὸς τὸ
φῶς. Πρός τὸ φῶς, τὸ ἐκ τῆς
πυρκαιᾶς, ὥστε φαίνεσθαι τοῖς
συγκαθημένοις καὶ πᾶσι τοῖς
ἐν τῇ αὐλῇ· εἴρηται*] καὶ
περὶ τούτων ἐκεῖ.

[14:53,54] "And they led [Jesus] away
—to the light." To the light, [i.e.] which
came from the fireplace, so as to be seen by
all those sitting together and all those in the
courtyard; but concerning these [matters] it
has been commented on there.

KEΦ. MZ'. Περὶ τῆς
ἀρνήσεως

Chapter 47:
"Concerning the Denial"

Καὶ ὄντος – λέγεις.
Εἴρηται ἐν τῷ ἑξηκοστῷ ἕκτῳ
χεφαλαιῳ τοῦ κατὰ Ματθαῖν.

[14:66,67] "And being—you are saying."
It has been commented on in the sixty-sixth
chapter of the [Commentary on the Gospel]
Accoring to Matthew.

Καὶ ἐξῆλθεν – ἐφώνησεν.
Ἀνάγνωθι ἐν τῷ ἑξηχοστῷ
τεταρτῳ κεφαλαίῳ τοῦ κατὰ
Ματθαῖον τὴν ἐξήγησιν τοῦ,
Πρὶν ἀλέκτορα φωνῆσαι, τρὶς
ἀπαρνήσῃ με.

[14:68] "And he went forth [a cock]
crowed." Read in the sixty-fourth chapter of
the [Commentary on the Gospel] According
to Matthew the exegesis of this: "before the
cock crows, you will deny me thrice."

Καὶ ἐφώνησε. Περὶ τῆς
παιδίσκης καὶ τῶν παρεστώτων
εἴρηται λεπτομερῶς ἐν τῷ
ἑξηκοστῷ πέμπτῳ κεφαλαίῳ
τοῦ κατὰ Ματθαῖον, καὶ
ἀνάγνωθι τὴν ἐξήγησιν ἐκεῖ
τοῦ, καὶ εἰσελθὼνεθω ἐκάθητο
μετὰ τῶν ὑπηρετῶν ἰδεῖν τὸ
τέλος. Περὶ δὲ τῶν ἄλλων
ἐλέχθη πάλιν ἐν τῷ ἑξηκοστῷ
ἕκτῳ καφαλαίῳ τοῦ τοιῦτου
Εὐαγγελίοο.

[14:69-72a] "And [a cock] crowed."
Concerning the servant girl and the bystanders it has been commented on briefly in the
sixty-fifth chapter of the [Commentary on
the Gospel] According to Matthew, and read
the exegesis of this there: "and entering
within [he] sat with the attendants [in order]
to see the end." But concerning the other
[matters] it has been commented on again in
the sixty-sixth chapter of the previous [?]
Evangelist.

Καὶ ἀνεμνήσθη – ἔκλαειν. Ἐν ἐκείνῳ καὶ περὶ τούτων ἐρρήθν. Οὐ μόνον δὲ τούτου τοῦ ῥήματος ἀπὸ τοῦ φόβου καὶ τῆς ἀσθενείας ἐπελάθετο, ἀλλὰ καὶ τοῦ· Ὅστις δάν ἀρνήσηταί με ἔμπροσθεν τῶν ανθρωπων, ἀρνήσομαι αὐτόν κάγω ἔμπροσθεν τοῦ πατρός μου τοῦ ἐν οὐπανοῖς.

[14:72b] "And [Peter] remembered--he wept." Concerning this and also the other [matters] it has been commented on. Not only [concerning] the statement [that] he forgot by reason of fear and weakness, but also this; "Whoever should deny me before men, him also will I deny before my Father who is in heaven."

The Greek text above is taken from Migne's *Patrologia Graeca*, vol. 129, columns 765-852. The English translation is my own.

Appendix G

JOHN CALVIN
on
Matthew 26:69-75, Mark 14:66-72, Luke 22:55-62

Peter's fall, here described, brilliantly mirrors our own infirmity. His repentance in turn is a memorable demonstration for us of God's goodness and mercy. The story told of one man contains teaching of general, and indeed prime, benefit for the whole church; it teaches those who stand to take care and caution; it encourages the fallen to trust in pardon. First, we must note that Peter acted without thought in entering the court of the high priest. It was the disciple's duty to follow his Master. But as he was warned of the lapse he would make, he should rather have hid in some corner and not run into an occasion of sinning. It often happens that the faithful throw themselves into temptations under the appearance of virtue. We must ask the Lord that the Spirit may hold us on firm rein, in case we go beyond the mark and at once pay the penalty. We must ask, as often as we undertake anything, that He may not allow us to fall in the midst of our efforts or at the outset of the task, but may supply from heaven strength to the end. A sense of our weakness should not be a reason for doing nothing, for not going wherever God calls us, but it should check our rashness, in case we attempt more than our calling. It should prompt us to pray, that God who gave a right beginning, may add the grace of perseverance.

Matt. 26.69. *A maid came unto him.* Here we see that it does not take a heavy fight to break a man, nor many forces and devices. Whoever is not dependent on God's hand will soon fall, at a breath of wind or the noise of a falling leaf. Peter certainly was no less brave than any of us, and had already given no ordinary proof of his high courage (though his boldness was excessive). Yet he does not wait to be brought to the tribunal of the Pontiff, or until the enemy threatens his violent death, but, at the voice of a young woman, he is scared, and straight out denies his Master. A moment ago he had seemed to himself a soldier, even unto death. Let us remember that our powers are so unequal to bearing large-scale attack that they fail even at the mere shadow of a fight. So God gives us a due reward for our treachery, in disarming us and stripping us of all virtue, till we tremble at nothing at all, once we have cast off our fear for Him. If a lively fear of God had dwelt in Peter's heart, it would have been an insuperable rampart. But now, stripped and defenceless, he panics when danger is still far off.

Matt 26,70. *He denied before them all.* This is a circumstance that aggravates the offence; Peter, in denying his Master, did not take note of the crowd of witnesses in his fear. The Spirit precisely wishes to impress on us that the sight of men should

166

embolden us to hold firm to our faith. If we deny Christ in the sight of the weak, they may be shocked and cast down by our example, and thereby we destroy all the souls we can. If, in the presence of wicked scorners of God and enemies of the Gospel, we cheat Christ of His due testimony, we expose His sacred name to the ridicule of all. As a bold and free confession builds up pious minds and puts the unbeliever to shame, so defection involves a public collapse of faith for the Church and a shaming of sound doctrine. The higher a man stands the more he should take care to himself, for he cannot fall from his rank without doing greater damage. The form of denial set down here shows sufficiently that wretched sophists gain nothing by their ingenuity, when with ambiguous and smart-spoken tricks they make evasions, if they are called to give an account of their faith. Peter does not explicitly deny the whole teaching of the Gospel. He only denies he know the man, but because under Christ's person he buries indirectly the light of the offered redemption, he is condemned as a foul and base betrayer. He had just heard from the Lord's mouth that a confession of faith was a pleasing sacrifice in God's sight, so his denial is quite beyond excuse, robbing God of His due service and Christ of His honour. Take this point; as soon as one departs from a simple and sincere profession of Christ, one robs Him of His rightful witness.

Matt. 26.71. *Another maid saw him.* We tend to guess, from Mark's account, that it is the same maid: he certainly does not say she is a different one. There is nothing contradictory, in fact it is likely, that one girl's remark went round them all, the first pointing him out to many over and over again, the others going up to find out for sure and spreading the discovery further still. John says that the second questioning came not from the maid, but from a crowd of men. Obviously the report that started with the girl was picked up by the bystanders, who turned it against Peter. There is another difference between Mark and the other three. He mentions the cock crowing twice, the others say that it only crowed when Peter had denied the Lord for the third time. This problem too has an easy solution, since Mark says nothing to contradict the report of the others. What they pass over in silence, he relates explicitly. I have no doubt when Christ said to Peter, 'Before the cock crows', He meant the cock-crowing in its various repetitions. Cocks do not only crow once but repeat their calls several times, yet all the cock-crows of one night are called the cock-crowing. So Matthew, Luke and John say that Peter denied the Lord thrice before the end of the cock-crowing. Mark gives the greater detail, that Peter came in quite a short space of time to his third denial, and did not repent at the first cock-crow. We do not say profane historians are in disagreement if one of them tells a thing the others leave unmentioned. Although Mark's narrative is different it is not at odds with the others. It is to be noted that once Peter found he could not slip out of it with a simple denial, he doubles his crime by putting in an oath. A little later when he is pressed more strongly he goes as far as cursing.

We see how once a sinner has fallen he is rapidly taken into worse plight. Those who begin with minor faults rush from them headlong into the foulest crimes, which at first they would have abhorred. This is God's just punishment, once we deprive ourselves of the assistance of the Holy Spirit, that He allows Satan to work his power on us with violence, tossing us this way and that in our utter addiction and slavery. This is particularly the case with denial of the faith. When a man, for fear of the cross, turns aside from the pure profession of the Gospel he goes further if he sees he has not satisfied his enemies. And what he had not dared to make a simple confession of, he must now adjure outright without the chance of concealment. Then this also must be observed, that virtually in one moment of time Peter defected three times over: when it appears how slippery and steep is the slope on which we fall, whenever Satan drives us. There will certainly be no limit to our fall unless the Lord reach out His hand to hold us. When the vigour of the Spirit of grace died in Peter, as often as he was asked about Christ, whoever approached, he was ready to deny with a hundred, yes a thousand denials. Disgraceful as it was for him to fall three times, yet the Lord spared him, and checked the mouths of the enemies, in case they made more attacks. So the Lord must daily bridle Satan, or he would overwhelm us with temptations beyond number. Though he does not cease to come against us with all kinds of trickery, unless the Lord had regard for our weakness and held off the brunt of his rage, we should have to encounter a vast onslaught of temptation. In this respect we must glory in the Lord's mercy, that He allow no more than the bare hundredth part of our enemy's evil purpose to make way against us.

Matt. 26.74. *Then began he to curse.* At the third denial Peter's faithlessness towards his Master reached its highest peak. Not content with an oath, he passed to cursing, calling damnation on his body and soul. He wills himself cursed of God, if ever he knew Christ. This has the force of saying, 'May I perish, if I have any part in the salvation of God.' Christ's goodness is the more wonderful, that He healed the disciple brought forth from such a pit. This passage teaches that it is not direct blasphemy against the Spirit for a man fallen through weakness of the flesh to deny the truth he knows. Peter had certainly heard from the Lord's mouth what a detestable treachery it was to deny Him before men, and what a terrible vengeance awaits them, at the hand of God and the angels, who desert their confession of faith in cowardly fear of the cross: not for nothing, a little before, had he preferred death and torment to denial of Christ. Now in full knowledge and after due warning, he comes to grief, yet wins pardon afterwards. It follows that he sinned from weakness, and not from incurable malice. He would willingly have offered to Christ the due devotion that he owed, but fear had extinguished his sparks of right desire.

Matt. 26.75. *And Peter remembered.* Besides the cock-crow Luke tells us there was the sight of Christ: for he had first ignored the cock's crow, as we have learned from Mark. So he had to meet Christ's eyes to come to himself. This is the experience of each one of us. Which of us does not neglect with deaf ear and unconcern—not the many and various songs of birds (and yet they prompt us to glorify God)—but the actual voice of God, which in Law and Gospel clearly and distinctly resounds for our learning? And it is not for one day only that our minds are seized with this dumb stupidity, but on and on, until He grants us a sight of Himself. This alone converts the hearts of men. It is well worth noting, that it was no ordinary look (since He had already looked on Judas, who became none the better of it), but with the turning of His eyes on Peter, there went the secret power of the Spirit that as often as a man has lapsed, repentance for him only starts from the look the Lord gives. *Wept bitterly*. It is likely that Peter went out through fear, not daring to weep where witnesses could see: again he displayed his weakness. We gather that he did not win pardon by any satisfaction, but from the kind fatherly affection of God. The example teaches us that however lame our repentance, yet we may have good hope. As long as it is sincere, God scorns not even feeble repentance. Peter's secret tears testified in the Face of God and of the angels that his sorrow was true. Hidden from the eyes of men he puts before him God and the angels: from the inmost feelings of his heart flow those tears. We should note this, since we see many in floods of tears, as long as there is someone to watch, eyes are dry as soon as they are by themselves. No doubt tears that are not forced from us by God's judgments, spring from self-seeking and hypocrisy. It is asked whether true penitence requires weeping. I answer that the faithful often sigh unto God with dry eyes, and confess their fault, to obtain pardon: but in the graver sins it is too stupid and unfeeling not to be wounded with grief and sorrow to the point of shedding tears. Scripture, after convicting men of their crimes, urges them to sackcloth and ashes.

The above text is from D. W. and T. F. Torrance, eds. *Calvin's Commentaries: A Harmony of the Gospels: Matthew, Mark and Luke and The Epistles of James and Jude,* translated by A. W. Morrison, 3 Vols., Grand Rapids: Wm. B. Eerdmans, 1972, III: 169-73, and is reprinted with permission.

Appendix H

CORNELIUS À LAPIDE
on
Mark 14:54, 66-72

Ver. 68. *And the cock crew.* Hear S. Chrysostom on S. Matt. xxvi. 70, "Mark signifies that neither by the crow of the cock was he led to remember, nor did it keep him from denial." Chrysostom adds, "Mark only has written thus, most accurately detailing the gracious care of the Master for His disciple, and Peter's weakness. Wherefore we ought especially to admire him, because he not only did not hide his master's fault, but wrote the account of it in greater detail than the others, for this very reason that he was Peter's disciple."

Ver. 70. *For thou art also a Galilaean.* That is, by speaking in the idiom of the Galilaeans thou showest thyself to be a Galilaean. The Arabic adds, *And thy speech is similar to their speech.*

Ver. 72. *And he began to weep:* Gr. [*epibalon eklaie*], i.e., literally, *adding he was weeping*; which you may translate, 1st, *he began to weep*; 2nd, *he added to weep,* i.e., "he began to weep very violently," says Theophylact. The Arabic is, *and the betook himself to tears,* not in the court before the Jews, that he might not betray himself to them, but when he was alone, having gone out of it as appears from S. Matt. xxvi. 75.

The above text is from Thomas W. Mossman, translator. *The Great Commentary of Cornelius à Lapide.* 8 Vols. Edinburgh: John Grant, 1908. III: 438-9.

Appendix I

PASQUIER QUESNEL
on
Mark 14:54, 66-72

[54] A man never exposes himself to temptation without danger. Human engagements are attended with great difficulties, and the indiscreet advance of one false step has very often dreadful consequences. Peter has rashly boasted of his courage, his honour is at stake, he will by no means go back, and nothing is wanting on his part to his destruction. But it is much better for a man to retreat and humble himself for his fault, than thus blindly to pursue it to the last.

[66] Presumption, curiosity, and unprofitable conversation draw Peter into the occasion of his fall. When a man can be serviceable to his friends under their disgraces and persecutions for religion, he may then expose himself to some danger upon their account; but to do it when he cannot serve them in the least is to forget that he is weak, and that he ought, out of humility, to avoid danger as much as possible, and not to expose himself thereto out of curiosity or presumption.

[67-68] What! not know him, who, by the eucharist, had just given himself to him, and was at that very time sacrificing himself for him? There are but too many who imitate Peter, in denying Christ by their works as soon as ever they leave the holy table, and in being ashamed before men of his truths, his gospel, and his friends. Men look upon it as a small thing, under the fair and specious pretexts of wisdom, advantage, and other prudential considerations, to dissemble the knowledge which they have of the innocency of those who are rendered odious to the world, or their agreement with them in the same sentiments and opinions. We shall one day see what judgment God will pass upon this conduct. The silence of a good man and a friend is a piece of treachery, which is sometimes more prejudicial and of more pernicious consequence than the accusation of a declared enemy.

[69-70] The experience of a first, and even of a second fall, is not sufficient to convince a presumptuous person, or to make him sensible of his danger. The danger is never small when the weakness is great, and a man depends upon himself. A silly woman, a word, or even a look, is able to overturn the chief pillars of the church, if they are not well founded upon the love of God and the contempt of the world, and of all its false advantages.

171

[71] Is this the man who said, "Lord, to whom shall we go? thou hast the words of eternal life. And we believe, and are sure that thou art the Christ, the Son or the living God." What knowledge, what faith, what zeal soever a man has, he may lose it all in a moment, and become like Peter. Presumption was the cause of his fall: let humility support us, and conserve in us the gifts of God.

[72] In vain does the cock crow to the ears of Peter; in vain do all preachers cry aloud to awaken the sinner, unless the grace of Christ open his understanding, his memory, and his heart, and draw from thence the tears of repentance. Peter's tongue utters not a word, but his heart speaks by his eyes. A true penitent ought to begin by silence, especially if his tongue has been the instrument of his sin. Such a person should speak to God by his love, and to men by his tears. It is to his heart that God speaks, when it is touched with a sense of his sins; and it is his heart which must speak to God, if it desires to be cured.

The above text is from Pasquier Quesnel. *The Gospels: with Moral Reflections on Each Verse*. 2 Vols. Philadelphia: Parry & McMillan, 1855. I: 531, 534-6.

Appendix J

JOHN ALBERT BENGEL
on
Mark 14:54, 66-72

54. [*Meta ton upereton*], *with the attendants*) Often a fall is incurred more easily in the presence of such as servants, who are less feared, than among their masters, [the great].—[*thermainomenos*], *warming himself*) Often under care for the body the soul is neglected.—[*phos*], *the light*) Apparently *light* is the expression used instead of *fire*: Peter was recognised by the *light*, when under other circumstances he might have been safer: comp. ver. 67.

66. [*Kato*], *beneath*) There seem to have been a flight of steps there.

69. [*H paidiske*], the maid [not as Engl. Ver *a* maid]) That same maid: or else a second one, so that the [*palin*], *again*, may be connected with the participle alone, [*idousa*], *having seen* him.—[*tois parestekosin*], *to them that stood by*) She said it then in the spirit of joking, not with the intent to hurt him [Comp. note on Matt. xxvi. 69].

[*ex auton*], *of them*) The expression, *of them* shows, that speaking against Jesus and His disciples was most common and frequent.

72. [*Epibalon eklaie*], *he betook himself*) To weeping, or as Stapulensis interprets it, *He broke forth into weeping*. The French happily express it, *il se mit à pleurer.* Theophr. charact., [*peri logopoiias; euthus erotesai—kai epibalon erotan:* as to which see Casaubon [Engl. Ver., *When he thought thereon.*]

The above text is from John Albert Bengel. *The Gnomon of the New Testament.* [Notes on St. Mark translated by Andrew Robert Fausset]. 5 Vols. Edinburgh: T. & T. Clark, 1859. I: 567-8.

Abbreviations

AnBib	Analectica biblica
ANF	The Ante-Nicene Fathers
ASTI	*Annual of the Swedish Theological Institute*
AusBR	*Australian Biblical Review*
AusCR	*Australian Catholic Record*
BAGD	W. Bauer, W. F. Arndt, F. W. Gingrich, and F. W. Danker, *Greek-English Lexicon of the NT*
BBB	*Bonner biblische Beiträge*
BFER	*British and Foreign Evangelical Review*
Bib	*Biblica*
BibToday	*Bible Today*
BJRL	*Bulletin of the John Rylands University Library of Manchester*
BR	*Biblical Research*
BRPR	*The Biblical Repertory and Princeton Review*
BSac	*Biblotheca Sacra*
BTB	*Biblical Theology Bulletin*
CBQ	*Catholic Biblical Quarterly*
CBTEL	M'Clintlock, *Cyclopaedia of Biblical, Theological, and Ecclesiastical Literature*
CCSL	Corpus Christianorum Series Latina
CovQ	*The Covenant Quarterly*
CT	*Christianity Today*
CTJ	*Calvin Theological Journal*
CurTM	*Currents in Theology and Mission*
DCB	Smith, *Dictionary of Christian Biography*
DRev	*Downside Review*
EHR	*The English Historical Review*
ETL	*Ephemerides theologicae lovanienses*
EvQ	*Evangelical Quarterly*
EvT	*Evangelische Theologie*
ExpTim	*Expository Times*
HibJ	*Hibbert Journal*
HTR	*Harvard Theological Review*
Int	*Interpretation*
JAAR	*Journal of the American Academy of Religion*
JBL	*Journal of Biblical Literature*
JBR	*Journal of Bible and Religion*
JDT	*Jahrbücher für deutsche Theologie*
JEH	*Journal of Ecclesiastical History*
JETS	*Journal of the Evangelical Theological Society*
JR	*Journal of Religion*

JSNT	*Journal for the Study of the New Testament*
JTS	*Journal of Theological Studies*
KD	*Kerygma und Dogma*
LB	*Linguistica biblica*
LS	*Louvain Studies*
NedTTs	*Nedelands theologisch tijdschrift*
NICNT	New International Commentary on the New Testament
NovT	*Novum Testamentum*
NPNF	Nicene and Post-Nicene Fathers
NTS	*New Testament Studies*
ODCC	Cross, *The Oxford Dictionary of the Christian Church*
PG	J. Migne, Patrologia graeca
PL	J. Migne, Patrologia latina
PRS	*Perspectives in Religious Studies*
RB	*Revue biblique*
RefR	*Reformed Review*
RelS	*Religious Studies*
RelSRev	*Religious Studies Review*
RevExp	*Review and Expositor*
RTAM	*Recherches de theologie ancienne et medievale*
SacEr	*Sacris erudiri: Jaarboek voor Godsdienstwetenschappen*
SBB	Stuttgarter biblische Beiträge
SBLASP	Society of Biblical Literature Abstracts and Seminar Papers
SBLDS	Society of Biblical Literature Dissertation Series
SE	Studia Evangelica
S-HRE	*The New Schaff-Herzog Encyclopedia of Religious Knowledge*
SJT	*Scottish Journal of Theology*
SNTSMS	Society for New Testament Studies Monograph Series
SPCK	Society for the Promotion of Christian Knowledge
SWJT	*Southwestern Journal of Theology*
TDNT	G. Kittel and G. Friedrich (eds.), *Theological Dictionary of the New Testament*
TGl	*Theologie und Glaube*
TLZ	*Theologische Literaturzeitung*
TS	*Theological Studies*
TSK	*Theologische Studien und Kritiken*
TToday	*Theology Today*
TTZ	*Trierer theologische Zeitschrift*
TU	Texte und Untersuchungen
TZ	*Theologische Zeitschrift*
WMANT	Wissenschaftliche Monographien zum Alten un Neuen Testament
WS	*Word & Spirit: A Monastic Review*
ZMR	*Zeitschrift für Missionskünde und Religionswissenschaft*
ZNW	*Zeitschrift für die neutestamentliche Wissenschaft*
ZTK	*Zeitschrift für Theologie und Kirche*

Bibliography

Auerbach, Eric. *Mimesis: The Representation of Reality in Western Literature.* Princeton: University Press, 1953.

Aune, D. E. "The Problem of the Messianic Secret." *NovT* 11 (1969) 1-31.

Baldermann, Ingo. *Biblische Didaktik. Die sprachliche Form als Leitfaden unterrichtlicher Texterschirssung am Beispel synoptischer Erzählungen.* Furche-Verlag, 1966.

Barbour, Robin S. "Recent Study of the Gospel According to St. Mark." *ET* 49 (1968) 324-329.

Bede. *In Marci Evangelium Expositio.* In *Patrologia Latina,* xcii, columns 131-302. Edited by J. P. Migne.

_____. *In Marci Evangelium Expositio.* In *Corpus Christianorum, Series Latina.* Vol. 120. Turnhout, Belgium: Brepols, 1960. Edited by D. Hurst.

Bellenger, Aidan. "Bede: Monk of Wearmouth-Jarrow." *WS* 7 (1985) 23-33.

[Bengel, Johann Albrecht.] *Bengelius's Introduction to His Exposition of the Apocalypse: With His Preface to that Work, and the greatest Part of it: And also his Marginal Notes on the Text, which are A Summary of the Whole Exposition.* Translated by John Robertson. London: J. Ryall and R. Withy, 1757.

_____. *Critical English Testament.* Edited by W. L. Blackley and James Hawes. 3 Vols. London: A. Strahan, 1872-76.

_____. *Gnomon Novi Testamenti.* Tübingen, 1742. English translation, Edinburgh, 1877.

Best, Ernest. "Discipleship in Mark: Mark 8:22-10:52." *SJT* 23 (1970) 323-37.

_____. *Following Jesus: Discipleship in the Gospel of Mark.* Sheffield, England: JSOT, 1981.

_____. "Mark 3:20, 21, 31-5." *NTS* 22 (1975-6) 309-19.

_____. *Mark: The Gospel as Story.* Edinburgh: T & T Clark, 1983.

_____. "Mark's Use of the Twelve." *ZNW* 69 (1978) 11-35.

_____. "Markus als Bewahrer der Überlieferung." In *Das Markus-Evangelium,* 390-409. Edited by R. Pesch. Darmstadt, 1979.

_____. "Peter in the Gospel According to Mark." *CBQ* 40 (1978) 547-558.

_____. "The Role of the Disciples in Mark." *NTS* 23 (1977) 377-401.

_____. *The Temptation and the Passion.* SNTSMS 2. Cambridge, 1965.

Betz, Otto. "The Concept of the So-called 'Divine Man' in Mark's Christology." In *Studies in New Testament and Early Christian Literature: Essays in Honor of Allen P. Wilgren,* 229-40. Edited by David Edward Aune. Leiden: E. J. Brill, 1972.

Birdsall, J. Neville. *"To rhema hos eipen auto ho Iesous:* Mk xiv. 72." *NovT* 2 (1958) 272-275.

Black, Carl Clifton II. *An Evaluation of the Investigative Method and Exegetical Results of Redaction Criticism of the Gospel of Mark: The Role of the Disciples As A Test Case in Current Research.* Ann Arbor, MI: University Microfilms International, 1986.

Blevins, J. L. "Seventy-two Years of the Messianic Secrect." *PRS* 1 (1974) 187-194.

Bonner, Gerald I., ed. *Famulus Christi, Essays in Commemoration of the Thirteenth Centenary of the Birth of the Venerable Bede.* London: S.P.C.K., 1976.

_____. *Saint Bede in the Tradition of Western Apocalyptic Commentary.* n.p.: Jarrow Lecture 1966.

_____. "The Saints of Durham." *Sobornost* 8 (1986) 34-46.

Boobyer, G. H. "The Secrecy Motif in St. Mark's Gospel." *NTS* 6 (1960) 225-35.

Boomershine, Thomas Eugene. *Mark, The Storyteller: A Rhetorical-Critical Investigation of Mark's Passion and Resurrection Narrative.* Ann Arbor, MI: University Microfilms, 1974.

_____. "Mark 16:8 and the Apostolic Commission." *JBL* 100 (1981) 225-39.

Boomershine, T. E. and G. L. Bartholomew. "The Narrative Technique of Mark 16:8." *JBL* 100 (1981) 213-23.

Bouchier, E. S. *A Short History of Antioch, 300 B.C.–A.D. 1268.* Oxford: Basil Blackwell, 1921.

Boyd, W. J. Peter. "Peter's Denial: Mark 14:68, Luke 22:57." *ExpT* 67 (1956) 341.

Brady, David. "The Alarm to Peter in Mark's Gospel." *JSNT* 4 (1979) 42-57.

Brecht, M. "J. A. Bengels Theologie der Schrift." *ZTK* 64 (1967) 99-120.

Bristol, Lyle O. "New Testament Textual Criticism in the Eighteenth Century." *JBL* 69 (1959) 101-12.

Brown, George Hardin. *Bede the Venerable.* Boston: Twayne Publishers, 1987.

Brown, Raymond E. "The Passion According to Luke." *Worship* 60 (1986) 2-9.

_____. "The Passion According to Matthew." *Worship* 58 (1984) 98-107.

_____. Review of *The Passion in Mark,* ed. by Werner Kelber. *CBQ* 39 (1977) 285.

Brown, S. Review of *Mark—Traditions in Conflict,* by T. J. Weeden. *TS* 33 (1972) 754-756.

Bruce, Alexander Balman. *The Gospel According to St. Mark.* Vol 1 in *The Expositor's Greek Testament.* Edited by W. Robertson Nicoll. Grand Rapids: Wm. B. Eerdmans, 1976.

Buchanan, G. W. "Mark xiv. 54." *ExtT* 68 (1956) 27.

Bultmann, Rudolf. *The History of the Synoptic Tradition.* New York: Harper & Row: 1976.

Burgon, John W. *The Last Twelve Verses of the Gospel According to S. Mark.* Oxford and London: James Parker and Co., 1871.

Burk, Johann Christian Friedrich. *Memoir of the life and writings of John Albert Bengel.* Translated by Robert Francis Walker. London: Wm. Ball, 1837.

Burkill, T. A. "The Hidden Son of Man in St. Mark's Gospel." *ZNW* 52 (1961) 189-213.

_____. *Mysterious Revelation.* New York, 1963.

_____. "Strain on the Secret: An Examination of Mk 11:1-13:37." *ZNW* 51 (1960)

Burkitt, F[rancis] Crawford. *The Book of Rules of Tyconius. Text and Studies* iii. I. Cambridge: University Press, 1894.

_____. *The Gospel History and its Transmission.* Edinburgh: T. & T. Clark, 1911.

Butterworth, G. W., tr. & ed. *Origen. On First Principles.* New York: Harper & Row, 1966.

Calvin, John. *A Harmony of the Gospels Matthew, Mark, and Luke.* 3 Vols. Translated by A. W. Morrison. Edited by David W. Torrance and Thomas F. Torrance. Grand Rapids: Wm. B. Eerdmans, 1972.

_____. *Commentary on a Harmony of the Evangelists, Matthew, Mark and Luke*. Translated by William Pringle. Grand Rapids: Wm. B. Eerdmans, 1949.

Campbell, J. "Bede," in *Latin Historians*, ed. by T. A. Dorey. London: Routledge & Kegan Paul, 1966.

Caplan, Harry. "The Four Senses of Scriptural Interpretation and the Mediaeval Theogy of Preaching." *Speculum* 4 (1929) 282-90.

Carroll, Sister M. Thomas Aquinas. *The Venerable Bede: His Spiritual Teachings*. The Catholic University of America Studies in Mediavel History New Series, Vol. IX. Washington, D.C.: The Catholic University of America Press, 1946.

Catania, F. J. "A Bibliography of St. Albert the Great." *The Modern Schoolman* 37 (1959) 11-28.

Colgrave, B. *The Venerable Bede and his Times*. Jarrow Lecture 1958. Gallowgate, Newcastle: J. & P. Bealls Limited, 1958.

Corwin, Virginia. *St. Ignatius and Christianity in Antioch*. New Haven: Yale University Press, 1960.

Cowdrey, Herbert E. J. "Bede and the 'English People.'" *The Religious History* 11 (1981) 501-23.

Cramer, J. A. *Catenae Graecorum Patrum in Novum Testamentum. Tomus I: Catenae in Evangelia S. Matthaei et S. Marci*. Oxford, 1840.

Cranfield, C. E. B. *The Gospel According to Saint Mark*. Cambridge: University Press, 1966.

Croinin, O Daibhi. "'New Heresy for Old': pelagianism in Ireland and the Papal Letter of 640." *Speculum* 60 (1985) 505-16.

Cross, F. L. *The Oxford Dictionary of the Christian Church*. 2nd edition. Oxford University Press, 1977.

Cullmann, Oscar. *Peter: Disciple—Apostle—Martyr: A Historical and Theological Study*. London: SCM Press, 1953.

Daube, D. "The Responsibilities of Master and Disciples in the Gospels." *NTS* 19 (1972-3) 1-15.

Derrett, J[ohn] Duncan M[artin]. *The Making of Mark: The Scriptural Bases of the Earliest Gospel*. 2 Vols. Shipston-on-Stour: P. Drinkwater, 1985.

_____. "The Reason for the Cock-crowings." *NTS* 29 (1983) 142-144.

Dewey, Kim E. "Peter's Curse and Cursed Peter." In *The Passion of Mark: Studies on Mark 14-16,* 96-114. Edited by W. H. Kelber. Philadelphia: Fortress Press, 1976.

_____. "Peter's Denial Reexamined: John's Knowledge of Mark's Gospel." *SBL Seminar Paper* 16 (1979) 109-112.

Dibelius, Martin. *From Tradition to Gospel.* Cambridge: James Clarke & Co. Ltd., 1971.

Donahue, J. R. *Are You The Christ? The Trial Narrative in the Gospel of Mark.* SBLDS 10. Missoula, Montana: University of Montana, 1973.

Donaldson, J. "'Called to Follow'. A Twofold Experience of Discipleship in Mark." *BTB* 5 (1975) 67-77.

Dorey, T. A., ed. *Latin Historians.* Studies in Latin Literature and its Influence, eds. D. R. Dudley and T. A. Dorey. London: Routledge & Kegan Paul, 1966.

Downey, Glanville. *A History of Antioch in Syria from Seleucus to the Arab Conquest.* Princeton: Princeton University Press, 1961.

Eckenrode, T. R. "The Venerable Bede and the Pastoral Affirmation of the Christian Message in Anglo-Saxon England." *DRev* (1981) 258-78.

Ellwein, Eduard. "Das Rätsel von Römer VII." *KD* 1 (1955) 247-68.

Ernst, Josef. "Die Petrustradition im Markusevangelium—ein altes Problem neuangegangen." In *Begegnung mit dem Wort. Festschrift für Heinrich Zimmermann,* 35- 65. Edited by J. Zmÿewdki and E. Nellessen. BBB 53. Bonn: Peter Hanstein, 1980.

_____. "Noch einmal: Die Verleugnung Jesu durch Petrus (Mk 14, 54. 66-72)." *Catholica* 30 (1976) 207-226.

_____. "Simon—Kephas—Petrus. Historische und typologische Perspektiven im Markusevangelium." *TGl* 71 (1981) 438-456.

Euthymius, Zigabenus. *[Hermeneia tou kata Markon euaggeliou].* In *Patrologia Graeca,* 129, columns 765-852. Edited by J. P. Migne.

Evans, C. A. "'Peter Warming Himself': The Problem of an Editorial 'Seam.'" *JBL* 101 (1982) 245-249.

Farrer, Austin Marsden. *A Study in St. Mark.* Westminster: Dacre Press, 1951.

_____. *St Matthew and St Mark.* London: Dacre Press, 1966.

Fitzpatrick, M. "Marcan Theology and the Messianic Secret." *AusCR* 59 (1982) 404-16.

Foakes-Jackson, F. J. *Peter: Prince of Apotles: A Study in the History and Tradition of Christianity.* New York: George H. Doran, 1927.

Foord, Bede, OSB. "Bede the Venerable and Venerable Women." *WS* 7 (1985) 47-61.

Fortna, Robert T. "Jesus and Peter at the High Priest's House: A Test Case for the Question of the Relation Between Mark's and John's Gospel." *NTS* 24 (1978) 371-383.

Frantzen, Allen J. "The Penitentials Attributed to Bede." *Speculum* 58 (1983) 573-97.

Frei, Hans. *The Eclipse of Biblical Narrative: A Study in Eighteenth and Nineteenth Century Hermeneutics.* New Haven and London: Yale University Press, 1974.

Freyne, S. "At Cross Purposes. Jesus and the Disciples in Mark," *Furrow* 33 (1982) 331-9.

_____. "The Disciples in Mark and the *maskilim* in Daniel. A Comparison." *JSNT* 16 (1982) 7-23.

_____. *The Twelve: Disciples and Apostles: A Study in the Theology of the First Three Gospels.* London: Sheed & Ward, 1968.

Fritsch, Charles T. "Bengel, the Student of Scripture." *Int* 5 (1951) 203-15.

Froehlich, Karlfried, tr. and ed. *Biblical Interpretation in the Early Church.* Sources of Early Christian Thought, ed. William G. Rusch. Philadelphia: Fortress Press, 1984.

Gerhardsson, Birger. "Confession and Denial before Men: Observations on Matthew 26:57-27:2." *JSNT* 13 (1981) 46-66.

Gewalt, D. "Die Verleugnung des Petrus." *LB* 43 (1978) 113-44.

Giles, John Allen. *The Miscellaneous Works of Venerable Bede.* 6 vols. London: Whittaker, 1843.

Girard, Renè. "Peter's Denial and the Question of Mimesis." *Notre Dame English Journal* 14 (1982) 177-89.

Goguel, Maurice. "Did Peter Deny His Lord?" *HTR* 25 (1932) 1-27.

Goltz, Hermann Freiherr von der. "Die theologische Bedeutung J.A. Bengel's und seiner Schule." *JDT* 6 (1861) 460-506; Translated and reprinted "The Theological Significance of J.A. Bengel and his School." *BFER* 11 (April 1862) 304-42.

Gransden, Antonia. "Bede's Reputation as an Historian in Medieval England."
    JEH 32 (1981) 397-425.

Grant, Robert and Tracy, David. *A Short History of the Interpretation of the Bible.*
    Philadelphia: Fortress, 1984.

Hagenbach, K. R. *A History of Christian Doctrines.* 3 Vols. Clark's Foreign
    Theological Library, Vol. 3. Edinburgh: T. & T. Clark, 1883.

_____. *History of the Church in the Eighteenth and Nineteenth Centuries.*
    Translated by John F. Hurst. New York: Charles Scribner, 1869.

Harnack, Adolf von. *Petrus im Urteil der Kirchenfeinde des Altertums.* Tübingen:
    Mohr, 1922.

Haskin, Richard Webb. *The Call to Sell All: The History of the Interpretation of
    Mark 10:17-23 and Parallels.* Ann Arbor, MI: University Microfilms, 1971.

Hawkin, D. J. "The Incomprehension of the Disciples in the Markan Redaction."
    JBL 91 (1972) 491-500.

Hawkins, John Caesar. *Horae Synopticae: Contributions to the Study of the Synoptic
    Problem.* Oxford: Clarendon Press, 1909, 1968.

Hemphill, Robert. *The Diatessaron of Tatian. A Harmony of the Four Gospels
    Compiled in the Third Quarter of the Second Century; Now First Edited in an
    English Form with Introduction and Appendices.* London: Hodder &
    Stoughton, 1888.

Hengel, Martin. *The Charistmatic Leader and His Followers.* Edinburgh: T & T
    Clark,

_____. *Studies in the Gospel of Mark.* SCM Press, 1985.

Hennecke, Edgar. *New Testament Apocrypha.* 2 Vols. Philadelphia: Westminster,
    1964.

Henry, Patrick. *New Directions in New Testament Study.* Philadephia: Westmin-
    ster, 1979.

Herron, Robert W., Jr., Vernon D. Doerksen, Opal L. S. Reddin. *New Testament
    Study Bible: Mark.* Vol. 3 of *The Complete Biblical Library,* 16 vols. Editor,
    Ralph W. Harris. Springfield, MO: The Complete Biblical Library, 1988.

Herron, Robert W., Jr. "Mark's Jesus on Divorce: Mark 10:1-12 Reconsidered."
    JETS 25 (1982) 273-81.

_____. Review of *Beyond Biblical Criticism: Encountering Jesus in Scripture,*
    by Arthur Wainwright. *JETS* 26 (1983) 223-4.

_____. Review of *Call to Discipleship: A Literary Study of Mark's Gospel*, by Augustine Stock. *JETS* 26 (1983) 242-3.

_____. Review of *Following Jesus: Discipleship in the Gospel of Mark*, by Ernest Best. *JETS* 26 (1983) 241- 2.

_____. Review of *The Passion of Jesus in the Gospel of Mark*, by Donald Senior. *JETS* 28 (1985) 248-9.

Hickling, C. J. A. Review of *Mark—Traditions in Conflict*, by T. J. Weeden. *RelS* 10 (1974) 339-46.

Hodge, Charles, ed. [author's name omited] "Quesnel and the Jansenists." *The Biblical Repertory and Princeton Review* 28 (1856) 132-56.

Holladay, C. H. *Theios Aner in Hellenistic Judaism. A Critique of the Use of this Category in New Testament Studies.* SBLDS 40. Missoula, MT: Scholars Press, 1977.

Hurst, David, OSB. "Venerable Bede and the Scriptures." *WS* 7 (1985) 68-79.

Hurst, John R. *History of Rationalism: Embracing a Survey of the Present State of Protestant Theology.* London: Trübner & Co., 1867.

Jackson, Samuel Macauley, ed. *The New Schaff-Herzog Encyclopedia of Religious Knowledge.* 12 Vols. Grand Rapids: Baker Book House, 1957.

James, Montague Rhodes. *The Apocryphal New Testament.* Oxford: Clarendon Press, 1924, 1975.

Jedin, Hubert, and Dolan, John, eds. *History of the Church.* 10 Vols. New York: Crossroads, 1981. Vol. 6: *The Church in the Age of Absolutism and Enlightenment,* by Wolfgang Müller et al. Translated by Gunther J. Holst.

"John Albert Bengel." *BFER* 2 (1853) 1-41. No author cited.

Jones, Charles W. "Some Introductory Remarks on Bede's Commentary on Genesis." *SacEr* 19 (1969-70) 115-98.

Kalin, E. R. "Early Traditions About Mark's Gospel: Canonical Status Emerges, the Story Grows." *CurTM* 2 (1975) 332-41.

Kealy, Sean P. *Mark's Gospel: A History of Its Interpretation.* New York: Paulist Press, 1982.

_____. "Reflections on the History of Mark's Gospel." *Proceedings: Eastern Great Lakes Biblical Society,* ed. by P. Sigal (1982) 46-62.

Keck, Leander. "Will the Historical-Critical Method Survive? Some Observations." *Orientation by Disorientation: Studies in Literary Criticism and Biblical Literary Criticism, Presented in Honor of William A. Beardslee.* Editor, Richard A. Spencer. Pittsburgh: The Pickwick Press, 1980.

Kee, Howard Clark. "Mark as Redactor and Theologian: A Survey of Some Recent Markan Studies." *JBL* 90 (1971) 333-6.

_____. "Mark's Gospel in Recent Research." *Int* 32 (1978) 353-68.

Kelber, Werner H. *The Kingdom in Mark: A New Place and A New Time.* Philadelphia: Fortress, 1974.

_____. "Mark 14:32-42: Gethsemane. Passion Christology and Discipleship Failure." *ZNW* 63 (1972) 166-87.

_____. *The Oral and the Written Gospel. The Hermeneutics of Speaking and Writing in the Synoptic Tradition, Mark, Paul, and Q.* Philadelphia: Fortress, 1983.

_____. *The Passion in Mark: Studies on Mark 14-16.* Philadelphia: Fortress, 1976.

Khoury, A. T. "Gespräch über den Glauben zwischen Euthymios Zigabenos und einem sarazenischen Philosophen; übers von A. Antweiler." *ZMR* 48 (1964) 192-203.

King, Margot H. and Stevens, Wesley M., eds. *Saints, Scholars and Heroes. Studies in Medieval Culture in honour of Charles W. Jones.* Collegville, MN: Hill Monastic Manuscript Library. Saint John's Abbey and University, 1979.

Kingsbury, J. D. "The 'Divine Man' as the Key to Mark's Christology—The End of an Era?" *Int* 35 (1981) 243-57.

_____. "The Gospel of Mark in Current Research." *RelSRev* 5 (1979) 101-7.

Kirby, D. P. "Bede, Eddius Stephanus and the 'Life of Wilfrid.'" *EHR* 98 (1983) 101-14.

Klein, Günther. "Die Berufung des Petrus." *ZNW* 58 (1967) 1-44.

_____. "Die Verleugnung des Petrus. Eine traditionsgeschitliche Untersuchung." *ZTK* 58 (1961) 285-328.

Klostermann, Erich. *Das Markusevangelium.* Tübingen: J. C. B. Mohr, 1950.

Knigge, H. D. "The Meaning of Mark." *Int* (1968) 53-70.

Kosmala, H. "The Time of the Cock-Crow." *ASTI* 2 (1963) 118-20.

_____. "The Time of the Cock-Crow." *ASTI* 6 (1968) 132-34.

Kraeling, Carl H. *A Greek Fragment of Tatian's Diatessaron From Dura*. London: Christophers, 1935.

Kraus, Hans Joachim. "Calvin's Exegetical Principles." *Int* 31 (1977) 8-18.

Kuby, A. "Zur Konzeption des Markus-Evangeliums." *ZNW* 49 (1958) 52-64.

Kugel, James and Greer, Rowan. *Early Biblical Interpretation*. Edited by Wayne A. Meeks. Vol. 3: *Library of Early Christianity*. Philadelphia: Westminster Press, 1986.

Kümmel, W. G. *The New Testament: The History of the Investigation of its Problems*. London: SCM, 1972.

Laistner, M. L. W. "Antiochene Exegesis in Western Europe during the Middle Ages." *HTR* 40 (1947) 19-31.

_____. "Source-Marks in Bede MSS." *JTS* 34 (1933) 350-4.

Lampe, G[eoffrey] W[illiam] H[ugo]. "St. Peter's Denial." *BJRL* 55 (1973) 346-68.

Lane, William L. "From Historian to Theologian: Milestones in Markan Scholarship." *RevExp* 75 (1978) 601-17.

_____. *The Gospel According to Mark: The English Text with Introduction, Exposition and Notes*. NICNT. Grand Rapids: Wm. B. Eerdmans, 1974.

_____. "The Gospel of Mark in Current Study." *SWJT* 21 (1978) 7-21.

_____. "*Redaktionsgeschichte* and the De-Historicizing of the New Testament Gospel." *Bulletin of the Evangelical Theological Society* 11 (1968) 27-33.

Lapide, Cornelius à. *The Great Commentary of Cornelius à Lapide*. 8 Volumes. Translated by Thomas W. Mossman. Edinburgh: John Grant, 1908.

LaVerdiere, E. "The Passion-Resurrection of Jesus according to St. Luke." *Chicago Studies* 25 (1986) 35-50.

Leclercq, Jean, OSB. "Saint Bede and Christian Expansion." *WS* 7 (1985) 3-22.

Lee, G. M. "Mark 14, 72: *[epibalon eklaien]*." *Bib* 53 (1972) 411-12.

_____. "St. Mark xiv. 72: *[epibalon eklaien]*." *ET* 61:160.

Lewis, C. S. *Surprised by Joy, The Shape of My Early Life*. New York: Harcourt, Brace & World, 1955.

Lightfoot, R. H. *The Gospel Message of St. Mark*. Oxford: Clarendon Press, 1950, 1958.

Linnemann, E. "Die Verleugnung des Petrus." *ZTK* 63 (1966) 1-32.

Longenecker, Richard N. *Biblical Exegesis in the Apostolic Period.* Grand Rapids: Wm. B. Erdmans, 1975.

Luz, U. "Das Geheimnismotiv und die markinische Christologie." *ZNW* 56 (1965) 9-30.

Lynch, Kevin M. "The Venerable Bede's Knowledge of Greek." *Traditio* 39 (1983) 432-39.

Manschreck, Clyde L[eonard], ed. *A History of Christianity: Readings in the History of the Church from the Reformation to the Present.* Englewood Cliffs: Prentice Hall, 1964.

_____. *A History of Christianity in the World.* Englewood Cliffs: Prentice Hall, 1974.

_____. *Melanchthon: The Quiet Reformer.* New York: Abingdon Press, 1958.

_____., trans. and ed. *Melancthon on Christian Doctrine.* New York: Oxford University Press, 1965.

_____. *The Reformation and Protestantism Today.* New York: Association Press, 1960.

Mansfield, M. Robert. *"Spirit and Gospel" in Mark.* Peabody, MA: Hendricksen, 1987.

Marcus, Joel. "Mark 4:10-12 and Markan Epistemology." *JBL* 103 (1984) 557-74.

Marshall, I. Howard, ed. *New Testament Interpretations.* Exeter: Paternoster Press, 1977.

Martin, J. P. Review of *Mark—Tradtions in Conflict,* by T. J. Weeden. *Int* 26 (1972) 361-2.

Marxsen, Willi. *Mark the Evangelist: Studies on the Redaction History of the Gospel.* Nashville: Abingdon Press, 1969.

Mayo, C. H. "St. Peter's Token of the Cock Crow." *JTS* 22 (1921) 367-70.

M'Clintock, John, and Strong, James, eds. *Cyclopaedia of Biblical, Theological, and Ecclesiastical Literature.* Grand Rapids: Baker Book House, 1968.

McNally, Robert E., S.J. *The Bible in the Early Middle Ages.* Maryland: The Newman Press, 1959.

McNamara, M. *The Medieval Irish Contribution.* Dublin: Dominican, 1976.

Menzies, Allen. *The Earliest Gospel: a historical study of the Gospel According to Mark.* London: Macmillan, 1901.

Merkel, H. "Peter's Curse." *The Trial of Jesus.* Ed. by E. Bammel. London, 1970.

Meye, R. P. *Jesus and the Twelve: Discipleship and Revelation in Mark's Gospel.* Grand Rapids: Eerdmans, 1968.

Michiels, R. "Het passieverhaal volgens Lucas" [The Passion Narrative according to Luke]. *Collationes* 30 (1984) 191-210.

Mitton, C. L. "Some Further Studies in St. Mark's Gospel." *ExpTim* (1976) 297-301.

Moloney, F. J. "The Vocation of the Disciples in the Gospel of Mark." *Salesianum* 43 (1981) 487-516.

Murphy, Roland G. "Patristic and Medieval Exegesis—help or hindrance." *CBQ* 43 (1981) 505-16.

Murray, G. "Saint Peter's Denials." *DRev* 103 (1985) 196-8.

Neale, John Mason, gen. ed. *A History of the Holy Eastern Church.* Vol. 5: *The Patriarchate of Antioch.* New York: AMS Press, 1976.

_____. *A History of the So-Called Jansenists Church of Holland; With A Sketch of its Earlier Annals, And Some Account of the Brothers of the Common Life.* Oxford: John Henry and James Parker, 1858; reprint ed., AMS, 1970.

Nineham, D. E., ed. *The Church's Use of the Bible.* London: S.P.C.K., 1963.

O'Collins, Gerald, S.J. *What Are They Saying About Jesus?* New York: Paulist Press, 1977.

Olsen, Glenn. "Bede as Historian: The Evidence from his Observations on the Life of the First Christian Community at Jerusalem." *JEH* 33 (1982) 519-30.

Osborne, B. A. E. "Peter: Stumbling-Block and Satan." *NovT* 15 (1973) 187-90.

Pelikan, Jaroslav. J. "In Memoriam: Johann Albrecht Bengel, June 24, 1687 to November 2, 1752." *Concordia Theological Monthly* 23 (1952) 785-96.

Pesch, R. "Die Verleugnung des Petrus: Eine Studie zu Mk 14,54. 66-72 (und Mk 14,26-31)." *Neues Testament und Kirche: Für Rudolf Schnackenburg.* Ed. by Joachim Gnilka. Freiberg/Basel/Vienna: Herder, 1974.

_____. *Simon-Petrus: Geschichte und Geschichtliche Bedeutung der ersten Jüngers Jesu Christi.* Stuttgart: Anto Hiersemann, 1980.

Petersen, Norman. *Literary Criticism for New Testament Critics*. Philadelphia: Fortress, 1978.

_____. "When is the End not the End? Literary Reflections on the Ending of Mark's Narrative?" *Int* 34 (1980) 151-66.

Plummer, C., ed. *Historica Ecclisiastica*. Oxford, 1896.

Quesnel, Pasquier. *The Gospels with Moral Reflections on Each Verse*. Philadelphia: Parry & McMillan, 1855.

_____. *The New Testament with moral reflections*. Translated by Richard Russel. 8 Vols. in 4. London: R. Bonwicke, 1719-25.

Quesnell, Q. *The Mind of Mark*. AnBib 38. Rome: Biblical Institute, 1968.

_____. Review of *Mark—Traditions in Conflict*, by T. J. Weeden. *CBQ* 35 (11973) 124-5.

Ramsay, W. M. "The Denials of Peter." *ExpTim* 28 (1916-17) 297.

Rawlinson, Alfred Edward John. *The Gospel According to St. Mark*. London: Methuen & Co., 1925 (1st ed.), 1960.

Ray, Roger. "What Do We Know About Bede's Commentaries?" *RTAM* 49 (1982) 5-20.

Rhoads, David and Michie, Donald. *Mark as Story: An Introduction to the Narrative of a Gospel*. Philadelphia: Fortress Press, 1982.

Robbins, Vernon K. *Jesus the Teacher: A Socio-Rhetorical Interpretation of Mark*. Philadelphia: Fortress, 1984.

Robinson, J. Armitage, gen. ed. *Texts and Studies: Contributions to Biblical and Patristic Literature*. Cambridge: University Press, 1895. Vol. 3, no. 1: *The Book of Rules of Tyconius*, by F. C. Burkitt.

Robinson, James M. *The Nag Hammadi Library*. San Francisco: Harper & Row, 1977.

Robinson, John A. T. *Redating the New Testament*. London: SCM, 1976.

Robinson, W. C., Jr. "The Quest for Wrede's Secret Messiah." *Int* 27 (1973) 10-30.

Roelofsma, Derk Kinnane. "A Tug-of-war with Biblical Scholars." *Insight* (March 21, 1988) 60-1.

Runia, Klaas. "The Hermeneutics of the Reformers." *CTJ* 19 (1984) 121-52.

Schaff, Philip. *History of the Christian Church*. 8 Vols. Grand Rapids: Wm. B. Eerdmans, 1950.

Schmahl, G. "Die Berufung der Zwölf im Markusevangelium." *TTZ* 81 (1972) 203-13.

_____. *Die Zwölf im Markusevangelium*. Trier: Paulinus, 1974.

Schweitzer, Albert. *The Quest of the Historical Jesus*. London: Adam & Black, 1954.

Schweizer, E. "Neuere Markus-Forschung in USA." *EvT* 33 (1973) 533-7.

Screiber, Johannes. "Die Christologie des Markusevangeliums." *ZTK* 58 (1961) 154-83.

Seal, Welton O., Jr. "Norman Perrin and His 'School': Retracing a Pilgrimage." *JSNT* 20 (1984) 87-107.

Seitz, O. J. F. "Peter's 'Profanity': Mark 14:71 in the light of Mt. 16:22." SE, TU 73 (1959) 516-19.

Senior, Donald. *The Passion of Jesus in the Gospel of Mark*. Wilmington, Delaware: Michael Glazier, 1984.

Smalley, Beryl. *The Study of the Bible in the Middle Ages*. Notre Dame: University of Notre Dame, 1964.

Smart, James D. *The Strange Silence of the Bible in the Church: A Study in Hermeneutics*. Philadelphia: Westminster Press, 1970.

Smith, Harold. *Ante-Nicene Exegesis of the Gospels*. London: SPCK, 1928.

_____. "The Sources of Victor of Antioch's Commentary of Mark." *JTS* 19 (1918) 350-70.

Smith, R. H. "Darkness at Noon: Mark's Passion Narrative." *CurTM* 44 (1973) 325-338.

Smith, Terence V. *Petrine Controversies in Early Christianity*. Tübingen: Mohr, 1985.

Soards M. L. "'And the Lord Turned and Looked Straight at Peter': Understanding Luke 22,61." *Bib* 67 (1986) 518-9.

Stead, Julian, OSB. "The Inspiration of Bede." *WS* 7 (1985) 62-7.

Steinmetz, David C. "The Superiority of Pre-Critical Exegesis." *TToday* (1980) 27-38.

Stock, Augustine. *Call to Discipleship: A Literary Study of Mark's Gospel*. Wilmington, Delaware: Michael Glazier, 1982.

_____. "Literary Criticism and Mark's Mystery Play." *BibToday* 100 (1979) 1909-15.

Stock, Klemens. *Die Boten aus dem Mit-Ihm-Sein*. AnBib 70. Rome: Biblical Institute, 1975.

_____. "Gliederung und Zusammenhang in Mk 11-12." *Bib* 59 (1978) 481-515.

Strabi, Walafridi. *Glossa Ordinaria*. *PL*. Vols. 113-114, ed. by J. P. Migne.

Streeter, B. H. *The Four Gospels*. London: 1953.

Sutcliffe, Edmund F., S.J. "Quotations in the Ven. Bede's Commentary on S. Marc." *Bib* 7 (1926) 428-39.

Tannehill, Robert C. "The Disciples in Mark: The Function of a Narrative Role." *JR* 57 (1977) 386-405.

Taylor, Edward Lynn, Jr. *The Disciples of Jesus in the Gospel of Mark*. Ann Arbor, MI: University Microfilms International, 1980.

Taylor, Vicent. *The Gospel According to St. Mark: The Greek Text with Introduction, Notes and Indexes*. Grand Rapids: Baker Book House, 1981.

Theophylact. *[Hermeneia eis to kata Markon euaggelion]*. *PG*. Vol. 123, ed. by J. P. Migne.

Thompson, A. Hamilton, ed. *Bede. His Life, Times and Writings. Essays in Commenoration of the Twelfth Centenary of his Death*. New York: Russell & Russell, 1966.

Turner, C. H. *The Gospel According to St. Mark*. London: S.P.C.K., n.d.

Turner, H. E. W. "Modern Issues in Biblical Studies: The Tradition of Mark's Dependence upon Peter." *ExpTim* 71 (1960) 260-3.

Tyson, Joseph B. "The Blindness of the Disciples in Mark." *JBL* 80 (1961) 261-8.

van Iersel, B. M. F. "The Gospel According to St. Mark—Written for a Persecuted Community?" *NedTTs* 34 (1980) 15-36.

van Walt, A. G. P. "Reflections of the Benedictine Rule in Bede's homilary." *JEH* 37 (1986) 367-76.

Wainwright, Authur. *Beyond Biblical Criticism: Encountering Jesus in Scripture*. Atlanta: John Knox Press, 1982.

Wallace, R. S. "Calvin the Expositor." *CT* 8 (May 22, 1964) 8-10.

Walter, N. "Die Verleugnung des Petrus." *Theologische Versuche VIII*. Edited by Joachim Rogge and Gottfried Schille. Berlin: Evangelische Verlagsanstalt, n.d.: 45-61.

Ward, Benedicta, SLG. "Bede and the Conversion of the Anglo-Saxons." *WS* 7 (1985) 34-46.

Weborg, C. John. "Pietism: A Question of Meaning and Vocation." *CovQ* 41:3 (1983) 59-71.

_____. "The Eschatological Ethics of Johann Albrecht Bengel." *CovQ* 36:2 (1978) 31-43.

Weeden, Theodore J. "The Heresy that Necessitated Mark's Gospel." *ZNW* 59 (1968) 145-58.

_____. *Mark—Traditions in Conflict*. Philadelphia: Fortress Press, 1971.

_____. "The Conflict Between Mark and His Opponents Over Kingdom Theology." SBLASP 2. Edited by G. MacRae. Cambridge, MA, 1973.

Weiss, Johanness. *Das älteste Evangelium*. Göttingen: Vandenhoeck und Ruprecht, 1903.

Wellhausen, *J. Das Evangelium Marci*. Berlin: Georg Reimer, 1909.

Wenham, J. W. "How Many Cock-Crowings? The Problem of Harmonistic Text-Variants." *NTS* 25 (1979) 523-5.

Wierenga, Robert. "Calvin the Commentator." *RefR* 32 (1978) 4-13.

Wilcox, M. "The Denial Sequence in Mark xiv. 26-31, 66-72." *NTS* 17 (1971) 426-36.

Wink, Walter. *The Bible in Human Transformation: Toward a New Paradigm for Biblical Study*. Philadelphia: Fortress Press, 1973.

Wood, Susan. "Bede's Northumbrian dates again." *EHR* 98 (1983) 280-96.

Index

A

Ambrose 39, 46
Angelom of Luxeuil 118
Anselm of Laon 49
Anti-Marcionite Prologue 16, 28
Arnauld, Antoine 76
Arndt, J. 78
Auerbach, Eric 2
Augustine 7, 39, 44, 47, 49, 55, 71, 89, 118, 125
Augustine (of Canterbury) 35

B

Bauer-Arndt-Gingrich 53
Bede, The Venerable 35ff, 67, 117, 123, 125
Bengel, John Albert 53, 77ff
Birdsall, J. Neville 138f
Bogomiles 53
Böhme, J. 78
Boomershine, T. E. 134f, 143
Bornkamm, Günther 99
Brown, G. H. 36, 40
Bruce, A. B. 91
Bultmann, Rudolf 93f
Burgon, John W. 19, 30

C

Calvin, John 6, 26, 63, 66ff, 81
Cassian 37, 118
Chrysostom 18ff, 31, 71f
Clement 16, 19
Clement (of Alexandria) 21
Conzelmann, Hans 99
Culpepper, Raymond A. 126
Cyril of Alexandria 17, 18, 31

D

Dewey, Kim 104f, 132f
Dibelius, Martin 90, 93f

E

Eichorn, J. G. 89
Enthusiasts 65
Erasmus 62
Ernst, Josef 3
Eucherius of Lyons 118
Eusebius 16, 29
Euthymius Zigabenos 53ff

F

form criticism 7
Fuller, R. H. 134

G

Gallicanism 73
Georgi, Dieter 101
Gieseler, J. L. 89
Glossa ordinaria 48ff, 117, 123
Goguel, Maurice 94f
Grant, Robert M. 25, 64f, 122
Gregory the Great 35, 39, 41, 49
Grynaeus 63
Gunkel, Hermann 93

H

Hadrian of Africa 35
Hagenbach 54
Hauck, Albert 48
Hawkin, D. J. 9
Hawkins, John C. 90
Hengel, Martin 17
Henry, Patrick 5
Holtzmann, H. J. 6, 7, 90
Hurst, David 58

I

In Marci euangelium 36ff
Irenaeus 16, 28
Isidore 47, 49

192

About the Author

Robert W. Herron, Jr. was born and raised in Louisiana. After a conversion to Pentecostal Christianity at the age of 16, he attended Lee College in Cleveland, TN where he earned a B.A. in Biblical-Historical Studies. From there he took an M.A. in Humanities from Western Kentucky University, and an M.A. and a Ph.D. in Religious Studies from Rice University in Houston, TX.

While pursuing his doctoral studies he served as Vice President of Academic Affairs at Southern Bible College in Houston, TX, Research Fellow at the Institut zur Erforschung des Urchristentums, in Tübingen, Germany, and Assistant Professor of Religion at Lee College. He presently serves at his alma mater, Lee College, as Associate Academic Dean. He is a minister in the Church of God, Cleveland, TN.

He is married to Diane, and they have two children, Robert Wilburn III, and Tiffany Danielle.

195